CONSTRUCTING
THE SELF
IN A
MEDIATED
WORLD

Inquiries in Social Construction

Series Editors
Kenneth J. Gergen and John Shotter

Inquiries in Social Construction is designed to facilitate across disciplinary and national boundaries, a revolutionary dialogue within the social sciences and humanities. Central to this dialogue is the idea that all presumptions of the real and the good are constructed within relations among people. This dialogue gives voice to a new range of topics, including the social construction of the person, rhetoric and narrative in the construction of reality, the role of power in making meanings, postmodernist culture and thought, discursive practices, the social constitution of the mental, dialogic process, reflexivity in theory and method, and many more. The series explores the problems and prospects generated by this new relational consciousness, and its implications for science and social life.

CONSTRUCTING THE SELF IN A MEDIATED WORLD

EDITED BY
DEBRA GRODIN AND THOMAS R. LINDLOF

INQUIRIES IN SOCIAL CONSTRUCTION

SAGE Publications
International Educational and Professional Publisher
Thousand Oaks   London   New Delhi

AGD7366

For information address:

 SAGE Publications, Inc.
2455 Teller Road
Thousand Oaks, California 91320
E-mail: order@sagepub.com

SAGE Publications Ltd.
6 Bonhill Street
London EC2A 4PU
United Kingdom

SAGE Publications India Pvt. Ltd.
M-32 Market
Greater Kailash I
New Delhi 110 048 India

Printed in the United States of America

Library of Congress Cataloging-in-Publication Data

Main entry under title:

Constructing the self in a mediated world / editors, Debra Grodin,
    Thomas R. Lindlof.
        p.   cm.—(Inquiries in social construction ; no. 18)
    Includes bibliographical references and index.
    ISBN 0-8039-7011-0 (cloth : acid-free paper).—ISBN
    0-8039-7012-9 (pbk. : acid-free paper)
        1. Self.   2. Self—Social aspects.   3. Identity (Psychology).
    4. Individuality.   I. Grodin, Debra.   II. Lindlof, Thomas R.   III. Series.
    BF697.C583   1996
    155.2—dc20

                                                                        95-32497

This book is printed on acid-free paper.

96 97 98 99 10 9 8 7 6 5 4 3 2

Sage Production Editor: Astrid Virding
Sage Typesetter: Andrea D. Swanson

Contents

Preface

Several years ago, when we began this project on self and media, we did so with enthusiasm for this promising area of interdisciplinary investigation. As communication researchers, we observed how our mediated world has challenged assumptions about the self, both academically and in the popular imagination. That's what led to the development of this book. A tip-off for us about the saliency of a project on self and media came by way of nonscholarly responses to our topic. The mention of this book to friends and others who were not academics was met with uniform enthusiasm, indicating to us that issues of self and media need more articulation, not only in scholarly circles but in the culture "outside" of the academy.

Notions of the self as highly contained and stable have historically dominated research approaches in the social sciences, including the study of media. This means that many studies about the human experience of media decontextualize the self and do not emphasize socially constructed aspects of identity and experience. Over the past 20 years, the socially constructed nature of the self has been the premise of many important research projects, but during that time relatively little attention has been given to the relationship between self and media.

Although there has been some significant theoretical work in the area of self and mediated communication, there are still few actual research projects, particularly those involving research participants. This volume is a first attempt to bring together some of the original research that is currently being done in this area. In addition, several chapters are theoretical. In working together as editors, we found ourselves deepening our interests in the topic of self and media, and also recognizing how far-reaching a topic it is. For example, during this project, we both developed a strong interest in issues of mediated communication and community. Many of the pieces we've collected for this volume are not just about the self but about self in relation to others, and in context.

A number of people contributed their expertise toward the development and completion of this book. Conversations with Mick Presnell, Nina Gregg, Andrea Press, and Kelly Coyle helped with the initial development of the project. Autumn Grubb-Swetnam was a sounding board along the way. The University of Louisville (Debra Grodin's academic home when the project began) supported a leave that enabled work on this book, and the Northwest Center for Research on Women at the University of Washington offered an academic affiliation.

Pulling together an edited volume is a social experience. The book evolved as a result of our contributors, and we are grateful for their interest in the project.

Sophy Craze, our editor at Sage, has been a calm and encouraging voice during the course of the project, steering us efficiently and thoughtfully and deeply understanding our purposes. We also thank Astrid Virding at Sage for her guidance during the production process. Our series editor, Ken Gergen, provided needed critiques in the beginning and later phases of our work.

We also want to thank our partners. Bill Mowat provided unstinting support for the project, including computer assistance in difficult moments and a genuine interest in the topic. Joanne Popa Lindlof, as always, gave wonderful advice and encouragement and helped secure the moments and places in which the work got done. We are grateful for their help.

Part I

Introduction

1

The Self and Mediated Communication

Debra Grodin
Thomas R. Lindlof

A recent plot in the popular soap opera *All My Children* involves a burgeoning romance over the Internet, where two people engage in discourse about themselves. Using e-mail pseudonyms, these individuals share information about self on a daily basis. When they arrive at the office each morning, they look forward to going "on-line" and learning about one another's passions, dislikes, and so forth. The twist is that in life off the Internet, these romancers actually know each other. In fact, unknown to them, they are office mates whose desks are within 10 feet of one another. As they court in cyberspace (sitting at their office desks), they sometimes observe each other using the computer in real time, without knowing that they are actually corresponding with one another. They become intrigued with one another in a way that has not yet happened during their everyday face-to-face interactions. This plot, however unlikely in everyday life, does raise questions about the role of mediated communication in our lives and its relationship to self. How is discourse about the self over electronic mail different from what occurs in face-to-face interactions? Does cyberspace allow for an experience of self in relationships that is not available to us in nonmediated forms?

Discourse about the self and about self experience is, of course, not limited to soap operas or cyberspace courtship; it is a major currency of contemporary culture. Self-help books, talk shows, advertising, therapy sessions, and parenting workshops are just a few domains where talk about the self flourishes. Terms such as *self-esteem, self-denial, self-fulfillment,* and *self-centeredness* constitute a common vocabulary that is shared among those living in the United States. This far-ranging discourse reveals something about contemporary life: what constitutes self, how self is experienced, and what pulls and supports there are in the negotiating of self in everyday experience.

Discourse about the self is an everyday phenomenon; it is also a key preoccupation of scholars who examine human lives. Communication researchers, sociologists, psychologists, educators, and social critics have long viewed issues of self and identity as critical to explaining human behavior. In this volume, we bring together the realm of the everyday and the realm of scholarship in presenting pioneering efforts that examine the self in the context of mediated communication. Specifically, we are interested in what happens to notions of self, on many levels, in the context of changing and proliferating systems and forms of mediated communication.

Our interest in self in the context of mediated communication largely stems from postmodern ideas regarding the expansiveness of media imagery and talk in everyday life, and the development of assorted media technologies that by now are a hallmark of our contemporary period. Destabilization of the self is one characteristic of postmodernity. Mediated communication enables us to encounter many diverse people representing different social enclaves and ethnic or religious backgrounds. In this way, it challenges the validity of singular perspectives and calls into question the hegemony of rational choice and the belief in one truth or univocal judgment (Gergen, 1991). Self becomes multivocal as we carry a number of voices with us. Individuals, then, may find that they no longer have a central core with which to evaluate and act, but instead find themselves "decentered." Decenteredness is also linked to a sense of dislocation, not only in the sense of not being strictly tied to physical space because of mediated opportunities but also in the way self may be mobilized and dispersed. An individual calling up an advice expert on a radio talk show carries on a conversation with someone who may be broadcasting from another state or perhaps another country, *and* he or she will also be listened to by large numbers of people, all of whom are scattered geographically. The constitution of self for the caller is quite literally mobilized electronically, and in turn is implicated in the way listeners construct self.

It is important to understand that mediated communication shapes experience of self not only in its capacity as a purveyor of content that might influence self-definition but also because media are technologically circumscribed forms. In other words, it is not just program content that affects identity but also the use and presence of various technologies. For example, the placement of television in public spaces such as restaurants, malls, and airports changes the nature of social interaction and, consequently, the way individuals experience themselves in relation to others. Therefore, the increase in numbers of mediated experiences individuals are having, as well as the mobility and interactivity of media technologies, serves to undermine many notions of self and identity that have endured during the modern period (Gergen, 1991). Thus, both technological and content qualities of mass communication are shaping the experience of self and are interrelated.

Poststructuralist ideas about the discursive nature of human experience are also key to appreciating how and why the mediated environment is so influential. From a poststructuralist position, language is the site where subjectivity is constructed. Language is also the place where "actual and possible forms of social organization and their likely social and political consequences are defined and contested" (Weedon, 1987, p. 21), thereby making the activity of self-construction socially specific and conflicted. The linguistic derivation of notions of self makes suspect the idea of a fixed, stable, and unified identity. The cultural and discursive contingencies of our notions of self and identity are laid bare.

Constructing the Self in a Mediated World looks at self in myriad ways, and indeed the notion of construction is itself a kind of play on words. Although writing from varied theoretical perspectives, many contributors to this volume rely on theories of social construction in the formulation of their research. Social constructionist perspectives, stemming from the work of Mead, Berger and Luckmann, and others, have emphasized the relational and linguistic embeddedness of our experiences of self. As Sampson (1989) points out, social constructionism argues that "selves, persons, psychological traits, and so forth, including the very idea of individual psychological traits, are social and historical constructions, not naturally occurring objects" (p. 2). In addition, personhood occurs in concert with others through conversation, and is not an autonomous project. It is not a matter of simply choosing a role that one somehow becomes aware of. In this volume, several contributors from a range of disciplines are interested in social constructionism as a perspective compatible with postmodern awareness (Kvale, 1992). Social constructionist perspectives challenge dominant and historically entrenched notions of the American self as autonomously engineered or "constructed."

Self in a Cultural Context

Examining notions of self in the American historical and cultural context offers one way of understanding why self is a contested area in today's mediated environment. By situating a discussion of self within the framework of dominant American ideology, we can better appreciate the various ways that postmodern ideas challenge extant notions of self, and why discourse about the survival and enactment of self is so pervasive in our culture.

A belief in self-determination has always been part of the ideology of the United States. The quest for freedom in the realm of self and identity has complex historical roots, and the texture of it was, of course, vastly different for African slaves, men and women who emigrated from Ireland during the potato famine, and the pilgrims, for example. But as a dominant theme in American culture, freedom in the realm of self and identity has referred to freedom from the restrictions of political worlds where social milieu, religious affiliation, property ownership, gender, and, later, race were viewed as detriments to living one's life. *Autonomy* has also been a term closely tied to the dream of self-determination. Being autonomous suggests separation from restrictive conditions that had for many centuries determined the course of everyday existence. *Autonomy* also referred to the idea of "going at it alone." In America, it was thought, one could "help oneself" (Benjamin Franklin's notion of self-help) to shape a life uniquely satisfying and unfettered.

The ideology of self-determination was not without its difficulties. For many, the idea of crafting a self was exhilarating, frightening, and for some disappointing. By the late nineteenth century, anxiety about self-image as well as hunger for self-expression characterized daily life (Ewen, 1988). These feelings were manifested in everything from the widespread malady of neurasthenia (the loss of equipoise regarding self; Lears, 1981) to preoccupation with selecting clothing that would be viewed as socially acceptable (Ewen, 1988). Freedom associated with forging the self coincided with the growth of cities and the diminishment of traditional communities. These changes, along with many other social shifts, are often described as engendering *anomie,* a loss of personal meaning. Anomie, in turn, has been linked to the growing importance of psychotherapeutics in contemporary American culture (Reiff, 1966).

According to sociologist John Hewitt (1989), struggling with identity is a key cultural theme in American life:

> There seems to be a persistent impulse among Americans to worry about whether they are what they should be, whether they have the sort of personal traits, abilities, skills, social manners, or inner strength they should have. The sense of ambiguity does not stem from individual lack of adjustment to social life, but is an inherent part of the culture and its system of meanings. (p. 38)

If concerns about self are an integral part of American culture, what then happens to that preoccupation in the context of ever-changing systems and forms of communication? What does it mean for self-experience that we can now form relationships over electronic mail with those whom we may never meet? Do we think of ourselves differently than those of the previous century because we are exposed to multifarious personalities and lifestyles through use of television, radio, and newspapers (Gergen, 1991)? What images of self are portrayed in film, television, and magazines, and to what ideological perspectives are these images aligned? For example, are we a culture dominated by images of self as autonomous and self-determining, or are other images emerging and in what contexts? What do talk shows and other media that focus on self-expression and healing tell us about the condition of self and identity in contemporary times?

This volume raises some of these questions, and in doing so reflects a key characteristic of the self in contemporary times: its reflexivity. Modernity, as the posttraditional order, has been characterized by questions that were unprecedented in premodern times; for example, "How do I raise my child?" or "How do I treat my spouse?" (van den Berg, 1961). This reflexivity is not the normal monitoring of action that is part of human activity but refers to "chronic revision in the light of new information and knowledge" (Giddens, 1991, p. 30). Such revision is an ironic product of Enlightenment thought. Giddens points out that the Enlightenment offered both freedom from arbitrary (and irrational) rule but also the promise of certainty of knowledge that would guide human action. Yet principles of scientific doubt embedded in the Enlightenment also paved the way for a radical questioning of the expectation of certitude, of singular truths. Modernity became increasingly marked by uncertainty yet remained entwined with the goal of establishing Truth.

Modernity/Postmodernity and Mediated Experience

According to Douglas Kellner (1992): "In modernity, identity becomes more mobile, multiple, personal, self-reflexive, and subject to change and innovation. Yet the forms of identity in modernity are also relatively substantial and fixed; identity still comes from a circumscribed set of roles and norms" (p. 141). Thus, identity maintains a high degree of stability. One may develop a unique identity as a professor who is a mother, daughter, Kentuckian, and recreational mountain climber, but identity here largely comes from these established roles. One may creatively make and remake one's identity in modernity, but "modernity also increases Other-directedness . . . for as the number of possible identities increases, one must gain recognition to assume a stable, recognized identity" (Kellner, 1992, p. 142).

In the view of some scholars, we are now in a postmodern condition, suggesting that somehow we are leaving behind or have left behind the characteristics and prescriptions of modernism. Self, as we've already described, becomes destabilized. According to other scholars, the term *post* is perhaps misleading. Scholars such as Kellner and Giroux make the case that postmodernism is an intensification of modernist experience. Yet they also make distinctions. Postmodernism seems to call for more awareness than modernism regarding self and identity formation, more experimentation, and, ultimately, more risk (Kellner, 1992). Whether one describes our contemporary period as modernity, postmodernity, or something of a blend, postmodern thought has presented a challenge that asks us, among other things, to reexamine the premises of modernism as well as its application to current experience.

In the postmodern/modernist discussion, there has been great emphasis on the limitations of the modernist notion of self that emphasizes individualism, autonomy, and self-containment. There are feminist theorists, for example, who find the model of the self-contained individual to be morally problematic; it ignores the political and social contingencies of behavior, both in the development of self and in the therapeutic issues related to self. Another objection to the notion of self-contained individualism, one voiced by feminists and others, is to the dominance of a notion of self that does not adequately explain human experience. Many of our contributors dwell on the limitations of the stable and autonomous self and, not surprising, a number of authors do research in areas explicitly related to using mediated forms in the construction of self: talk shows, self-help books, magazines, and so forth.

In the area of cultural studies, scholars have begun to examine various aspects of self, identity, subjectivity, and mediated communication. For example, essays about fandom collected by Lisa Lewis (1992) include discussions of identity construction and popular music, television, and film. The emphasis is on how fans make "meanings of social identity and social experience from the semiotic resources of the cultural commodity" (Fiske, 1992, p. 37). Cathy Schwichtenberg's (1993) *The Madonna Connection* covers ground in the area of identity politics, particularly with reference to the postmodern condition of the destabilized self. Other examples of scholarship exploring self and mediated communication are Ewen's (1988) work on consumerism and identity, studies of the use of mediated texts that focus on self and identity (Grodin, 1991; Simonds, 1992), and examinations of the enactment of self on confessional television programming (White, 1992). Adding to these studies, a primary purpose of this volume is to continue the investigation of how media forms and content, as well as audience experience with media, shape the way self and identity are experienced and understood. Although the larger challenge of postmodern theory serves as a backdrop for the book, the volume includes an assortment of research approaches and purposes, not all of which explicitly reference postmodern agendas.

In This Volume

This volume focuses on four themes of self and mediated communication: self and media content, self and media use, the relational self in the mediated context, and self in inquiry. Part II, "Self and Media Content," focuses on how self is presented and treated in specific mediated texts such as film, television, magazines, and books. In Part III, "Self and Media Participation," audiences of media, as well as those who have performed or presented themselves in mediated contexts, are featured as the subjects of analysis. Part IV, "Relational Selves and the Mediated Context," includes theoretical work and original research, all of which emphasizes notions of self as less autonomous and more relational. The last part, "The Mediated Self and Inquiry," poses questions about notions of self in communication research, both theoretically and from the perspective of research practice.

Part II, exploring self and media content, features two chapters that look closely at how notions of self are represented in various forms of mass mediated popular culture. Examining representations of self in mediated sources turns our attention to the discourse on self that shapes our social experience. Both chapters in this part look at media content that is focused on women's lives and experience, and both authors point to limitations in the representations of self that they uncover. Wendy Simonds's chapter on self-help books targeted at women examines the various meanings connected with the notion of constructing self. Simonds's interest is in cultural contradictions regarding self and identity. She argues that, on one hand, self-help manuals promote an ideal of self as well integrated and highly individualistic. Furthermore, self-help authors typically speak of finding a true and core self—an essential self. Yet these promises and values are made in the wake of what Simonds considers to be a social constructionist method. Readers are asked to "make themselves over" using the ideas of the texts, of psychotherapists, and others. For Simonds, the contradiction sets up an untenable dichotomy. We cannot be restored to absolutist notions of self while also engaging in the kind of social construction that self-help books urge.

From a historical and feminist perspective, Suzanna Walters explores representations of the mother-daughter relationship in film, television, and magazines. She describes the variations in narrative presentation of mother-daughter relationships but finds a predominant thread: Sense of self for women is profoundly shaped by the notion that their identities will develop in opposition to their mothers. Her chapter raises important questions regarding issues of autonomy and connection in the lives of women, and suggests through reference to media texts that interdependence and independence in relation to mothers does not have to be viewed dichotomously in the development of a mature self.

Communication researchers have been increasingly interested in how individuals engage with media, make sense of media content, and use media experience to meet a variety of needs. In the next part, on self and media use, our contributors examine specifically how audiences and "participants" of specific media construct self and identity. This concentration on experience with media focuses the lens of inquiry beyond media content and the critics' interpretations of content, to include the perspective of media participants. In the first chapter of this part, Mary Ellen Brown examines a postmodern television program, *Twin Peaks*, and the experience of identification and subjectivity in the "reading" strategies of viewers. Given the postmodern qualities of *Twin Peaks,* its shifting discourses, its fragmented presentation, and its discontinuities, one might expect a consonant subject position. Instead, Brown discovers that individual subjects incorporate elements of postmodernism, modernism, and realism in their sense-making strategies. Notably, this incorporation also suggests the presence of multiple subject positions.

In the next chapter, Patricia Priest presents a unique piece of research that examines the experiences of talk show participants as featured guests. Focusing on those members of her sample whom she describes as marginalized, Priest is interested in how participants manage to negotiate a position of self-enhancement as a result of a talk show appearance, despite the context of commodification. She relies on concepts of status conferral to describe the nearly celebrity rise of these participants in the eyes of viewers they later meet "on the street." Extending her findings, Priest suggests that TV appearances offer a Baudrillardian sense of reality and experience that is not available offscreen. Her chapter raises important questions about the functions of talk shows that are rarely acknowledged or discussed by critics or supporters.

Donal Carbaugh's examination of a segment of the *Donahue* show taped in the (former) Soviet Union with Soviet guests and audience focuses on a sequence of interaction in a televisual text. Carbaugh analyzes program content regarding what transpired in conversation between Donahue and his guests. But the content itself is a commentary on the experience of being on *Donahue.* What emerges is a fascinating description of cross-cultural communication in a televisual context that compares the American notion of self with the Soviet notion of soul. Carbaugh's analysis offers insight into the American idea of self and its expression in mediated forums. Soviet discomfort and reaction to this expression expose cross-cultural differences.

In the last chapter of this part, Timothy Simpson takes us on his journey as a fan of rap music. His autobiographical approach is a good example of research practice and reflection invited by postmodern thought. Following Henry Giroux's lead, Simpson is interested in how his own subjectivity and practices are present "in the construction of the margins." Simpson looks at a genre that appropriates materials and memories from others so as to form, through repetition, "a place from which to speak." In his examination of the style of "mix" that shapes the rap artist's self-expression, he finds the metaphor of mix a useful one to explain his own relationship to the music. His relationship is one that illuminates aspects of identity as a white male enjoying the creations of "underclass, urban, black revolutionary nationalism."

In many of the chapters in this volume, there is an explicit or implicit reference to changing notions of self in contemporary culture. One of the more prominent themes of this volume is that conditions of our mediated culture engender experiences of self that are not fixed and self-contained but more fluid and relational. In the next part, on the relational self and the mediated context, our authors focus on how the mediated world has illuminated and influenced a less essentialist and more relational notion of self. In Chapter 8, Kenneth Gergen outlines how discursive homogeneity has supported the notion of the essentialist self in recent history, and why this notion is now undergoing deterioration. He describes a breakdown in homogeneity that has resulted from the proliferation of media and other technologies (such as airplane and automobile transportation) that have expanded our notion of physical boundaries. Gergen's perspective is not of Baudrillardian despair. Rather, he claims that the loss of the essentialist position now heralds an interest and commitment to more relational under-standings of self.

Sheila McNamee's provocative chapter is an examination of a more relational understanding of self in a specific domain of practice: psychotherapy. Although McNamee's chapter does not examine particular media use or content, she argues that differences between the modernist and postmodernist discourse regarding self and identity are deeply situated in our changing mediated world. McNamee's work is both descriptive and prescriptive; she not only examines how media have shaped changing notions of self but suggests how these notions need to shape domains of practice. As a communication scholar and trained therapist, she examines how a more fluid, relational, and less essentialist notion of self might be honored in the practice of psychotherapy.

In the next chapter, Sherry Turkle presents her research on virtual reality and the construction of self. In this piece, she examines how relationships forged through electronic mail shape identity. Based on extensive interviews and obser-vation, Turkle's chapter describes the way people use computing relationships to play with self-identity and to "try out" new identities. In particular, the use of MUDs (multiple-user dungeons) raises questions about personhood, agency, and the meaning of "I" as users become aware of their role in constructing the virtual world. Today, MUDding is a relatively unusual phenomenon that Turkle believes will become increasingly central in our psychological culture.

The last part, on self in inquiry, focuses on issues pertinent to communication research theory and practice. If the self is now conceived as constructions of a social or ideological type, then inquiry should try to account for the terms and processes of construction. Certainly researchers are also actors in the mediated environments they study, not neutral observers. Their first task in many cases, and often the longest and hardest, is in unlearning what they already know, and opening themselves to new ways of presenting and interpreting one's "self." Exploring modes of interplay between the worlds of theory and everyday popular culture presents a real challenge for future studies. Moreover, as paradigms for studying media continue to multiply, it becomes clear that at the heart of every theory lies a concept of the communicative self. A first step toward becoming better users of media theory is understanding the nature and effects of these epistemologies.

Thomas Lindlof and Autumn Grubb-Swetnam build a framework for a dia-logical practice of inquiry for investigating mediated experience. This approach conceives of research participants as investigative partners and regards the experience of the researcher "self" in relation to participants as primary data. The experimental and emergent quality of this approach to research is reflected in this chapter through dialogues between the authors as they discuss Grubb-Swetnam's dissertation research. These dialogues are reflections on the research process, exposing the vulnerability of self in the process of dialogic inquiry.

James Anderson and Gerald Schoening's chapter decodes some of the assumptions regarding self that underlie communication research and social research in general, but that are typically not made evident. What becomes apparent in their piece is that particular notions of self do particular epistemic work. Notions of self assumed by particular models of science shroud the individual in silence, give the individual voice, allow for individuality, deny individuality, and so forth. This chapter illuminates the contested character of concepts such as self, identity, and subjectivity that affect our work but that often go unexamined.

It is our hope that this volume will open up space for discussion and further development of projects that consider the complexities of self and mediated communication. There is much work to do, for example, in the realms of gender, class, and race, which have been only touched upon here. Issues of power and identity were not central to most of the pieces represented in this volume, but this indicates, again, what needs attention. New technologies also beckon the scholar; already, for example, the world of electronic mail is being used for the forging of marginalized identities. Through electronic mail, new identities are also constructed in such realms as family and friendship. Another area needing scholarly attention is that of children, media, and self-experience. As with all studies on self and media, this exploration may require greater interest in the affective side of self as well as the use of research methods (personal narratives, case studies) that tap felt experience. It may also need to bring together disparate literatures, such as developmental psychology and cultural studies. We view this integration of knowledge across disciplines to be crucial to the task of enhancing an understanding of self in a mediated world.

References

Ewen, S. (1988). *All consuming images: The politics of style in contemporary culture.* New York: Basic Books.

Fiske, J. (1992). The cultural economy of fandom. In E. Lewis (Ed.), *The adoring audience: Fan culture and popular media* (pp. 30-49). New York: Routledge.

Gergen, K. (1991). *The saturated self: Dilemmas of identity in contemporary life.* New York: Basic Books.

Giddens, A. (1991). *Modernity and self-identity: Self and society in the late modern age.* Palo Alto, CA: Stanford University Press.

Grodin, D. (1991). The interpreting audience: The therapeutics of self-help book reading. *Critical Studies in Mass Communication, 8*(4), 404-420.

Hewitt, J. (1989). *Dilemmas of the American self.* Philadelphia: Temple University Press.

Kellner, D. (1992). Popular culture and the construction of postmodern identities. In S. Lash & J. Friedman (Eds.), *Modernity and identity.* (pp. 141-177). Oxford: Basil Blackwell.

Kvale, S. (Ed.). (1992). *Psychology and post-modernism.* London: Sage.

Lears, J. (1981). *No place of grace.* New York: Pantheon.

Lewis, L. (Ed.). (1992). *The adoring audience: Fan culture and popular media.* New York: Routledge.

Reiff, P. (1966). *The triumph of the therapeutic.* New York: Harper & Row.

Sampson, E. (1989). The deconstruction of self. In K. Gergen & J. Shotter (Eds.), *Texts of identity: Inquiries in social construction* (pp. 1-19). Newbury Park, CA: Sage.

Schwichtenberg, C. (1993). *The Madonna connection*. Boulder, CO: Westview.

Simonds, W. (1992). *Women and self-help culture*. New Brunswick, NJ: Rutgers University Press.

van den Berg, J. (1961). *The changing nature of man: Introduction to a historical psychology*. New York: Delta.

Weedon, C. (1987). *Feminist practice and poststructuralist theory*. Oxford: Basil Blackwell.

White, M. (1992). *Tele-advising: Therapeutic discourse in American television*. Chapel Hill: University of North Carolina Press.

Part II

Self and Media Content

2

All Consuming Selves:
Self-Help Literature
and Women's Identities

Wendy Simonds

Sociological theory and philosophy seek programmatic methods for achieving "the good society"; self-help ideologies proffer ways of procuring good selves. In self-help books, readers are all cast as damaged merchandise, as potential insatiable consumers of new and presumably better identities, but also as redeemable from within. We can become who we *truly* are and achieve the good self, with training, practice, and techniques that self-help advisers teach us.

Within the self-help consumer marketplace, we are *all* consuming selves and we are *all-consuming selves*. In this chapter, I discuss how self-help books from the 1960s to the 1990s portray selfhood, how notions of mutable identities as well as discoverable "cores" are sold especially to women readers, and how the self-help genre's depiction of selfhood for women reflects and reinforces American cultural ideology about gender, sexuality, identity, and consumption. I draw examples from a systematic study of best-selling self-help books as well as from several self-help books that fall outside of the best-selling mainstream. I do not see texts as best understood through a reductive tallying of "messages"; thus, I do not mean the interpretations I offer here to be read as conventional content analysis. My aim is not to summarize what self-help authors intend but to construct my own persuasive reading of the literature as it works to reinforce cultural ideology (see Simonds, 1992, for a detailed discussion of the methodology of my reading).

I focus on self-help books for women written by authors who have either explicitly called themselves feminist or have become well known (within media culture) as experts with insights particularly enlightening to American women.[1] The books include Friedan's (1963) *The Feminine Mystique*, Greer's (1970) *The Female Eunuch*, Friday's (1977) *My Mother/My Self*, Dowling's (1981) *The Cinderella Complex*, Norwood's (1985) *Women Who Love Too Much*, Forward and Torres's (1986) *Men Who Hate Women and the Women Who Love Them*, Clunis and Green's (1988) *Lesbian Couples*, Penelope and Wolfe's (1989) *The Original Coming Out Stories*, Steinem's (1992) *Revolution From Within*, and hooks's (1993) *Sisters of the Yam*. These books represent, in many ways, the trends in self-help literature over the years, although they are not a representative sample.[2] All the books I write about here, except for *Sisters of the Yam, Lesbian*

Couples, and *The Original Coming Out Stories,*[3] have been best-sellers. I have included these three books in an attempt to examine what happens when self-help books explicitly address an audience outside the mainstream (white, middle class, heterosexual). All the best-selling authors, except Steinem (1992), write about gender through an (unstated) white, middle-class, heterosexual lens.

A few of the books I discuss here may not immediately appear to be obvious examples of the self-help genre (such as those by Friedan, 1963; Greer, 1970; and Penelope & Wolfe, 1989); that is, they do not necessarily rely on the standard expository formula that structures most advice books, in which an "expert" specifically describes a problem or set of problems and then sets out a program for resolution. But even books that don't follow the self-help formula explicitly may be *marketed* as self-help, and thus may be used as self-help.

Readers may be surprised that authors like Steinem (1992) and hooks (1993), who have become well known as political activists, follow a conventional self-help formula. Perhaps they have turned to the form of the self-help book precisely because they feel their ideas will gain a larger audience than in monographs that get marginalized as "women's studies."[4] Thus, self-help writing may be a strategy for these writers to gain access to more readers, including women who don't define themselves as feminist. Steinem and hooks may hope to spread feminist ideology via a more palatable genre that will not intimidate women who eschew the feminist label, and to encourage women to incorporate at least watered-down feminist ideas into self-making.

My analysis of self-help books reveals a central contradiction in the formulation of selfhood authors advance: Essentialist conceptions of "core"—real, true, and highly individualistic—selves are portrayed as realized through a construction process based on instruction by therapeutic experts, hard work, and interactive expression. We are encouraged to embark on the quest for ourselves, to dig ourselves out from under the layers of psychological malfunctioning that keep our "true" selves imperceptible. Yet, ironically, this is a process whereby we fashion our selves seemingly out of thin air. For women, who make up the majority of the targeted audience for self-help ideology, selfhood is ever so elusive; we are always at risk of "losing" our identities, authors warn us, especially as we engage in heterosexual interaction. Thus, self-help literature presents itself as a method for self-creation, damage control, and even revival, offering the woman reader an internal makeover—a buyable "new, improved" self—while at the same time, it promises her a revelation of essential reality (her "true" self).

This contradiction between a makable self and an innate one recurs in the literature and overshadows authors' presentations of selfhood as a *social* construction achieved through social relations. Self-help literature for women ostensibly claims to teach us how to dissect, decode, and remedy relationships. It positions readers as solitary travelers stumbling toward the nirvana of self-knowledge that will presumably solve all relational riddles, even though others—especially men—may not be engaged in the same quest. The self-help genre, as part of a web of advice-giving media products addressed to women, serves as one example of how American culture in general creates gender and en-genders identity. The genre displays an idealized consolidation process at the same time that it reflects postmodern notions of fragmentation and the impossibility of coherence in a consumer culture gone cynical. How can a distinctive central self be fashioned out of bought fragments?

Escaping the Mother

In her 1963 blockbuster, *The Feminine Mystique,* Betty Friedan writes that self-realization means realizing one's potential through psychological growth, an activity that she believes women "forfeit" when they engage in conventional caretaking activities like homemaking and mothering. Women in American culture and "in most countries of the world" are considered to be normal without achieving self-actualization (p. 312), but Friedan urges that (American) women protest against theories that normalize our lack of selfhood, and struggle to break the middle-class bondage of housewifery, or "the problem that has no name." Friedan presents both a social constructionist *and* an essentialist view of selfhood.

According to Friedan (1963), people have an innate need to realize motivated purposefulness, to shape the future; these qualities cannot be achieved by ministering to others: "Housewives who live according to the feminine mystique do not have a personal purpose stretching into the future. . . . Without such a purpose, they lose the sense of who they are" (p. 313). So although self-realiza-tion is an internal universal drive, it can be destroyed by social experience (experience that Friedan overgeneralizes to women). Women lose "access" to ourselves: Spending most of our time attending to the needs of others means self-abnegation and, ultimately, negation of self. Fortunately, though, we can always get back on track—as in all self-help tales—and repair stalled develop-ment and shattered identity. Potential does not disappear; it merely lies dormant, waiting for the proper spark to reignite it. In Friedan's view, getting out of the house and into college will generate new inroads to better identities, as women gain entry into the public (male) realm, the place where selfhood opportunities burgeon.

In the opening pages of *The Female Eunuch,* Germaine Greer (1970) sneers at liberal feminist rhetoric—such as Friedan's, although she does not name her until much later in the book—for advancing "vacuous" concepts of liberty, but asserts, similarly, that "the housewife who must wait for the success of world revolution for her liberty . . . could begin not by changing the world, but by reassessing herself" (p. 4). Greer then launches into an exploration of how women have been socially constructed as other, as deficient, as detestable. The reassessment of misogynist knowledge that Greer encourages will ultimately lead, she claims, to revolution. Women have participated in our own miscon-strual, misshaping ourselves. Greer (1970) states this in many ways and urges women to "stop panhandling," to eradicate the hegemony of patriarchy: "In their clothes and mannerisms, women caricature themselves, putting themselves across with silly names and deliberate flightiness, exaggerating their indecisiveness and helplessness, faking all kinds of petty tricks that they will one day have to give up" (p. 288). It is as if women cannot achieve social change without admitting our own guilt. Once Friedan and Greer turn in this direction, women seem the cause of our own most potent problems.

Greer and Friedan come down hard on mothers; mothering, to them, seems to offer women false selves that we would be well advised to shed, so as to liberate ourselves and our children. Greer calls the mother-child bond an "introverted relationship of mutual exploitation." The problem is "the massive, dominating figure of Mother" who forces her child into a "symbiosis" *he* (Greer's—1970, pp. 69-70—pronoun of choice in this discussion) cannot resist. Although dangerously powerful, this *motherself*—a term I use to denote how self-help authors encapsulate the activity of mothering into a concrete and (negatively) defining identity—is *not* seen as potential developed but, at its best, as good intentions gone seriously awry. Because she lacks good selfhood, the mother furiously seeks to control the identities of others. Both Friedan and Greer see mothering as a kind of forced transmission of bad selfhood from one person to another, like the spreading of a virus: The mother expresses her subconscious frustration with her thwarted selfhood by making the baby over in her own image, and deprives him or her of good selfhood, too.

Boys often escape suffocating mother bonds by gaining entry into the public (male) world of not-Mother. But when they do not, watch out! Both Friedan and Greer reaffirm conventional masculinity as central and necessary to men's self-actualization (perhaps, in part, to make their arguments more palatable to a male audience). In any case, too much motherself in a boy child results in his turning away in "hatred and revulsion for all women" (Friedan, 1963, p. 275); he is "kept from growing up, not sexually, but in all ways. . . . The shallow unreality, immaturity, promiscuity, lack of lasting human satisfaction that characterize the homosexual's life" are bequeathed him by his overconnection with The Mother (p. 276).[5]

Friedan and Greer do not devote much space to discussing lesbianism. Friedan sometimes uses "homosexual" as a gender-neutral label. She also writes at length about "sex-seeking" women and men, whose promiscuity "often seems to stem from an excessive mother-child attachment"; this immature "sex for lack of self," whether homosexual or heterosexual, can only compound the problems of which it is a symptom, Friedan feels (1963, p. 278). On a different note, Greer writes ruefully of adolescent girls leaving behind female-identified love relationships ("among the strongest and the most elevated that she will ever feel") to enter into the contrived and demeaning world of heterosexual practice:

> However innocently one girl caresses the body of another, she cannot escape the necessity of furtiveness which she intuits right from the birth of her love. Gradually she learns to consider her own feelings in the light of the common appraisal of them and to ridicule and disavow them. (Greer, 1970, p. 82)

Greer never overtly states that the denial of lesbian attachments is the first step in the process of becoming a "female eunuch," but the implications are evident. Mothers are indicted as maintenance workers for the villainous system, and Greer even cites her own mother as an example.

Oddly, though, Greer later dismisses Anne Koedt's assertions that lesbianism is a threat to patriarchy and a logical choice for feminists to make as "most peculiar." And anyway, Greer (1970) adds, "a clitoral orgasm with a full cunt is nicer than a clitoral orgasm with an empty one, as far as I can tell at least. In addition, a man is more than a dildo" (p. 326). Ultimately, despite her girlhood dalliances, Greer confirms heterosexual practice as the most sensible way of expressing sexual selfhood.

Sexuality, thus, is linked to selfhood—as a *variable* that Friedan and Greer see as being warped from its *true* manifestations (heterosexual) into deviance and perversion (Friedan) or a compensatory, less fulfilling activity (Greer's "tribadism"). Sexuality is but one manifestation of self-expression stunted by misguided mothering. The whole picture reiterates the same dynamics: The *core* self, the self's potential, is easily sent down the wrong path in Friedan and Greer's tales of why *socially constructed* womanhood ought to be revamped. Motherhood is depicted both as an empty identity and as such an overpowering female persona that its destructive capabilities are practically unstoppable.

The theme of mothers living vicariously through (hence) unindividuated daughters in a potentially endless cycle of damaging symbiosis continues in Nancy Friday's (1977) *My Mother/My Self* and Colette Dowling's (1981) *The Cinderella Complex.* Friday (1977) writes:

> Emotionally unseparated from mother, just as afraid as she was, we repeat the process with our own daughter. An unfortunate history, a way of growing up female that our society has amazingly left unchallenged. Being cute and helpless, clinging, clutching, holding on for dear life, becomes our method for survival—and ultimate defeat. (p. 61)

Both Dowling and Friday inject brief doses of constructionist thought into their psychoanalytic medicine, but not enough to enable either author to examine the ways in which the powerful profit from hegemonic patriarchy (otherwise Friday would not consider the situation she describes to be "amazingly . . . unchallenged").

Dowling (1981) writes of women made dependent on men by childhood incorporations of motherself. Women act out what Dowling takes to be a kind of internal self-destructing mechanism, "the desire to merge, symbiotically," which is rooted in "childhood and the deep desire for 'reengulfment' with the mother" (p. 145). Dowling reenacts Chodorow's (con)fusion of Freudian essentialism with a social constructionist explanation for the engendering of identity (see Chodorow, 1978). The child may be complicit, but mothers ought to know better, in Dowling's view—although how anyone could gain perspective in the weird circular world she presents remains a mystery. Sons are better able to escape than daughters because mothers allow boys more independence than girls. Heterosexuality becomes the stage for repeat performances of unhealthy "fusion." Dowling (1981) writes:

> Men, of course, are partly responsible for maintaining this bind, but women feel themselves in greater jeopardy and can be positively brilliant at keeping the balance struck. The more dependent they are, the more vigorous their efforts. . . . In varying degrees of extremeness, dependent wives try to construct of "family life" an elaborate social network, a web of children and relatives and carefully selected friends in which the husband is ensnared, a stiff and shiny-winged fly. (pp. 145-146)

Ironically, deprived of good selfhood, women become, like their dissatisfied mothers, omnivorously controlling.

Dowling (1981) recommends that women undertake intensive self-analysis, studying every detail of our personalities, "and your inconsistencies, if you track them down . . . will lead you to the mother lode of underlying conflict," she writes, no pun intended I presume (p. 218). Dowling alleges that diligent self-study will, like magic, pave the way to improved identity: "By facing and accepting these hidden parts of yourself, you will ultimately discover a new, integrated, and forceful self" (p. 219). We may shed our mothers, paradoxically, only by accepting them.

Because our mothers teach us how to interact, we are bound to repeat what we have learned in our involvements with others. We may be lucky, and Friday (1977) offers a rare acknowledgment that mothers *can* do good:

> We get our courage, our sense of self, the ability to believe we have value even when alone, to do our work, to love others, and to feel ourselves lovable from the "strength" of mother's love for us when we were infants. (p. 55)

The gist of Friday's book, however, makes it clear that if women do not emerge from childhood with such positive attributes, mothering is responsible. Basically, in these self-help authors' view, women absorb motherself, a symbiotic negating power, and replay the mother-pattern with everyone in their wake, especially our children and lovers.[6]

Robin Norwood (1985) popularizes the notion that heterosexual love ought to be seen as an addiction in *Women Who Love Too Much*. And Susan Forward and Joan Torres (1986) adjust the focus (and slightly shift the allocation of responsibility) for bad heterosexual relationships in *Men Who Hate Women and the Women Who Love Them*. "Whatever the apparent cause of death, I want to reiterate that loving too much can kill you," Norwood (1985, p. 218) writes; thus man addiction both literally and figuratively negates self-realization. Norwood prescribes a recovery program modeled on the Alcoholics Anonymous Twelve Step groups "for those of you who really do want to change *yourself*" (p. 219).

Motherself recurs in these texts as a powerful predictor of disastrous heterosexual relations. For example, although Forward and Torres (1986) write about misogyny, quite a bit of men's hatred can be traced back to all-powerful mothers of sons: "The suffocating mother . . . restrains and constricts her son's development by overcontrolling him and by making him feel inadequate and helpless," they write (p. 111); they reiterate Friedan's contention that motherself warps men, but show how mother-damaged boys may grow up to wreak heterosexual havoc instead of turning out to be gay women-haters.

As self-help authors invoke psychoanalytic theories to explain women's problems, they tend to efface the power of the social constructionist elements of their own arguments, and ultimately rely on what they see as fundamental universals, which, if not based in biology, may as well be because they are seen as so intractable. Lynn Chancer (1992) demonstrates how psychoanalytic principles may contribute to a sociological argument without undercutting it. She writes of gender relations as exemplifying sadomasochistic principles of (not necessarily sexual) domination and submission.

> Paradoxically . . . deference to other's power and ability to affect one's life may become
> the only means for forging a vicarious, if estranged, relationship to self. To undergo
> self-subordination may become habitual, ringing with the ambivalent comfort of the
> familiar and potentially rewardable. (Chancer, 1992, p. 27)

Most self-help authors describe heterosexual relations as psychologically sadomasochistic without expressly linking them "to a more generalized [socially
constructed] sadomasochistic dynamic," Chancer (1992, p. 29) writes. Emphases
on individual action to accomplish change do not confront the enormity of social
problems, such as the persistence of "male domination of institutions of coercive
power" (p. 30), Chancer shows.[7]

Lesbian Affirmations

Most best-selling self-help authors presume heterosexuality and, as I have
shown, confirm heterosexual interaction as essential—albeit often troubling—
self-making practice. Looking at self-help manuals geared to a lesbian audience
reveals an alternative approach to conceptualizing selfhood, but one still rooted
in the notion of realizing true identity or attaining the good self.

In their introduction to the first edition of *The Original Coming Out Stories,*
Penelope and Wolfe (1989) write that "however we have arrived at our Lesbian
identity, whatever labels we have donned and shed in the process, we have
eventually discovered ourselves in a society that denies our existence" (p. 5).
Lesbian women's quest for selfhood may be stymied, delayed, or derailed by
discrimination, fear of stigma, and pervasive heterosexism:

> The barriers to self-realization for the Lesbian are so thoroughly entrenched in and
> supported by contemporary social values that the conceptual leap from heterosexually-
> oriented definitions to womon-identified [sic] relationships requires a highly creative
> imagination and a will to self-determinism that many wimmin [sic] cannot yet conceive
> of. (p. 6)

The Original Coming Out Stories offers lesbians a method for self-affirmation
through the words of others: selfhood that one accomplishes "in a community of
wimmin" (Penelope & Wolfe, 1989, p. 4).

Guides for heterosexual women often warn against connection with or depend-
ency upon men; lesbian self-help authors are less wary of strong ties. For
instance, in *Lesbian Couples*, Clunis and Green (1988) write: "In large measure
it is in our relationships that we learn who we are. It is here that we discover the
joy and exhilaration of loving women; here that we experience the magic and
rightness of being lesbians" (p. 3). These lesbian self-help writers see lesbianism,
at least in part, as a political identity. They also describe overcoming internalized
homophobia as a requisite step in the self-realization process. Clunis and Green
(1988) write about maintaining nonsymbiotic connectedness: "To have intimacy,
each of us must allow her partner to be herself"; we must protect and respect "the
personal boundary" of another, "the imaginary bubble that surrounds each of us
at our core . . . [that] contains our sense of self" (pp. 29-30). Women's boundaries, and thus our identities, may have been "interfered with by [childhood]

experiences such as physical abuse, sexual abuse," and so forth (Clunis & Green, 1988, p. 32); and detrimental influences mean unhealthy self-development, a damaged core. One possible result may be that women look to relationships to fill the gaps in our broken boundary bubbles. Clunis and Green write that the circle of self must be restored for relationships to work: "Shared intimacy . . . requires an equitable power balance" (p. 33).

Clunis and Green borrow from the language of the codependency and recovery trend in self-help writing and cite Janet Woititz (1983) and Claudia Black (1990), well-known recovery writers.[8] The resulting advice is similar to that offered by self-help writers steeped in psychoanalysis. Clunis and Green (1988) claim—as is popular in the recovery strain of self-help—that "although the term *recovery* has come to be associated with addiction, all of us, in a sense, are recovering from something" (p. 190). Recovery means, basically, rescuing one's self from the past: preserving the core and ridding one's self of the deleterious residue of traumatic experience and/or bad parenting. Despite Clunis and Green's insular psychological focus, *Lesbian Couples* still delivers somewhat socially conscious advice, although it lacks the political edge that recurs in the narratives Penelope and Wolfe have compiled in *The Original Coming Out Stories*. Clunis and Green (1988) describe friendship networks and lesbian communities as sources of "support" and "nurturance" for individual lesbians rather than as actions against patriarchal oppression, while they also acknowledge implicitly that such unions have political power: "The heterosexual world is not going to build a community for us. We need to do it for ourselves" (p. 111).

These two popular books for lesbian readers present a view of selfhood as growing out of (core) lesbian identity. Penelope and Wolfe's coming out story-tellers don't invoke the recovery movement, but they write about recovering or reconstituting selfhood, saving and protecting lesbian selfhood from the hostile reproaches of a heterosexist culture. Writers describe their discomfort with societal norms about gender and sexuality. The narratives are politically charged; realizing lesbian wholeness means engaging in resistance. The writers allude to, but do not name, a core self; they carefully avoid any biological essentialist claims abut sexual orientation. Lesbian identities seem to always have *been* there, and yet the process of self-creation in which the writers are all engaged enables the naming of past existence as "lesbian." Unlike Clunis and Green's discussion of selfhood, here the core may be read as deconstructed by the recurrent descriptions of the *process* of coming out, the process of achieving lesbian selfhood.

Saving the Child

Gloria Steinem's (1992) *Revolution From Within: A Book of Self-Esteem* exemplifies the reification of selfhood as redeemable, as innocent and childlike, as the requisite quest for everyone who wants to live a happy life or to accomplish social change of any kind. The book opens with a "Buddhist Aphorism": "You have come here to find what you already have." Steinem appropriates a variety of philosophical maxims from around the world, crafting an emphatic multicultural definition of self that knows no boundaries and can seemingly break through any barriers, solve any problems:

> The idea that self-knowledge was God-knowledge . . . was central to the origins of Hinduism, and thus to Buddhism, Sufism, and the many other religions that sprang from it. Self-realization became a goal placed over . . . everything. (p. 32)

> "When we realize the universal Self in us," ask the Upanishads defiantly, "when and what may anybody fear and worship?" (p. 33)

> "If you bring forth what is within you, what you bring forth will save you" . . . Jesus, *The Gnostic Gospels.* (p. 153)

Steinem (1992) seeks to synthesize the personal with the political; she recounts her own experiences to show that too much outer-directed political activism led her to neglect herself. A transforming therapeutic experience reunited her with—yes—her inner child, and helped her to regain what she now considers the cornerstone of social change, her self-esteem. "Self-esteem starts out as a personal blessing, but it becomes nothing less than an evolutionary force" (p. 322). Past selves must be integrated into the new (good) self: "We are so many selves. . . . What brings together these ever-shifting selves of infinite reactions and returnings is this: There is always one true inner voice" (p. 323). Evil becomes a shield people use against each other when our true inner voices have been silenced—trapped under unhappy childhoods, insecurities, and so forth. Layers of false self must be shed in one's self-renewal project; Steinem encourages readers to make haste in forging an improved identity. For instance, she includes a "meditation guide" in her book to help readers meet our inner children:

> Invite the child to be with you—but respect the child's response. . . . Explain that this is a special place where you do only what you wish. . . . Try waiting until the child speaks to you—and if the child isn't ready yet, just stay there quietly. . . . As your time together ends, remember that whatever you have thought, learned, or felt here is now a part of you. The child is . . . part of you. You will come to know, trust and help each other. (p. 367)

In Steinem's portrayal, we can go far beyond the analytic reappraisal of our pasts proffered as examples of self-revival, as in the coming out stories. We can actually conjure up our past selves and heal their wounds to gain ultimate selfhood. When we achieve the feats of self-integration and self-esteem, we will be unfettered in our quest to save the world from inequality, discrimination, poverty—problems that are denied a social dimension when Steinem describes them as initiated by individuals who do not enjoy positive self-esteem.

Revolution From Within did not overwhelm reviewers with its single-handed resolution of dilemmas of the self and the universe. In an afterword to the paperback edition, Steinem (1992) recounts the bad press the book received, discusses her reactions to it, and reaffirms her "radical thesis"—"that systems of authority undermine our self authority to secure obedience, thus self-esteem becomes the root of revolution" (p. 327)—with the laudatory testimony of lay readers and "less prestigious publications" (p. 328).[9]

In *Sisters of the Yam* (published the same year as Steinem's rebuttal to the critics who sneered at her for writing a self-help book), bell hooks (1993) writes that she has "tremendous respect for this literature [self-help] whatever its limitations" (p. 4). She affirms Steinem's "radical thesis," that self-esteem is the necessary foundation for social action, writing: "We cannot fully create effective movements for social change if individuals struggling for that change are not also self-actualized or working toward that end" (pp. 4-5).

Like Steinem, hooks often echoes earlier self-help works, discussing problems such as overly authoritarian and overinvesting mothers, addiction and codependency, body image, sexuality, and spirituality. hooks's book is different because hooks specifically addresses black women. Also, despite her uncharacteristic descent into self-help lingo and her endorsement of self-centered strategies for problem solving, hooks repeatedly stresses the structural nature of the problems she discusses and endorses radical societal change along with the self-work she suggests.

For instance, in her chapter on sexuality, "Moved by Passion," hooks (1993) writes, "All our eroticisms have been shaped within the culture of domination" (p. 114). Many African Americans grow up without enough touching—parents deny children sensual pleasure. hooks provides an anecdote: A mother reprimands her little girl for wanting to touch merchandise in a shop. The mother fears other people will think her daughter is stealing. hooks (1993) links this mother's restraint to general sensual repression: "Taught not to reach out and touch objects in the world that invite interest and bring pleasure, many black children are socialized to think that this desire is 'bad' and brings punishment" (p. 117). Sexuality is enacted—as are all modes of expression—in a social world warped by the racist domination of whites over people of color, and by the sexist domination of men over women. Thus, black women have quite often been denied life-affirming erotic experiences; not touching is a defense mechanism against a powerful reality of denial and abuse. hooks (1993) writes: "Should we be surprised that a people whose bodies have been perpetually used, exploited and objectified should now seek to turn flesh into armor?" (p. 119). She encourages black women to strive for "sacred sexuality":

> Recovering a healthy passion, black women discover that we can pause in the midst of everyday activities and feel again the sense of wonder, of pleasure that we are flesh, that we are one with the universe, that there is a life-force within us charged with erotic power that can transform and heal our lives. (p. 127)

More emphatically than Steinem, hooks connects selfhood with social change while asserting, as Steinem does, that a common internal good self exists for all of us ("a life-force within us . . . that can . . . heal our lives"). hooks's book, like Steinem's, seems grounded in some kind of spiritual awakening; an optimistic zest recurs throughout *Sisters of the Yam* that contrasts with the sharp social criticism for which hooks has become well known (see, e.g., *Ain't I a Woman*, 1981; *Black Looks*, 1992). She urges black women to eschew bitterness and "practice forgiveness" to "cleanse our spirit of negative clutter and leave our souls free" (hooks, 1993, p. 171). hooks, like Steinem, sees properly realized selfhood leading directly to godliness:

Living a life in the spirit, a life where our habits of being enable us to hear our inner voices to comprehend reality with both our hearts and our minds, puts us in touch with divine essence. Practicing the art of loving is one way we sustain contact with our "higher self." (hooks, 1993, p. 185)

Through divine selfhood, through benevolent, bitterness-free and all-encompassing generous love, "black women have the potential to be a community of faith that acts collectively to transform our world" (p. 190), hooks concludes.

Many self-help writers urge readers to find ourselves through a spiritual quest, recommending a variety of New Age practices such as guided meditations or affirmations, and sometimes proselytizing the AA credo that one must recognize a higher power as a basis for self-formulation. Readers are told we have ultimate responsibility for realizing ourselves *and* that we are powerless to achieve good selfhood unless we recognize higher powers.

Autonomy, or independence, becomes a method for achieving individualistic identity: This is the American way. Yet, simultaneously, women are pulled in another direction by how we have been taught to "do gender," to borrow West and Zimmerman's (1987) compelling phrase, and connectedness (women's supposed forte) stands in dualistic opposition to self-realization in this culture. Steinem and hooks attempt to bridge this gap by positing a spiritually pure selfhood as the basis for any meaningful community.

Conclusion: Self-Consuming Selves

The steps toward self-knowledge (and thus self-improvement) advocated by self-help authors for women have changed very little since Friedan published *The Feminine Mystique* in 1963: Women have been encouraged to place less value in our involvements with others and to pay more attention to our own personal development. In American culture, selling masquerades as service, self-help books propose to help women find out about ourselves, to teach us effective ways of being for our own good (which we cannot yet know, being incomplete selves).

Self-acceptance becomes a paradoxical basis for accomplishing change. Identity becomes a messy compilation of past experiences that need to be sorted through and reprioritized; this activity will—allegedly—show women who we really are. Self-help authors urge women to make ourselves into objects to be scrutinized, worked into shape, remade (into whatever ideal is prescribed). Through consumption, we take action; we buy ourselves better selves. Christopher Lasch (1984) writes that uncertainty about identity is part of participating in consumer culture; it makes women make ourselves into commodities "offered up for consumption on the open market" (pp. 30-31). Self-help teaches women marketing strategies to use on ourselves.

The imperative to self-promote, to do interior remodeling, conjures up images from girls' and women's magazines. Take limp, stringy, greasy hair, add product X, and make it full-bodied and luxuriant. See the transformation of a grubby fat woman—via diet pills or exercise machine—into a slender fashion plate. Self-help

literature offers a psychic makeover. Take alienated selfhood—pernicious nega-
tivity—read a book, and achieve glorious, beautiful, even world-changing, true
identity.[10]

The message being conveyed by media that tell women how to make ourselves
over is not covert: Self-help books, magazines, television, and advertisements
all encourage women to see ourselves as mutable, correctable, a product of
various influences in constant flux. And yet, underneath, there we are: There we
have always been. We are like Dorothy discovering the secret of her magic shoes
at the end of *The Wizard of Oz*. Kansas was waiting inside us the whole time, or
something like that: The true selves we read about in self-help books are very
reassuringly midwestern-white-bread American in style. (Even hooks's forgiv-
ing spiritualized black womanliness renounces confrontational power because it
leads to bitterness.) The new selves are nonthreatening, nonexotic, kindly,
innocent—just like Dorothy, who prevailed despite all the possible pollutants
she encountered on *her* journey. In that tale of self-discovery, experts compete:
The wizard is shown up by Glinda the good witch for wanting to do Dorothy's
self-work for her (telling her *he* will bring her back to Kansas). Like self-help
authors everywhere, Glinda tells Dorothy she had to find out the secret of
self-return (nostos, anagnorisis) on her own, but then the good witch herself tells
Dorothy what to do (click her heels . . .). We find ourselves: We are returned to
ourselves via expert insights, and part of the task is affirming that we have chosen
to attend to the correct expert rather than the faux wizards.

Wendy Kaminer writes that the self-help world's insistence on readers' reliance on experts and "higher powers" is a toned-down example of what goes on
in cults, when people abdicate responsibility for their own actions. Thus, to
Kaminer (1992), self-help literature encourages intellectual laziness, makes
self-actualization into a farce. "Reading itself," she writes, "is becoming a way
out of thinking" (p. 8). Studies of actual—as opposed to academic or journalistic—readers, and of cultural consumers of a variety of media, show that whether
or not Kaminer has accurately described the intent of self-help authors, those
who use self-help books for their own personal edification (as opposed to critics)
do not merely uncritically, unthinkingly, slurp up what they find within its pages.

Reader- and viewer-oriented studies reveal that women, in particular, resist
some cultural scripts while accepting others, even in seemingly contradictory
ways (see, e.g., Brown, 1990; Grodin, 1991; Lewis, 1990; Press, 1991; Radway,
1984; Simonds, 1992). Grodin (1991) writes, for example:

> The women I interviewed state that a major reason for reading self-help is to establish
> autonomy. Yet, readers also have a sense of the self as socially constructed through
> contact with others who have similar problems. Their sense of self pivots upon a desire
> for autonomy and a desire for connection to a world beyond the self. (p. 416)

Reading, then, may be a quest for self *and* other (autonomy) as well as a quest
for self *through* other (community).

In opposition to Kaminer's assertion that self-help media deify authority,
Mimi White (1992) writes about talk shows as therapeutic discourse that verge
on postmodern decenteredness of authority, although "the process of confession

is linked in its discursive archaeology to the Western self, with all its integrity and sincerity, maintaining the dichotomies between mind and body, animal and human, public and private, nature and culture, men and women" (p. 23). I believe that what happens in self-help books—and self-help culture, as a whole, including television talk shows—reveals a schizophrenic decenteredness (which may be the same thing as unself-conscious postmodernism!): Oppositional relationships and dichotomous theories are maintained and deconstructed at the same time. We consume ourselves; we are consumed. We start all over again.

Jane Flax (1990) urges feminist theorists to ally ourselves with postmodernist philosophers and to "throw into radical doubt" ideas about knowledge, reason, and selfhood originating in the Enlightenment and still pervasive in American culture today, such as belief in the "the existence of a stable, coherent self" (p. 41). The self ought to be seen as process, and gender as a defining (but not static or universally equivalent) element; in Elspeth Probyn's (1993) words: "The self is an ensemble of techniques and practices enacted on an everyday basis and . . . it entails the necessary problematization of these practices" (p. 2).

Feminists have long argued that femininity and women's activities are a social construction, the result of inequitable gender relations, and, thus, women would be well advised *not* to posit notions of unsocially constructed selves. Flax (1990) writes:

> We cannot simultaneously claim (a) that the mind, the self, and knowledge are socially constituted and that what we can know depends upon our social practices and contexts and (b) that feminist theory [or any philosophy] can uncover the truth of the whole once and for all. (p. 48)

What Flax warns against is what the self-help authors I've discussed want to do: They want to combine a social constructionist argument with absolutist notions of selfhood, spirituality, knowledge, and power. Women may feel, as self-help narratives illustrate, that we *are* diminished, even made invisible to ourselves, by relationships or situations. But remedying our problems cannot mean we are restored to some omnipresent core self, made one with universal knowledge, or reunited with pristinely preserved "inner children." Ameliorating the ties that bind us into identities we find unsatisfactory, even abhorrent, can mean that we *change,* that we become different than what we were before, that we are agents in socially grounded self-construction. Finally, though, to change what is objectionable within our culture, we must do more than revamp ourselves.

Notes

1. Obviously, there would not be agreement among all feminists that all these writers are feminist; some feminists may even consider some to be antifeminist. I will not engage in such a debate here, nor will I devote any space to establishing a definition or definitions of feminism. I do believe that these writers all support at least the values of liberal feminism, and that adherence to liberal values frames their notions of selfhood and self-help.

2. For a systematic examination of the genre of best-selling self-help literature on psychological and sexual self-improvement, see Simonds (1992, chaps. 5 and 6).

3. Thanks to Jill Marsh, at Charis Books, for recommending popular advice books outside the mainstream self-help genre.

4. Thanks to students in my graduate seminar, "Women and American Popular Culture" in fall 1993, for these speculations about why feminist writers have embraced self-help.

5. Greer (1970) adds anti-Semitism to her homophobic attack, explaining boys' and girls' destruction when overmothered:

> What happens to the Jewish boy who never manages to escape the tyranny of his mother is exactly what happens to every girl whose upbringing is "normal." She is a female faggot. Like the male faggots she lives her life in a pet about guest lists and sauce béarnaise, except when she is exercising by divine maternal right the same process that destroyed her lusts and desires upon the lusts and desires of her children. (p. 74)

6. The flip side of this pattern—the neglectful mother—is also described in self-help literature, including the texts I've been discussing. She seems to be less pervasive as a societal problem, but plays an equally important role in making identity formation problematic for her children, according to self-help authors.

7. Not all self-help authors work to uncover the psychological roots of behavior. *You Just Don't Understand* by Deborah Tannen (1990) stands apart as a book relatively free of the psychological dramas I have been illuminating thus far. Tannen focuses on one method of self-presentation, conversation, and its relevance to gender. But Tannen presents the power imbalances in women's and men's relationships as benign; in fact, she rarely mentions power, although she treats it euphemistically in a variety of ways. Tannen asserts that miscommunication in conversation results from disparate gender training, which creates an "asymmetry" between men and women; as she puts it, "they are tuned to different frequencies" (p. 288). Despite the deeply ingrained trouble between couples that Tannen reports, everyone seems to be well meaning when she reveals what couples *really* intend to say: Tannen reduces power imbalances to misunderstandings. Men and women are simply inclined to use different conversational gender-based "styles."

8. Black (1990) has written a self-help manual specifically for gays and lesbians, titled *Double Duty,* in which she writes that lesbians and gay men experience "Dual Identity," which "often magnifies one's Adult Child issues" (p. 45). The task of the Adult Child, as Black defines it, is to restore the "inner child," who "needs to be recognized, validated, and healed" (p. 1). Lesbians' and gay men's task is complicated mainly because of homophobia; "When one can get beyond the societal fears and stigmas, being gay or lesbian becomes as normal to the homosexual as being heterosexual is to those who are straight" (p. 117). Black adheres to a "liberal humanist" approach, which, as explicated by Kitzinger (1987), paints lesbianism and gayness as an individualistic condition, and thus strips it of its political potential.

9. As she has done throughout the text, she reinscribes herself in the afterword as just a regular Glo—friend to a rainbow coalition of ordinary Americans who have been transformed by her cogent advice and who flock to tell her so. Critics, as Steinem portrays them, are clearly mired in sardonic condescension and snooty intellectualism; they scorn her, and because she is so popular with the common folk, they must scorn them by association.

10. Susan Bordo (1993) presents a compelling analysis of how current cultural images shape women's *bodies,* both imagistically and in reality; she links eating disorders to the requirements of a consumer culture that also stresses self-control and self-denial, especially for women.

References

Black, C. (1990). *Double duty gay or lesbian: Dual dynamics within the chemically dependent home.* New York: Ballantine.

Bordo, S. (1993). *Unbearable weight: Feminism, Western culture, and the body.* Berkeley: University of California Press.

Brown, M. E. (Ed.). (1990). *Television and women's culture: The politics of the popular.* London: Sage.

Chancer, L. (1992). *Sadomasochism in everyday life: The dynamics of power and powerlessness.* New Brunswick, NJ: Rutgers University Press.

Chodorow, N. (1978). *The reproduction of mothering: Psychoanalysis and the sociology of gender.* Berkeley: University of California Press.

Clunis, M., & Green, G. D. (1988). *Lesbian couples: Creating healthy relationships for the '90s.* Seattle: Seal.

Dowling, C. (1981). *The Cinderella complex.* New York: Pocket Books.

Flax, J. (1990). Postmodernism and gender relations in feminist theory. In L. J. Nicholson (Ed.), *Feminism/postmodernism* (pp. 39-62). New York: Routledge.

Forward, S., & Torres, J. (1986). *Men who hate women and the women who love them: When loving hurts and you don't know why.* New York: Bantam.

Friday, N. (1977). *My mother/my self: The daughter's search for identity.* New York: Dell.

Friedan, B. (1963). *The feminine mystique.* New York: Dell.

Greer, G. (1970). *The female eunuch.* New York: Bantam.

Grodin, D. (1991). The interpreting audience: The therapeutics of self-help book reading. *Critical Studies in Mass Communication, 8,* 404-420.

hooks, b. (1981). *Ain't I a woman: Black women and feminism.* Boston: South End.

hooks, b. (1992). *Black looks: Race and representation.* Boston: South End.

hooks, b. (1993). *Sisters of the yam: Black women and self-recovery.* Boston: South End.

Kaminer, W. (1992). *I'm dysfunctional, you're dysfunctional: The recovery movement and other self-help fashions.* Reading, MA: Addison-Wesley.

Kitzinger, C. (1987). *The social construction of lesbianism.* London: Sage.

Lasch, C. (1984). *The minimal self: Psychic survival in troubled times.* New York: Norton.

Lewis, L. A. (1990). *Gender politics and MTV: Voicing the difference.* Philadelphia: Temple University Press.

Norwood, R. (1985). *Women who love too much: When you keep wishing and hoping he'll change.* New York: Pocket Books.

Penelope, J., & Wolfe, S. J. (Eds.). (1989). *The original coming out stories* (expanded ed.). Freedom, CA: Crossing Press.

Press, A. L. (1991). *Women watching television: Gender, class and generation in the American television experience.* Philadelphia: University of Pennsylvania Press.

Probyn, E. (1993). *Sexing the self: Gendered positions in cultural studies.* London: Routledge.

Radway, J. A. (1984). *Reading the romance: Women, patriarchy, and popular literature.* Chapel Hill: University of North Carolina Press.

Simonds, W. (1992). *Women and self-help culture: Reading between the lines.* New Brunswick, NJ: Rutgers University Press.

Steinem, G. (1992). *Revolution from within: A book of self-esteem.* Boston: Little, Brown.

Tannen, D. (1990). *You just don't understand: Women and men in conversation.* New York: Ballantine.

West, C., & Zimmerman, D. (1987). Doing gender. *Gender and Society, 1,* 125-151.

White, M. (1992). *Tele-advising: Therapeutic discourse in American television.* Chapel Hill: University of North Carolina Press.

Woititz, J. (1983). *Adult children of alcoholics.* Deerfield Beach, FL: Health Communications.

3

Terms of Enmeshment:
The Cultural Construction of
the Mother-Daughter Relationship

Suzanna Danuta Walters

In a film called *'night, Mother*, a mother is trying to prevent her thirtyish daughter from shooting herself. During the climactic scene, the mother, clutching her breast and trying to comprehend her daughter's decision, screams in anguish, "I don't know what I did but I know that I did it!" In an otherwise forgettable film, these few words stand out as poignant and resonate with what we take to be the "truth" about relationships between mothers and daughters. For, whatever else occurs between these two women during the evening of the daughter's death, we know—like Mother—that somehow, in some way, she *was* responsible.

In a world saturated, perhaps even dominated, by the image, it is close to impossible to understand any given interaction without reference to the multitude of mass-produced images that often seem like only so much background noise to the "real" business of "social forces." Mothers and daughters come to understand their relationship not only through the exigencies of family life, economic survival, and social policies but through the systems of representation and cultural production that help to give shape and meaning to that relationship. For the relationship of mother and daughter does not simply materialize onto the social field, nor is it produced only through the machinations of explicit social policies and social theories. Rather, the mother-daughter relationship is formed, at least in part, by the cultural images that give it meaning. Indeed, when we go to the movies, read a novel, see a television sitcom, or open the pages of a women's magazine, we are presented with vivid and often contradictory images that provide us with a variety of messages concerning our behavior and self-image as mothers and daughters. Films like *Terms of Endearment*, television programs like *Maude*, and popular books like *My Mother/My Self* (Friday, 1977) furnish us with examples of mother-daughter interactions that contribute to our understanding of our own affiliations.

The terms we use to describe the mother-daughter relationship are inextricably linked to a psychological framework: *bonding, symbiosis, separation, differentiation, autonomy.* But the mother-daughter relationship needs to be described, understood, and analyzed in fully social and historical terms. The ways we understand and talk about mothers and daughters are structured by our own unconscious acceptance of certain concepts and paradigms that are not innocent

30

but are, in fact, often destructive to the possibility of mother-daughter intimacy and continuity. The themes that we take to represent psychological truths about the relationship need to be seriously and rigorously questioned; they need to be deconstructed to uncover and reveal the ideological agendas inscribed within many commonsense understandings of this relationship.

Many of these "commonsense" ideas are manifested in popular culture, particularly in the narrative forms of popular culture such as film, literature, and television. How the relationship is represented there will tell us a great deal about how we think about the relationship in our own everyday lives, for there is no greater index of practical knowledge than popular culture. This is not to say that popular images of mothers and daughters are a simple reflection of already existing ideas that come from psychology or sociology. Rather, these popular images both reflect and construct; they *reproduce* existing mainstream ideologies as well as help to *produce* those very ideologies. And those psychological "truths" are themselves made apparent to the population through the mediation of popular forms: If we live in a Freudian culture, it is not because most people have studied Freud but because the institutions of cultural production have so absorbed Freudian thinking that it has become part of the foundation of how we tell a story or perceive a character's motivation.

What is important to recognize is that the ideas we have with us today about mothers and daughters (for example, that conflict between mothers and daughters is inevitable and in fact essential to the full development of the daughter into an adult; that too much closeness between mother and daughter is unhealthy beyond a certain age, and signals "immaturity" in the daughter and "clinging" or "possessiveness" or "overprotectiveness" or "living through" on the part of the mother; that separation from the mother, both literally and developmentally, is the hallmark of mature individuation) were not always with us. Ideas about "good" mother-daughter relationships have changed throughout history, and it is important not only to recognize those changes but to see how those different ideas relate to significant changes and developments in the society at large.

This study starts from a conviction that we live in a society that, through the mechanisms of the mass media as well as through the more traditional agents of socialization (family, church, education, politics), compresses the mother-daughter relationship into the narrow vision of psychology, framing it within the dichotomous boundaries of "bonding" and "separation" and thus actively constructing a relationship to be inherently conflictual, forcing women apart and rendering this prophesy self-fulfilling. This can have—and has had—a profound impact on women's sense of self. To the extent that a woman understands her identity as necessarily constructed in opposition to the identity of her mother, she will be in conflict about the very role she will someday probably assume. Thus, she becomes more vulnerable to larger, more socially inscribed messages of female self-deprecation (e.g., the dichotomous formations endemic to a patriarchal society, such as that between motherhood and career, between family and public life). This dichotomy structures, in various guises throughout the life cycle, an ambivalent self that underlies much of what has come to be identified as "feminine."

The narrative of mothers and daughters has largely been portrayed in terms of conflict and the ambivalent struggle of separation. Indeed, just a brief glance at popular images of mothers and daughters would bear this out. We might find Bette Davis as the dominated daughter in *Now, Voyager* struggling to overcome her mother, the incarnation of repression and sexual denial. It is no accident, of course, that Bette is "saved" by the dual efforts of a male psychiatrist and a dashing lover. Or there is the classic film noir *Mildred Pierce*, where the desire of Mildred (Joan Crawford) to provide for her daughter backfires because she is, well, too self-sacrificing. Or there is Lana Turner as the perennially guilty mother in *Imitation of Life* whose adolescent daughter fancies her lover while Mom is away making a film, thus indirectly chastising her mother for her neglect. Lana finally sees the light when an angry Sandra Dee tells her that nothing can replace a mother's love and round-the-clock attention—not horses, or cars, or the finest education. Lana weeps, quits the world of work, goes to her daughter's graduation, and marries the simple but decent man of her dreams.

In the dubiously "postfeminist" 1980s, we have Shirley MacLaine and Debra Winger in *Terms of Endearment* as a mother and daughter locked in a repetitive cycle of mutual need and denial, resolved only by the daughter's tragic death and relinquishment of *her* children to her newly maternal Mom, already "saved" by the lecherous but loving spaceman, played by Jack Nicholson; or the eerie recent film *The Stepfather*, where a single mother and her daughter living without a man become perfect targets for a crazed killer stepfather; or the 1990s tell-all Hollywood saga *Postcards from the Edge*, in which former movie queen Mom virtually causes her cynical daughter's drug overdose by her early maternal neglect and bossy grandstanding.

These are but a few of the mainstream images of mothers and daughters in our culture. The message, contradictory as it sometimes is, comes through loud and clear: Too much mother love can lead to symbiosis; too little to maternal deprivation. The daughter's mandate to separate from her mother is represented not as a natural process of growth and maturation but as a wrenching experience that must be gone through to reach the "other side" of men and marriage. It is no accident that in almost every mother-daughter film where this struggle for autonomy is the central theme, a man (either in the figure of a lover, future husband, or, more ominously, a psychiatrist) frees the daughter from the maternal grasp and leads her into the world of adult femininity. The option presented to these fictional daughters is to sink even further into the domestic and nonsexual world of their mothers or to fly bravely from the maternal nest into the waiting arms of a strong man.

In almost all cultural representations, mothers and daughters are caught in a double bind. If mother does too much for her daughter, if she is self-sacrificing, she will spoil the daughter and lose her own independence and vitality; if she does too little, or is too involved with her own adult life, she is neglectful and damages her daughter. The scenario is typically one of a battle, with a necessary and unambiguous victor.

In what follows, I briefly trace the history of representations of the mother-daughter relationship from the 1930s to more contemporary images, focusing particularly on the shift from the 1930s to the postwar years, as these years offer the most vivid example of a "sea-change" in cultural constructions of the mother-daughter relationship.[1]

From Sacrificial *Stella* to Maladjusted *Mildred*: De(class)ifying Mothers and Daughters

Representations of the mother-daughter relationship have survived many permutations to arrive at the classic juncture of blame and guilt. Yet it is possible to locate a specific moment when this new paradigm of inevitable conflict took hold in the popular imagination. Here I will focus primarily on two films, *Stella Dallas*, made in 1937, and *Mildred Pierce*, made in 1945, to examine the shift in discourses of the mother-daughter relationship from the context of Depression-era America to a nation absorbed with the war effort and already deeply concerned about the implications of Rosie the Riveter.

This shift—from a sacrificial model of mothering a daughter to a model of psychopathology—speaks to an increasing anxiety toward the end of the war around the role of women, and the nature and status of "mothering" in a postwar society. Many historians have argued, convincingly, that the backlash that followed women's participation in the labor force had already begun midwar, and that ideologies of maternal neglect and the deprivation caused by working mothers began almost as soon as women entered the wartime economy. The change in representation also signals a broader postwar desire to move away from class-based discourses (so prevalent during the 1930s) and toward a sanitized version of the pluralistic American dream, replete with suburban idylls, postwar consumerism, and a rejuvenated familialism.

The film *Stella Dallas* signifies an end to a *social* representation of family relationships. Instead, what we increasingly see is the personalization and psychologization of the mother-daughter relationship, removing that interaction from the larger field of social and class relations, a field that continued to shape cultural production as late as the 1937 "weepie" *Stella Dallas*.[2]

In this film, Stella (played by Barbara Stanwyck), a fast-talking, upwardly mobile working-class girl from a small New England mill town, marries the upper-class and correct Steven Dallas. The birth of their baby girl, Laurel, signifies the real beginning of the narrative. Stella's husband quickly separates from the family in exasperation over her refusal to become appropriately upper class, and Laurel is brought up by her mother, although the father remains very much on the periphery.

Through a series of events, Stella "recognizes" that she is inadequate to bring up a "proper" girl and concocts an elaborate scheme to give Laurel away into the bourgeois family of her husband and his new wife. In the final scene, remembered by many spectators as both compelling and disconcerting, Stella stands in the rain outside the house where her daughter is being married, looking in on the scene of wedded bliss.

The mother-daughter theme in *Stella Dallas* is worked through, or intersects with, a pronounced class theme, something that should not be surprising given the Depression era in which it was filmed, an era when questions of equality, class mobility, and governmental responsibility came to the fore. It is this linking—of class and motherhood—that has disappeared in more recent films, as the mother-daughter relationship has increasingly come under the master discourse of popular psychology.

The central conflict in the film is not so much between Stella's desire to be a "woman" (defined as sexual, active, free, and so on) and her duties as a mother, but precisely between two different sensibilities about mothering itself: care and love as differentiated from social access and mobility. Stella explicitly resists the kind of "appropriate mothering" that her husband and the medical establishment try to force her into. In an early scene, when she returns from the hospital, she refuses to allow her maternity to be pathologized and it is in the taking control of her own maternity that Stella's real transgression can be seen:

> Why is it that doctors and nurses and husbands always seem to think they know more about this maternity business. Don't you think a mother learns anything in that little room they wheel her into? Or is that just a kindergarten class? Let me tell ya something, I picked up quite a little experience in that room, and it wasn't out of books either. Experience.

Here Stella, as her daughter does later in the film, validates her own *experience* of birth and mothering over the upper-class learning and establishment ways. So the first conflict we have in the film is a conflict between Stella's version of mothering ("experience," she tells us) and the version promoted by the nurse and her husband (an interesting alliance of male interests and the pathologizing medical establishment).

Laurel mirrors Stella's emphasis on everyday (coded here as both maternal and working-class) experience when she rushes home to her mother after she hears of Stella's sacrificial plan to "give her up" to Mrs. Morrison, the soon-to-be new wife of Steven: "But good times oh they aren't what make you belong, it's other kinds of times, it's when you've cried together and lived through things together, that's when you seem to love the most . . . it's different." Laurel here validates the routine, commonplace events in domestic life she shares with her mother. Yet "everyday life," familiarity, continuity lose out to social ascendancy. By discrediting that everydayness, the film invalidates women's social reality. Experience loses out to progress, familiarity to newness, the prosaic to the novel.

Nevertheless, we are invited to empathize with Stella's anguish and pain when she realizes that it was her lower-classness (Stella as embarrassment) that led Laurel to insist on leaving a resort where Stella had proved to be an embarrassment. One of the most poignant moments between mother and daughter occurs during the train ride home, a moment of mutuality, a glimpse of a *shared* love—a love that is nevertheless doomed as Stella begins to see herself through her daughter's eyes and see the social situation as insurmountable.

The daughter feels the mother's hurt, the mother translates her own hurt into the implications for her daughter: The sacrifice theme is initiated. But it is also at this moment, the moment of their greatest shared pain (for themselves, for each other), that they seem most intimate, most deeply connected. The kind of image seen here—the soft music, the daughter stroking the head of the mother lovingly, the daughter's head on the mother's shoulder as they sleep together on the train bunk—creates a mise-en-scène usually reserved for lovers.

Not coincidentally, it is following this intimate love scene between mother and daughter that the mother's attempt to propel the daughter into the father's world is launched. Stella must try several times; her daughter will not leave willingly. To do so would render the daughter less likable and the relationship itself more conflictual, thus deemphasizing the sacrifice theme and replacing it with a more tortured, psychodrama motif.

The mother in *Stella Dallas* can't win: She is bad because she wanted more (whether some form of sexuality, or to retain her class identity, or merely to have an intimate and passionate life with her daughter), but good because she didn't get it. The triumph in her eyes in the last scene is the triumph of sacrifice, a dubious triumph indeed.

By the time we get to the 1940s, the mildness of women's magazine articles and the gentleness of the maternal melodrama begin to recede. Forties films were either filled with wartime propaganda or, as the war began to come to a close, filled with the urgent need to return women to acceptable postwar family life.

As early as 1942, a year that witnessed the publication of Philip Wylie's *Generation of Vipers*, one of the most virulent attacks on women in the past 50 years, we get a very different type of representation of mothers and daughters than in the prewar years. Wylie's book remains one of the most astoundingly misogynist tomes in recent memory. His basic thesis—that America was being weakened from within by a horde of omnipotent "moms" who turned men into sniveling company dolts and women into awful moms-in-training—found a receptive audience in the mid- to late 1940s.

In 1945, another important mother-daughter film—with another powerful female star at its helm—emerges to complete the shift from benign to aggressive, from sacrificial to overpowering, from class conflict to psychopathology. *Mildred Pierce* operates very much within the "back to the kitchen" mode of the late-war and immediate postwar years. It is a harsh condemnation of working women. More precisely, it is a condemnation of working *mothers*, for it was this new labor pool (white, middle-class mothers) that provoked the greatest outcry during and after the war. Even the war propaganda in the women's magazines, while urging women to work as a patriotic duty, constructed a strict hierarchy of admissible female labor, with single women at the top of the list and mothers with young children at the bottom, as a kind of "last resort."

It is also a film about maternal sacrifice; as Mildred tells us in no uncertain terms, "I've done without a lot of things—including happiness sometimes—because I wanted her to have everything." Yet, while Stella's sacrifice pays off (Laurel marries the man of her dreams and enters into the upper-class world), Mildred's sacrifice not only backfires but is seen itself as slightly unhealthy. What was once a sign of love and devotion is now a sign of smothering, overinvolvement, and, ultimately, pathology.

The way these two discourses—of maternal sacrifice and maternal deprivation—work hand in hand produces the ideological moment of the film. This moment speaks directly to the aggressive ideological work of the late-war and early postwar years, a work predicated on the disjuncture between the rise in working women and developing images of domesticity. The media were actively *working* to construct an ideological edifice that would safely enthrone Rosie the Riveter as a patriotic heroine while at the same time curtailing the radical potentials embodied in both the image and the reality of "Rosie."

Mildred Pierce is the story of a woman who moves up from slaving housewife to owner of a chain of restaurants. But Mildred's rise to the top is only one part of the narrative. It is Mildred's relationship with her greedy and malicious daughter Veda that moves the narrative and is the catalyst for the climactic finale. Almost every motivation for Mildred's actions—from leaving her husband to marrying the aristocratic moocher, Monty—originates with her devotion to this daughter, above all else in her life. Yet this is no straightforward maternal sacrifice film, where the mother's sacrifice is at least rewarded (à la *Stella Dallas*). Mildred's daughter ends up going to jail for the murder of Mildred's second husband, Monty. Ironically, it is the mother who goes off into the sunset in this film, reunited now with her original husband, Burt.

Indeed, Mildred's sacrifice seems to backfire, seems to spoil and warp the very child she purports to adore. Even Mildred's vapid husband wonders if it isn't perhaps a bit "abnormal" that Mildred is so devoted and sacrificing for Veda. In this first flashback scene with Mildred and Burt, he tells us that she's "trying to buy love from those kids and it won't work."

This film is responding to the growing trend in popular psychology to place the full responsibility for the psychological health of the child firmly on the mother's shoulders. Motherhood here is dangerous, suspect, almost unnatural. The men in the film repeatedly tell Mildred that "something is not quite right" with her doting closeness with Veda.

One question haunts the film: Why is Veda the way she is? Is she just a "bad seed" or does the film lead us to believe that Veda's greed and evil are directly attributable to her mother, a woman seemingly obsessed with giving the child "all that she never had"? The narrative works in such a way as to be critical of Mildred's status as businesswoman, without directly confronting the issue, a strategy perhaps more disturbing in its subtlety. Why does Mildred go out to work? She must support her family. And why must she support her family? Because she has kicked her husband out of the house. Why has she kicked her husband out of the house? Here again we return to Veda, for it is around a fight concerning her—and how Mildred is spoiling her—that Burt Pierce leaves. Indeed, even his involvement with another woman, which is also central to their breakup, can be seen as attributable to Mildred's overinvolvement with her daughter and subsequent neglect of her "wifely duties." Mother-daughter intimacy at the expense of husband-wife intimacy reinforces the Mother/Woman split that dominates the narratives of popular culture.

Mildred is not only punished by the loss of her daughter Veda at the end of the film, she is further punished as the daughter steals the mother's lover. The theme of mother-daughter sexual rivalry has been a staple of popular culture. But *Mildred Pierce* adds a strange twist: It is a completely one-sided rivalry. Seen in the context of 1940s ideologies of irresponsible mothering, Veda's involvement with Monty can be seen as an indication of maternal deprivation in two senses. First, if Mildred weren't so busy with "making money," she would be more aware of what was happening right under her nose. And, second, if Mildred were more of a mother, more *there*, more attentive to her daughter's emotional life, then the daughter wouldn't have to turn to Monty to get her mother's attention, and perhaps the murder wouldn't have taken place.

Clearly, then, we are getting a change here from a more complexly layered representation of the mother-daughter relationship where attachment *itself* was not suspect *(Stella Dallas)* to an image that presents intimacy and attachment as *inherently* debilitating and essentially unhealthy. The attachment was clearly *mutual* between Stella and Laurel, and the poignancy of the film, at least in part, derives from the very palpable and mutual love between mother and daughter. Mildred's attachment, conversely, is coded as "overinvolved" and rejected by the daughter, as she moves out of the house to live on her own and becomes a nightclub singer.

While, during the war years, women's magazines suggested mother-daughter togetherness, whether through war work or housework, by midwar, they had begun to express a more overt concern with the perils that the working mother offered to the smooth functioning of the family:

> The initial idea that working mothers could raise happy children was replaced by tragic portraits of families breaking under the strain of mother being away. By the spring of 1944, ads began dramatizing the unhappiness of children with war-working mothers. (Honey, 1984, p. 124)

This is not to say that the shift from the sacrificial model to the malevolent model was straightforward and without deviations. Indeed, although the shift remains a dramatic one, we do see a number of important exceptions, particularly in the war films of the mid-1940s. In both *Since You Went Away* and *The Best Years of Our Lives*, daughters are not the victims of maternal love gone awry but are instead helpful and nurturant mothers-in-training, keeping the home fires burning while dad is off making the world safe for democracy. As in much of the wartime advertising that depicted daughters side by side with valiant victory-gardening moms, these wartime films served to locate teenage and young adult daughters as mature and responsible apprentices to the arts of American domesticity. Often, mothers and daughters are shown sharing domestic tasks such as preparing a drunken returning soldier's breakfast in *The Best Years of Our Lives* or wearing matching aprons as they cook together in the kitchen of *Since You Went Away*. Indeed, mothers and daughters are here shown to be united in their war efforts and their desire to maintain a "haven" for the returning vets.

What emerges from this overall transformation, then, is twofold. On the one hand, the move from *Stella* to *Mildred* signifies a shift from a vision of all-giving motherhood that locates women as sacrificial caretakers who derive pleasure from sacrifice, to an image of unhealthy motherhood responsible for the psychic viability (or psychic trauma) of their offspring. The change, however, is not just in images of motherhood (from sacrificial and benign to overpowering and controlling) but in the way the discourses of motherhood interact with other significant social discourses.

The story of Stella's mothering is also a story of class, an uneasy story that applauds class ascendancy (and sees it as accessed through the father) but still maintains a sharp criticism of bourgeois "expert" values and modes. The story of Mildred's mothering, on the other hand, is a purely psychological story. Even Mildred's class ascendancy is directly tied to her unhealthy desire to "give her daughter all she never had," while Stella's original move up the class ladder was propelled by her own desires. Mildred is punished both for wanting too much for her daughter and for daring to think that a working mother/single parent can join the ranks of the entrepreneurial upwardly mobile. Class as providing the context for the mother-daughter interaction thus disappears as that relationship is increasingly portrayed as having no context other than itself.

But the most critical continuity, and the most lamentable one, is the legacy of loss in these films. In both of the films discussed here and, indeed, in most representations of the mother-daughter relationship, mother and daughter are split apart, forever to be deprived of each other's company. Stella's daughter is forever lost to her, and Veda goes off to jail. Narrative resolution is firmly anchored to a permanent separation of mother and daughter, a separation that is both psychic and physical.

At least with *Stella*, we experience the loss of mother to daughter (and daughter to mother) as sad, wrenching, unhappily necessary. And, as Andrea Walsh (1984) has pointed out, we do get some sense of Stella's activity, her decision making, her subjectivity:

> These *sacrifice* films, though rarely feminist in ideology, are based on a feminist assumption that women can make choices. . . . They are, to an extent, authors of their own destiny. The fact that they are depicted as choosing subjects may be as important as the *content* of the life styles they choose. (p. 26)

Conversely, in other films of the period, the loss is never depicted as loss, much less as choice, but as the *inevitable* liberation of daughter from mother. Clearly, though, neither option constructs a discourse of constancy and mutuality. In the move from sacrificing *Stella* to maladjusted *Mildred*, we may have relinquished class and acquired psychoanalysis, but one thing remains constant: We have lost each other.

Father Knows Best About the Woman Question: Familial Harmony and Feminine Containment

From the 1930s through the wartime years, the representations of mothers and daughters underwent profound shifts—from an idealized mother as sacrificial lamb to her daughter's social ascendancy, to a much harsher nightmare of the mother as malevolent force on her daughter's struggling psyche. If the war brought women into the workforce and into public life with a vengeance, then the postwar period attempted to shunt them back off into the domestic, familial world from which they had been recently liberated.

Certainly, the 1950s are most often remembered as the period in which the ideal of the traditional nuclear family, with 2.4 kids, a suburban tract home, station wagon, and assorted barbecue grills, domestic pets, and home appliances, restructured the social and cultural terrain. The mass media played a central role in this restructuring. For not only was the new medium of television filling up the family living room and occupying a larger space in the social body,[3] the images themselves were crucial to orienting both women and men to the new social and sexual order, an order organized to a great extent around the new consumerism born of the postwar economic boom.

If previously women had been targeted by the mass media as potential workers, "Rosie the Riveters" hammering away at fighter planes while their menfolk were fighting fascism, then now they were targeted as "happy homemakers," suburban wives and mothers keenly attuned to the newest home products, eagerly reading their Dr. Spock and supporting their husbands' climb up the company ladder.

At the same time that these ideologies of maternal beneficence were blossoming, the specter of Philip Wylie's malevolent mom reared her ugly head. Wylie's description of a society gone soft, ruined and shriveled by the effects of hordes of devouring, emasculating moms, is as much a part of the familial discourse of the 1940s and 1950s as are the happy homemakers and cake-baking mothers.

These two aspects of postwar ideology—the glorification of motherhood and its simultaneous denigration by the exponents of "Momism"—may seem to be in contradiction. But it is this double message that itself is the defining discourse of mothering in the 1950s, and most especially of mothering daughters. The image of the devouring mother and of the virtuous mother are part of the same double bind. Both are mystifications—the idealization and the demonization— that serve to further distance mothers and daughters from their own complex, lived reality. The misogyny found in popular texts such as Wylie's *Generation of Vipers* and in many of the melodramas of the period is not an aberration. Rather, the attempt to erase mom, to find her guilty and responsible not only for her children's failures but for the failures of a society as well, is part of the same ideological moment that locates June Cleaver and Mrs. Anderson as the ultimate examples of virtuous motherhood.

There were two primary and simultaneous responses to the changing roles of women in the postwar world of the 1950s. The first response can be seen in such films as *I Remember Mama* and *Little Women* and such TV shows as *Father Knows Best, Mama*, and *The Donna Reed Show*. These images yearned for the (always fictional) good old days when mothers were all-tolerant and all-sacrificing. In many ways, these nostalgic images of traditional family life refer back to the Depression-era films such as *Stella Dallas* in that they posit a benign and all-loving mother who is unproblematically governed by a maternal instinct of sacrifice and familial devotion. And women's magazines consistently advocated not only the psychological dictum of maternal responsibility for the growth and development of husband and children but the social doctrine of maternal responsibility for the growth and development of Western civilization.

In these nostalgic representations, mothers and daughters are seen as united in their domestic orientation as well as in their position within the family. In both

Father Knows Best and *The Donna Reed Show*, the teenage daughters are seen as extensions of the mother—they help out in the kitchen, participate in mother's household chores, and laugh knowingly along with mother when dad and the boys act up.

The *second* response was far more interesting, in that it obliquely acknowledged that women were not solely domestic, and set out to explore the issues that arose from this "new paradigm" of work and family for women. This would include such films as *Imitation of Life* and *Peyton Place* and, a surprise, many articles in women's magazines, which began to discuss the new working mother and often (tentatively) supported women in their desire to remain in the labor force after the war ended. But, more significantly, this second line of response continued the often vitriolic attacks against working mothers found in films of the 1940s (such as *Mildred Pierce*), and popular texts helped to exacerbate this anxiety about working women.

It is this tension, between the nostalgic image of the domestic mother and daughter and the tormented image of the working mother and neglected daughter, that characterizes this period. Yet these seemingly disparate representations are united not only by their shared hyperbole but by their insistent emphasis on domesticity as the happiest possible route for women. And, importantly, both sets of representations convey the feeling of a familial world in crisis. Even classic 1950s "happy family" sitcoms such as *Father Knows Best*, while ostensibly benign in their depiction of the mother-daughter relationship, clearly created an ideological context where the attempts of either mother or daughter to escape the confines of suburban domesticity were rejected. The tendency toward a more refined and glitzy version of "Momism" was stronger than its nostalgic counterpart.

In an era that both celebrated and derided the mother, it was the *father* (or often the symbolic father figure in film melodramas such as 1959's *Imitation of Life*) not only who reigned as head of household but whose interaction with the children proved the most substantive and important, in terms of both narrative structure and ideological weight. Fathers seem to have been brought back into the picture as a result of the "realization" (promoted by Wylie et al.) that mothers were ruining their children. If maternal instinct was now aggressive and predatory, if "moms" ruled the earth and made their children rue the day, then fathers needed to reenter the family fray and set things straight. *Father Knows Best*, for all its innocuousness, implied in its very title that moms may be cute and addle-brained (or mean and malevolent) but, when it really comes down to the important issues of child rearing and family life, father really *does* know best.

Imitation of Life (1959) exemplifies the double bind mothers in the 1950s faced both in the narratives of popular culture and in the experience of their everyday lives. Here again we see the construction of ambivalence as fundamental to female identity, setting the stage for a whole series of myths about woman's inability to "make up her mind."

Imitation of Life is the story of two mother-daughter couples: one black and one white. This racial theme is vitally important here, not only for what it reveals about the racial dynamics of 1950s society but for the part it plays in this specific narrative and in the melodrama genre in general. In the 1930s, films such as *Stella Dallas* played out class conflict through the mother-daughter relationship as metaphor; in the 1950s, a film like *Imitation of Life* represents the racial "issue" through familial interactions.

Imitation of Life is an exceedingly complex and contradictory melodrama, although its glitzy style often obscures the more explicit ideological implications: the routine story of a mother's climb up the ladder of success and the havoc it wreaks on her home life. As another example of a film highly critical of "career women," particularly as parents, the very title and theme song—*Imitation of Life*—attests to the "falseness" of a working woman's life ("What is love without the giving? Without love, you're only living . . . an imitation, an imitation of life").[4]

Lana Turner plays Lora Meredith, a widow who recently moved to New York and is trying to make it in the theater and raise her daughter Susie (played by Sandra Dee). The story of Lora's rise is joined early on with the story of another mother and daughter, Annie and Sara Jane Johnson (played by Juanita Moore and Susan Kohner[5]), who come to live with/work for "Miss Lora" before she has made it, and stay on with her through her success. Certainly, this success and its repercussions construct a central ideological moment of the film. Lora, like Mildred, wants to give her daughter everything, and it backfires, as Annie lets Lora know after they've moved into a glamorous new house and Susie has been sent to boarding school:

Annie: Did you see those bills from Susie's new school?
Lora: Uh huh. And it doesn't matter.
Annie: But Miss Lora —
Lora: No matter what it costs, Susie's going to have everything I missed.
Annie: From her letters, she misses you more than she'd ever miss Latin.

As in *Mildred Pierce* and even *Stella Dallas*, mothers cannot access upward mobility: that is the province of fathers. Later, Annie reveals to Lora that Susie is in love with Steve, Lora's hardworking but unglamorous lover. Lora, in shock, says, "Why didn't I know about this, why didn't she come to me?" and Annie replies, "Maybe you weren't around." Lora, of course, gets the message: "You mean I haven't been a good mother." The next scene reiterates the evil career mother theme, with an angry and love-struck daughter Susie further condemning the mom who "gave me everything, but herself." Even Lora's dramatic attempt to make amends with her daughter by sacrificing Steve for the sake of their relationship backfires, as Susie pleads with her mother not to "act" because Susie is not "one of her fans."

The difference between the original 1934 version and the 1959 remake is instructive. In the original, Claudette Colbert plays a working mother, carrying on her dead husband's syrup business in a valiant attempt to support her daughter. Her rise to success is predicated on the pancake recipe of Delilah, the obsequious black maid who pleads to work for "Miss Bea" and stays with her until her own death, many years later. The work that propels Miss Bea to the top is thus domestic in origin, beginning in a do-it-yourself diner and moving up to a nationally famous pancake recipe (with Delilah's "Aunt Jemima" picture on the box). This, in itself, places the film on radically different ground, as the 1959 version turns the white mother into a glamorous actress, whose neglectfulness as a mother is linked to her own ostentation and narcissism as a (sexualized) "star." Claudette Colbert, as Bea Pullman, is a paragon of virtue: Not once do we doubt her motherliness or compassion.

The differences between the two films can be understood as exemplifying precisely that shift away from discourses centered on extrafamilial realities (race, class) to a psychologically centered melodramatic crisis. Although the racial theme is certainly more vividly and candidly expressed in the 1959 version (and, one could argue, is more socially responsive), it is narratively in the service of the repetitious discourse of bad working mothers. Indeed, the 1934 version, although more explicitly racist in its blatant and appalling use of stereotyped images of black women, refuses the indictment of the working (white) mother and rather foregrounds her working-classness (as in *Stella*) and her motherly devotion. And the figure of the male savior, so crucial to the reconstruction of the domestic unit in the 1959 version (particularly in his alliance with the black mother), is almost incidental in 1934, peripheral to the narrative and, really, to the women's lives.

Containing the Crisis, Domesticating Dissent

In the 1950s, popular culture was passionately enjoined in the effort to acclimate and orient Americans to the "brave new world" of mass consumption, tract housing, and ideological homogeneity. Conflicts between mothers and daughters were seen as manageable only through the reconstruction of the harmonious (patriarchal) nuclear family. Representations of the mother-daughter relationship in the postwar years presented a vision of an endlessly malleable nuclear family, able to withstand problems and disagreements, as long as the family structure remains intact. Although conflict between mother and daughter remained central, it was interpreted as part of a "life stage" or even generational rebellion. As in the films of the mid- and late 1940s (*Mildred Pierce; Now, Voyager*), class as a mediating theme is replaced by psychology—a psychology now searching for continuity and conformity, resolution and adjustment. So the mother and daughter are reunited in many of these 1950s images, yet it is a problematic reunion. First, class and history continue to disappear, rendering the reunion rather sterile. But, most important, the reunion in both films discussed depends on the reconstruction of the nuclear family and the reestablishment of a dominant male presence, a reestablishing that is also performed in terms of genre. Perhaps this reestablishing of the male presence signals the end to the female-centered "women's films" and a resurgence of more male-defined generic formulas, particularly in the "rebel" films of the 1950s and early 1960s.

The 1950s and early 1960s were marked by the rigorous attention of popular culture to an explicit and rarely wavering ideological agenda of familial harmony and feminine containment. An examination of a segment from the popular sitcom *Father Knows Best* reveals the extent to which an unambiguous ideological dialogue permeates the very fabric of cultural design. Mother *is* the family, yet she is strangely insignificant. Here again is that double message of the 1950s: on the one hand extolling the virtues of motherhood and domestic femininity while at the same time promoting fathers as primary socializers.

In a 1959 episode titled "Kathy Becomes a Girl," the role of the father as the figure of knowledge and moral guidance, as well as the educator into appropriate femininity, is made explicit. In a reversal of what would typically have been a dialogue between mother and daughter, father now supplants mother as the one most able to educate their daughter in the realities of adult femininity. The episode begins with Mother's concern about youngest daughter Kathy's tomboy-ish behavior ("Kathy, don't you think you're getting a little old to be wrestling boys and playing football?"). Kathy's initial resistance ("What else is there to do?") quickly turns into concern over her lack of girlfriends and her status as "oddball." Mother informs her that "there comes a time when girls like girls who act more, well, more like girls." Kathy continues objecting: "You mean I should act the way they do and be a stuffed shirt?" Mother replies, "No! Just be a normal, average girl," to which Kathy wonders, "I don't think I'm the type." Mother here is able to express the desire for conformity but has not the power to create it; that job is left to father.

The inculcation of Kathy into appropriate femininity is painful to watch. Kathy's inappropriateness is signified by her physicality: roughhousing with boys and swinging and hugging her girlfriends. Part of constructing the feminine in a little girl is related to a restriction of the body and the production of a repertoire of deceit and manipulation that is identified with female wiles.

This episode of *Father Knows Best* puts to rest any doubts concerning the authenticity of de Beauvoir's comment that "woman is made, not born." The entire family becomes engaged in the task of making a woman out of Kathy. When Kathy is ignored by her girlfriends as a party is being planned, the tension heightens and father legitimizes mother's exasperated (and rather comical) concern by pointing out the implications of this problem for Kathy's "develop-ment": "If she feels rejected at school this can become a big problem for her. We've got to find a solution." When sister Betty suggests that the solution lies in a gender switch, Kathy runs down the stairs to concur with her joking sister, "I wish I was a boy!"

While Mother buys Kathy a frilly dress in the hopes that it will "encourage her to be more careful and ladylike," and big sister initiates her into the wooly world of feminine appearance, it is Father who finally gets through to the still-reluctant Kathy in a little talk they have on the steps. The reference point in his pitch is Mother; he's going to let Kathy in on the little tricks Mother uses that make her so wonderful:

Father: Oh, I mean cute things. Like, uhh, being dependent, a little helpless now and then, expecting me to take over. You see, men like to be gallant. All you have to do is give them the opportunity.

He convinces Kathy that little tricks are a part of being a woman, and she concludes that, "We girls have got it made. All we have to do is sit back and be waited on." But Father is quick to point out (and here is the nod to the reality of women's lives, including participation in the labor force) that "it's very important for a girl to be capable and self-sufficient." But Kathy continues to get it wrong and more work is needed to set her straight:

Kathy: I am! I can beat Eroll wrestling any day!
Father: Worst thing you can do. Never try to beat a man at his own game. You
    just beat the women at theirs.
Kathy: I'll remember Daddy. But are you sure it'll work?
Father: Your mother's worked it on me for over twenty years.

In the end, Kathy accedes to her feminization. She successfully seduces the boys by acquiring the trappings of "girlness" and employing the womanly arts of deception. The final scenes show her rendered prone and helpless by a (false) broken ankle, and thus rewarded by the attention of admiring boys. Kathy wins over the girls as well, who now find in Kathy a successful sister who is finally able to attract the sought-after males.

This inculcation into appropriate femininity is also the subject of an appalling article written in 1956 by Constance Foster titled, "A Mother of Boys Says: Raise Your Girl to Be a Wife." The author here is clearly angry at the "confused" roles in contemporary society and wants to get wayward women back on the right path to wife-and-motherhood:

> The one essential qualification for a satisfactory daughter-in-law is the ability to be a real woman and like it. For such a girl having children is the most natural thing in the world because it's what everything is all about. (Foster, 1956, p. 44)

Foster cites venerable misogynists Lundberg and Farnham (1947) in stating her case against willful mothers who would lead their daughters into the never-never land of female independence:

> Long before it's time for Mom to help plan the wedding or Dad to give the bride away, it's time to be raising a future wife in your home. Because wives aren't born—they are made. Your daughter is born a female, but she has to learn to be feminine. (Foster, 1956, p. 43)

This strange twist on de Beauvoir, like its *Father Knows Best* counterpart, encourages mothers to be diligent in their education of their girl-children. Bolstering dads seems to be a principal ingredient in the construction of a wife:

> Sometimes a mother harms her daughter's chances of future happiness in marriage by deprecating men in general and the girl's father in particular. If she is the one who "runs" the family she then gives her daughter the feeling that men need to be managed. (Foster, 1956, p. 113)

One thing remains clear: The 1950s continued the process of constructing the mother-daughter relationship as a series of double-bind discourses. On the one hand, mothers are to be endlessly available and responsive to the caprices of their teenage daughters. Indeed, the inevitability of generational struggle is produced here as a natural category and a prerequisite for development. The theme in many women's magazine articles was one of a kind of benign, all-giving tolerance toward rambunctious daughters. Yet mothers were simultaneously condemned for *not* being attentive and diligent enough with their kids (maternal deprivation/neglect) and thus urged to exert a more substantial maternal influence, on their wayward youth as well as on their wayward society.

The double binds continue. Mrs. Anderson is held up as the epitome of well-adjusted womanhood, yet she is not even deemed competent enough to teach her daughters the "necessary" lessons of womanhood. Mothers are to initiate their daughters into appropriate femininity, but how can Mrs. Anderson reproduce herself if Dad has taken over that job as well? Mothers continue to be held responsible for their daughters' psyches and personalities yet are given little narrative power to make that meaningful.

These double binds help to maintain a no-win situation that continues to plague contemporary representations of mothers and daughters and, I believe, lived experience as well. The daughters of these 1950s mothers are led to believe that working mothers, if depicted at all, will imply for them the experience of deprivation. And the alternative image of the period—the Margaret Andersons and Mama Hansens and June Cleavers—offers daughters a model of sappy, happy serfdom and sacrifice, completely negating any path for these daughters other than an endless reproduction of the same. The closeness of some of these 1950s mothers and daughters is not an intimacy built on the richness of human experience but a cloying attachment firmly anchored to the patriarchal constraints of female domesticity.

The Turning Point: Mothers and Daughters at the Birth of Second-Wave Feminism

In 1963, Betty Friedan published *The Feminine Mystique* and echoed torch singer Peggy Lee when she asked American women, "Is that all there is?" After over a decade spent amidst the eerie cheerfulness of the domestic fantasy, the facade was beginning to crack. Friedan's book spoke of this domestic ideology as both illusion and entrapment. She grieved for the days of valiant heroines and independent women that she had seen in images of the 1930s and during the war years, and tried to understand the "retreat to the home" that so characterized the period in which she both lived and wrote.

Clearly, the women's movement, much less feminism, did not emerge full blown the day after Friedan's tome hit the bookstores. Indeed, for a large part of the 1960s, it was business as usual. While the visual media of the 1960s retained a resolutely male (albeit often alienated and rebellious) outlook, the women's magazines, in their implicit targeting of a gendered audience, continued to explore issues of relevance to women's lives, including the relationship of mother to daughter. The women's magazines present a microcosm of the contradictory images of mothering and the mother-daughter relationship during the 1960s and 1970s. Beginning in 1963 with *The Feminine Mystique* are a series of highly truncated debates engaging the central challenges of Friedan's thesis. Importantly, Friedan was one of their own, not simply an outside "expert" who could be cited and then pressed aside in the service of a more homegrown editorial stance. As in the 1950s, the women's magazines expressed a wider variety of responses to the changing social/sexual situation than did film and television, and it is not until the mid-1970s that the visual media explored with the same vigor the "women's issues" explored early on in the women's magazines.

This is not to say that the magazines gave their full and unfettered support to the growing women's movement. In fact, there was a great deal of harshness from writers concerned about the "trend" toward liberation, a harshness that was magnified in other popular presses, such as *Time, Look,* and *Life.* Mothers are generally taken to task in relation to more traditional complaints from daughters, for example, maternal interference and the lack of separation. In the regular *Good Housekeeping* section called "My Problem and How I Solved It,"[6] a woman tells the story of how her mother came to live with her and her family, causing a breakdown in the woman, who finally realizes (with the help of the friendly psychiatrist) that it's because she can't grow up with her overinvolved mother:

> Most mothers know they must to some degree "lose" their children as they grow up. The best mothers, even at pain to themselves, try to help them to be independent. But my mother, I came to realize, had never accepted this idea. She fought to keep me from growing up, from growing away from her. ("My Problem," 1962, p. 17)

The good Doctor explains the woman's "fatigue" completely in relation to her mother's presence and her own failings:

> Dr. Harvey had been right. My fatigue had been a symptom of everything that had been bottled up inside me—resentment of Mother, a childish fear of her disapproval, anger at my own failings, and a lot of self-pity. Nowadays, I can do all the housework in half the time, with half the effort. ("My Problem," 1962, p. 17)

Given the later "problem-that-has-no-name" interpretation of housewives' depression, this passage has particular poignancy, and the resolution reasserts her *submission* rather than challenging it: "I'm still Mother's daughter, but I am even more Howard's wife, and Jill's mother" ("My Problem," 1962, p. 17).

Other authors continued to insist on the right of mothers to work and to do so not merely to maintain the family's level of consumption but for reasons of "personal satisfaction." Indeed, a specific discourse about the "problem that has no name" began even before the phrase was coined.

A 1966 *Look* article titled "The War Between Mother and Daughter" attempts to reassert both the language of biological determinism and the metaphors of war to describe the mother-daughter relationship. In this reading, mothers and daughters are drawn together via their biological destiny as mothers, yet, paradoxically, it is this sameness that initiates what the authors tellingly call the "cold war":

> And there is a rapport, an intimacy between women, which men can never achieve. Women are drawn together by a simple and complicated fact: Their bodies are designed to bear children, and they share an understanding of the physical changes and discomforts that accompany that privilege. The cold war starts when the little girl discovers she and her mother are of the same sex—and daddy is different. (Damon & Jabes, 1966, p. 30)

As penis envy creeps into the discourse of women's magazines, so does its ultimate Freudian purpose: the construction of an inevitable rift between women and the subsequent push toward an overriding male identification:

> I believe that no girl can ever become a whole woman unless she understands and has made a mature acceptance of her mother. . . . For if she still resents her mother and yearns for the kind of affection she thinks her mother denied her, she may have difficulty ever reaching a satisfactory relation with a man, leaning (consciously or unconsciously) toward women as mother substitutes. (Damon & Jabes, 1966, p. 34)

Coming to terms with mother is understood not in feminist terms (e.g., mother as another *woman*) but still in terms of how the mother-daughter relationship affects the "real" heart of women's existence: their relationships with men. It is precisely these discourses—of biology as bonding and bonding as healthy heterosexuality—that begin to change as feminism enters into the popular language of the women's magazines in the early 1970s.

Even more than in the 1960s, women's magazines in the 1970s continued to explore central issues of the mother-daughter relationship in the context of an ever-growing women's movement. The new concern about women's identity and sense of self produced a discussion of the possibility of mother as role model in a changing society. What was mother able to pass on to her daughter in the age of feminism?

> We all know that fathers pass their names and sometimes their ambitions along to their sons. But what do mothers pass on to their daughters? "My mother gave me recipes and the secret of how to endure," a friend told me. But like so many other daughters, she also feels she inherited many negative things from her mother—feelings of guilt, a tendency to martyrdom, a mistrust of men. (Schultz, 1976, p. 108)

Yet this aspect of the discussion—the inheritance of submission and domesticity—was more dormant in the 1970s than in earlier periods. Rather, the emphasis was much more on understanding commonalities and, more important, understanding the reality of mother's life and mother's options. Fundamental to this was an insistence, after so many years of relative silence, of the simple *importance* of a daughter's relationship to her mother in forming her own identity, an importance that was now being addressed with language that went beyond the 1940s bond/separate dichotomies.

It is hard to overestimate the importance of this shift. For the first time, the relationship between mother and daughter is placed within a social context that acknowledges the often painful reality of the "prefeminist" mother, which relieves her of some of the overwhelming responsibility for her daughter's psyche in the name of a more realistic appraisal of mother's life options and life limitations.

Sitcom Subversions: Working Daughters and Radical Mothers

One year after Spock bid farewell to his well-meaning paternalism, the wittiest matriarch ever to hit prime time emerged on CBS. The hit sitcom *Maude*[7] was a turning point for the representation of mothers and daughters in the medium of television. If Mary Richards used traditional feminine qualities to rethink office politics and women and work questions, and Edith Bunker was the stereotypical silly woman with a heart of gold, then Maude was the loud, brazen, brassy Bella Abzug of prime time. She was funny without being self-abnegating, smart without being coy, and contentious without being apologetic. She was, in other words, a radical woman.

Maude was also the first prime-time TV sitcom to portray an adult mother and daughter living together. In that, and in so many other ways, *Maude* was really a "social issue" sitcom with a sincerity and depth that surpassed that classic of social sitcoms, *All in the Family*. For there were no fools in *Maude*, no buffoons, no sitting targets waiting to be dissected with a dose of Learian liberalism. Even the right-wing character Arthur, though often buffoonish, was more often than not a relatively articulate spokesman for the small-minded Nixonian conservatism that Maude was always battling. No, the subject of *Maude* was not the single girl/big city, or working-class bigotry, or the hellishness of war, but the liberal, enlightened family itself. *Maude* represents the grand reversal of the domesticoms of the 1950s, in that it locates itself in terms of genre within that trusted environment of the family home and then proceeds to explore the new configurations and struggles engendered in that space since the late 1960s.

One of the significant dislocations of the traditional nuclear family has most certainly been the growing rates of divorce and single-parenthood, two issues that provide narrative grist for the mill of the social sitcom.[8] Maude was obviously no exception here: She had been married four times before she settled on her current mate, the wry appliance salesman Walter Findlay, and her daughter was a divorced, 27-year-old mother of an 8-year-old son when she came to live with Maude and Walter.

It is no exaggeration to say that the relationship between Maude and her daughter Carol is unlike any I have seen on TV—then or now. Unlike *Rhoda*, where the mother-daughter relationship is framed within the more traditional structure of old-fashioned, interfering Jewish mother and struggling-to-be-liberated daughter, both Maude *and* her daughter are feminists and "liberated women." Although Carol often plays the part of spokeswoman for the "new woman," she is by no means alone in this, and it is this *dialogue* between mother and daughter that is so refreshing and so enlightening. In one of the best (and most controversial) episodes, Maude has gotten pregnant at age 47 and is faced with the dilemma of whether to have this baby that she clearly doesn't want, or to have an abortion (legal by this time in the state of New York). Carol urges her mother on: "There is no earthly reason for you to go through this at your age" and is amazed at Maude's hesitancy given her politics:

Carol: . . . Mother, I don't understand your hesitancy. When they made it a law you were for it.
Maude: Of course, I wasn't pregnant then.
Carol: Mother, it's ridiculous, *my* saying this to *you*. We're free. We finally have the right to decide what we can do with our own bodies.

Maude does go on to have the abortion, with the support of her daughter and her husband.

Although struggle and conflict is openly and humorously acknowledged, it never entails a sense of the need for rift and separation: These two women obviously love each other and, in many ways, are much alike. Several episodes point this out clearly. In "Like Mother, Like Daughter" (1972), Carol has begun dating a man many years her senior and, importantly, a man Maude used to see before she met Walter. Maude is concerned that Carol will be jilted like she was and, after waiting up for Carol all night, confides her distress to Walter over breakfast:

Maude: Walter, I am going to put a stop to this right now!
Walter: Now look Maude, if you break this up Carol's going to think you're an interfering mother. You want that?
Maude: It's a hazard of the trade Walter. I didn't interfere when she eloped with Pete and it ended in divorce. I've never forgiven myself.
Walter: Then why didn't you interfere?
Maude: I was in Reno at the time divorcing Albert.

As in many such scenes, the explicit and humorous discourse of "the interfering mother" makes it less deadly, less *pre*scriptive and pathologizing. In addition, Maude's reference to her own divorce not only links the experience of mother and daughter but gives the mother a *life*, so that her interference is relativized.

In the next scene, Carol has come down the stairs and into the kitchen, clearly not eager to talk. Yet Maude persists, putting her hand on Carol's shoulders and facing her, a stance that is repeated time and time again between mother and daughter throughout the series:

Maude: I know you're going to tell me again to mind my own business. But look at it this way: God couldn't be everywhere, that's why he invented mothers.

But Carol is having none of it, and tells Maude that she doesn't intend to see him again anyway, as he called her "Maude" last night. Maude assumes it was during lovemaking, and is flattered, but it turns out that it was during an argument in which Russell (the lover) accused Carol of sounding just like her mother. When Russell emerges to make amends, he is placed physically in the middle of the two women, who proceed to castigate him and send him out the door. As Maude returns from the doorway, she walks over to Carol, "Good morning honey," "Good morning mother," and they smile and hug and kiss.

Importantly, the scene doesn't end on that note. Rather, Maude continues to tell Carol of *her* experience with Russell and Carol comforts her. When Walter walks in to apologize for his jealousy, Carol and Maude are seated on the edge of the couch, one slightly behind the other in a "matching" shot (similar clothes, hairstyles, position on couch, and so on) that is accentuated by the identical warm smile they give Walter during his speech. The women are brought together by a sense of wry sisterhood refracted through the egocentric man they both slept with and by a sense of mutual nurturing and caretaking.

Similarly, in a 1976 episode titled "The Election," both Maude and her daughter are working for Carter, and this shared work, while typically providing material for discourses of "enmeshment" and "lack of separation," is here expressed in terms of mutual pride and, always, humor:

Maude: Oh you know Carol, I just think you're wonderful. The way you have
   thrown yourself into this presidential campaign.
Carol: Well, after all, I am your daughter. You know what they say: the acorn
   doesn't fall far from the political nut.
Maude: Carol, you know you're getting to be more like me all the time. And
   some day we're both going to pay for it.

It sounds banal, but the simple statement from a mother to a daughter, "I think
you're wonderful," and its response, "I am your daughter," moves us decades
away from the agonizing ideologies of separation and struggle. To acknowledge
love, closeness, and sameness without being stamped as "overinvolved," "enmeshed," and "immature" is a major step in a feminist direction for the image of
the mother-daughter relationship.

Maude remains unique in that it acknowledges the scripts already written for
mothers and daughters (as Maude says to Carol, "Children resent and mothers
interfere. That comes with the territory.") while at the same time implicitly
challenging their authenticity. For the traditional scripts—with their emphasis
on separation and the inevitability of discord—certainly have no narrative space
for an adult mother and her adult daughter living and thriving together. The
difference with a series like *Maude* is that feminism and the women's movement
are *active* signifiers in the overall narrative. And, although no doubt Carol's life
is different than mother Maude's, it is a difference that they *share* rather than a
difference one owns at the expense of the other. Maude and her daughter are
represented equally as women warriors in the same suburban battlefield, turning
over the last remnants of charred domesticity in their march toward a feminist
future.

Nevertheless, in so many of these representations, mothers and daughters are
inevitably lost to each other, either through sacrifice, conflict, and death or
narcissism and neglect. In most of these popular images, there is a clear and
present victor, the daughter, and in the rest we are left with a promise of future
struggle and conflict. If resolution is reached, mother and daughter are torn
asunder. If no narrative conclusion exists, mother and daughter seem locked in
a repetitive cycle of confrontation and angst. In more recent years, the "maternal
sacrifice" genre—which at least put a "good face" on motherhood—has given
way to a more visceral depiction of a clearly evil mother *(Mommie, Dearest)* and
a victimized daughter, or, more generally, of a mother-daughter relationship that
is structured in terms of conflict.

Tellingly, in the films where we do see a line of continuity between mother
and daughter, like *I Remember Mama* or *Little Women* or even the wonderful
recent film *A World Apart*, both women are generally desexualized. The possibility of mother-daughter continuity that denies *neither* one their autonomy,
sexuality, or adulthood—that sees them in a relationship where neither one is
"all-powerful" or "all-victimized"—is an option rarely explored in popular
culture.

Television has provided a few glimpses into what this could be, with such
groundbreaking shows as *Maude* depicting adult mothers and daughters where

both were clearly sexual as well as being adult and independent. Not coincidentally, though, these shows were working within the sitcom format, itself a type of entertainment one was not supposed to treat very seriously. And, again, it is surely no accident that these sitcoms were produced at the height of the contemporary women's movement—the mid-1970s.

Representations that treat the familial as configured by the social; images that ground their narratives in the vagaries of class, race, ethnicity; narratives that break out of the psychological straitjackets and focus on the broader canvas of social relations—these are the images that give us pleasurable respite from the tedious tales of maternal martyrdom and motherly pathology. It is when the working-class mother in *A Tree Grows in Brooklyn* speaks to her own complicated location as mother and woman, when Maude and her daughter Carol become the shared signifiers for a changing generation of feminist and socially conscious women, when the daughter of the antiapartheid activist in *A World Apart* voices the complex emotions of political awakening and adolescent need, refusing the easy condemnation of the publicly involved mother. These are the kinds of images that can help construct a female identity that is not male defined and in opposition to other women but is autonomous *and* interdependent and, most important, feminist.

Notes

1. This work is taken from a much larger and more thorough study of mothers and daughters in popular culture. For a complete historical analysis, right up to the late 1980s, please see my *Lives Together/Worlds Apart: Mothers and Daughters in Popular Culture* (Walters, 1992).

2. *Stella Dallas* was first a 1915 popular novel that was then turned into a film by Henry King in 1925 and then later by King Vidor in 1937. In addition, it was one of the longest running radio serials, playing on NBC from 1937 to 1955. The early twentieth-century origins may have a great deal to do with the film's sympathetic rendering of maternal love, insofar as its reference is to a kind of preindustrial "Cult of True Womanhood" rather than psychoanalytic angst.

3. The number of television sets purchased is a good indication of the enormous expansion of TV as a form of popular entertainment: "Sales of sets jumped from three million during the entire decade of the 1940s to over five million *a year* during the 1950s" (Lipsitz, 1988, p. 83).

4. The title sequence, with the song in the background, depicts what appears to be diamonds dropping down and forming a pile, visualizing the falseness of Lora's fame and fortune.

5. Both actresses received Oscar nominations for Best Supporting Actress.

6. This section is, I believe, always written by anonymous editors, often with the aid of social service organizations, in this case the Family Services Association of America.

7. *Maude* was a consistently popular show—it ran from 1972 to 1978 and, except for its final two seasons, it always placed in the top 10 of the Nielsen ratings.

8. *Maude* is not alone in this. Many other sitcoms of the 1970s centered on divorced women—with or without children *(Rhoda*—post Joe—*Phyllis, One Day at a Time)*.

References

Damon, V. S., & Jabes, I. (1966, January 11). The war between mother and daughter. *Look*, pp. 30-34.

Foster, C. (1956, September). A mother of boys says: Raise your girl to be a wife. *Parents' Magazine*, pp. 143 ff.

Friday, N. (1977). *My mother/my self: The daughter's search for identity*. New York: Dell.

Friedan, B. (1963). *The feminine mystique*. New York: Norton.

Honey, M. (1984). *Creating Rosie the Riveter: Class, gender, and propaganda during World War Two*. Amherst: University of Massachusetts Press.

Lipsitz, G. (1988, January). The meaning of memory: Family, class, and ethnicity in early network television programs. *Camera Obscura, 16*, 79-116.

Lundberg, F., & Farnham, M. (1947). *Modern woman: The lost sex*. New York: Harper & Row.

My problem and how I solved it: Mother and daughter. (1962, June). *Good Housekeeping*, pp. 10-17.

Schultz, T. (1976, October). The feelings too many daughters are afraid to face. *Redbook*, p. 108.

Walsh, A. (1984). *Women's films and female experience, 1940-1950*. New York: Praeger.

Walters, S. (1992). *Lives together/worlds apart: Mothers and daughters in popular culture*. Berkeley: University of California Press.

Wylie, P. (1960). *Generation of vipers*. New York: Pocket Books. (Original work published 1942)

Part III

Self and Media Participation

4

Desperately Seeking Strategies:
Reading in the Postmodern

Mary Ellen Brown

Issues of the construction of the self in relation to postmodernity have been debated on a theoretical and philosophical level for some time. I suggest in this chapter that one meaningful site of struggle in relation to the construction of the self is at the level of reading practices. Some notions of subjectivity, or the construction of self by social forces, suggest that reading practices can structure subjectivity through the process of identification. Because postmodern notions of emphasis on consumption and surface qualities seem to negate the process of identification, there are questions regarding how, or if, the process of identification can take place in relation to a postmodern text. Accordingly, my research assistants and I looked at a postmodern television text, *Twin Peaks,* and some of its fans to theorize how, or if, a viewer might relate to such a text. In doing so, I have drawn upon the notion of the nomadic subject put forth by Grossberg (1988) and looked at focus group data collected from *Twin Peaks* fans. I suggest how ideology and subjectivity might be conceptualized as working together to construct a subject tied both to realism and to postmodernity.

In looking at the reading strategies employed by viewers of *Twin Peaks,*[1] my research assistants and I discovered that these reading strategies reflect a range of responses to the text, across the groups as well as within individuals. We have concluded that various positions are possible as readers negotiate ideas of the self in relation to a postmodern text. Traditional ideas about subject formation, based on the concept of identification (according to psychoanalytic critics) or of interpellation (the Althusserian and Marxist critics), inscribe the individual within the text through responses developed through experiences with realist texts. Postmodern texts seem to assert the emptiness of these realist conventions. Although one would, therefore, expect that the postmodern work would be powerless to affect the audience's security as subjects, I suggest that notions of self embedded in realism still exist in audience practices despite the presence of the postmodern text.

AUTHOR'S NOTE: This study was done with a grant from the State University of New York—Brockport and the help of research assistants Leslie Brugger, Eileen Button, Kathy Curran, Kimberly Holmes, Elizabeth Meyer, Judith Piere, Rae Rubly, and Bonnie Webster. Further support has been awarded by the University of Missouri Research Council. Research assistance at the University of Missouri has been provided by Sandra Camargo, Diane Tobin Johnson, Mehdi Semati, Jeff Shires, and Paul Summitt.

The Nomadic Subject

Some cultural studies audience theory has characterized the postmodern subject as nomadic (Grossberg, 1988). A nomadic subjectivity implies that a subject position, a way of reading and re-creating one's social relationship with the world, is constructed briefly at the intersection of various discourses but never comes to rest at either a particular place (an official designation) or a particular space, that is, a conceptual designation used by de Certeau (1986) and others (Morris, 1988; Radway, 1988) to suggest the moving or unstable cultural location of a specific subject. In the context of this theorization, it becomes almost impossible to ethnographically describe such a shifting subject. As Grossberg (1988) puts it:

> The task of cultural criticism is less that of interpreting texts and audiences than of describing vectors, distances and densities, intersections and interruptions, and the nomadic wandering (whether of people in everyday life or as cultural critics) through this unequally and unstably organized field of tendential forces and struggles. (p. 383)

In this chapter, I use the term *reading strategies* to suggest such temporary and fleeting subject positions, which, when united, contribute to the structuring of a postmodern self.

Thus, nomadic subjects construct their identities and subjectivities from various positions that change through time. Just as a nomadic wanderer cannot stay in one location for an extended length of time since the food sources soon are depleted, likewise a nomadic subject exhausts the sign system in any one text and must move on to the next. Grossberg (1992), however, describes such nomadic travels to be through a system of roads, stating that not "all roads are equally easy to travel" (p. 110). A road metaphor, however, indicates that the nomads are headed for a particular location or taking a particular route to an end. We believe that the nomadic analogy suggests more freedom for its subjects. For a subject to be truly nomadic indicates a higher degree of uncertainty than Grossberg ascribes. A road metaphor indicates a linearity, a movement from point A to point B, although Grossberg does allow for "stopping off" points. We believe a nomadic metaphor calls for a more circular and arduous route—and nomads may return when the food supply is replenished.

A television text can become a source needed by the self for continuation. It gives information and entertainment, nourishes, refreshes, and sustains the viewer. It is food for the mind. Certain types of texts, notably the postmodern text, provide a variety of stimuli that appeal to such nomadic subjectivities.

Subjects in/and Discourse

Because postmodern texts can have characteristics that were once obtained only through channel surfing, the postmodern text is fertile ground upon which the nomadic subject can graze. The postmodern nomadic self seems to follow Friedrich Nietzsche's idea of the active and passive self. Nietzsche (1964) states that active natures "act, not according to the maxim, 'Know Thyself,' but as if

always confronted with the command, 'Will a self, so you will become a self' "
(p. 168). Passive selves act as if "they have chosen their self 'once and for all'
at their entry in life" (p. 168). The nomadic self must continue to act and seek
out new representations to temporarily "complete" and center her- or himself.
This respite is only temporary, however, and after a short time, the nomadic
subject must continue to move.

Having described the possibility of the nomadic subject, what do we mean by
subject or *self*? Michel Foucault (1972) states that the term *subject* has two
definitions, "subject to someone else by control and dependence, and tied to his
own identity by a conscience or self-knowledge" (p. 212). Both of these are
accomplished through what Foucault refers to as *discourse,* for which he has two
distinct meanings. First is simple discourse (Foucault, 1970), a code language
formation that exists between *language* and *parole*—between the system of
language and individual utterance. He states:

> But between these two regions [*language* and *parole*], so distant from one another, lies
> a domain which, even though its role is mainly an intermediary one, is nonetheless
> fundamental. . . . It is here that culture, imperceivably deviating from the empirical
> order prescribed for it by its primary codes, instituting an initial separation from them,
> causes them to lose their original transparency. (p. xx)

Between the fundamental code of language (the primary code) and the scientific
theories (parole) lies an intermediary code. This code, which borrows from the
primary code, lays out the groundwork for what can be represented within a
culture, the language of everyday life. This is the language that a subject uses to
help construct a subject position.

The second definition that Foucault (1972) has for *discourse* is technical
language. This is the language of the scientist or the expert that subjects the
subject to its discourse. The "authorities of delineation" (p. 41) name the object
being studied and its attributes, which then is applied to society at large. Foucault
uses the example of madness, explaining that medicine "became the major
authority in society that delineated, designated, named and established madness
as an object" (p. 42).[2] After madness is established as a discourse, it is used to
label people who conform to a certain set of behaviors that describe madness.
The subject, then, is constructed within these two notions of discourse.

The two positions of subject, that involving being subject to someone and that
being tied to self-knowledge, can be said to leave a gap in the construction of the
self that must be filled. The self is constructed of what one says about oneself
and what is said about one. Because these two discourses are usually not the
same, a gap exists between self-constitution and self being constituted. It is this
gap that a person attempts to fill with what we usually call identification.

We have conceptualized identification as floating among various types of
reading strategies, which can take many forms. In the first form of reading
strategy, the audience member watches strictly for the surface pleasure. In a
second form, the viewer relates to the program as "art." Here the audience
member is looking at the series of conventions that structure the text. The third
type of reading strategy is group identification: The audience member watches

the program to belong to a larger group of fans. The final strategy considered here is the "That's me!" identification: The external image (a public figure, a television character, an authority figure) represents a synthesis of what is said about a person (the character) and what a person believes about him- or herself (the viewer).

The first two types of reading strategies, surface pleasure and the construction of the text as art, are relatively stable because they are structural identifications. These two are concerned with how the program is constructed and what surface elements are included in constructing the show. The last two types of identification, group membership and "That's me" identification, are not as stable. Because the audience member is surrounded by shifting discourses, identification cannot be maintained constantly but must be continually updated and redefined. This sets the subject to begin nomadic wandering.

The Postmodern Text

According to Fiske (1991), the postmodern text is fragmented; it is incoherent, disorganized, and unstable; its fragmentation overpowers attempts to provide coherence; it is known for its surface appeal. It refuses deep meaning underlying its surface qualities; it denies organizing structures that lie beneath our experience of both society and culture; it refuses the difference between signifier and signified and avoids the debate on which is more significant. It uses pastiche; it is not controlled by reality or ideology; it gives the audience the freedom to refuse social order. It also allows the audience to consume images without consuming their meaning (pp. 58-60).

Collins (1992) suggests that, in addition to stylistic elements, the postmodern television text incorporates and exploits the multiple subject positions for which television in the age of cable is famous. A postmodern television program approximates for the audience the rapidly changing multiple subject positions brought about by the use of the remote control to facilitate grazing and zapping, which causes changes in genres, narratives, styles of audience address, and degrees of involvement. A particular program that incorporates such shifts might also involve another subject-displacing form called *pastiche*, which, like parody, involves the imitation or mimicry of other styles, in particular their mannerisms and stylistic twitches. Unlike parody, whose purpose is to satirize another style or historical period, pastiche uses the imitated style without the satirical impulse, without the sense that there exists something normal with which it could be compared. Jameson (1985, pp. 113-114) calls pastiche *blank parody,* that is, parody that has lost its sense of humor.

The same divesting of meaning is suggested by the term *simulacra* (Baudrillard, 1983). Relating to postmodernism, *simulacra* suggests that there are only simulations with no real external to them, no original being copied. It is as if we were all reduced to exteriors, there being no longer any interiors (Kaplan, 1988, p. 155). Thus postmodern artifacts are thought to display a mass-produced surface quality without the sense of underlying meaning that we expect to find in the realist text or the sense of rebellion found in the modernist avant-garde.

The postmodern text is also decentered, particularly in terms of story line and characterization. This decenteredness is underscored in Jameson's (1985) references to the postmodern text as schizophrenic. Schizophrenia as a psychosis involves a person's not being able to conceptualize her- or himself over time. The schizophrenic has an undifferentiated vision of the world in which sensations become ever more brilliant, but ever more confusing (Jameson, 1985, p. 120). In such a postmodern visual example, each image is vivid but often only accidentally connected in a meaningful way with the images that come before or after it.

Some of the formal characteristics of postmodernism have been taken from those first developed by modernism. Modernist texts, however, self-consciously separate themselves from the mainstream and, unlike realist art forms, foreground their own artificiality. This aspect turns reading into a struggle or contest. Kellner (1992) argues that modernism, which had earlier attacked realism, never really took hold in television so that U.S. commercial television has most often consisted of images and stories that attempt to produce a reality effect. In contrast, postmodern television—such as MTV, *Miami Vice,* high-tech ads, or *Max Headroom*—presents

> a new look and feel: The signifier has been liberated and image takes precedence over narrative, as compelling and highly expressive and non-realist aesthetic images detach themselves from the television diegesis and become the center of fascination, of seductive pleasure, of our intense but highly transitory aesthetic experience. (p. 146)

Fiske (1987) has noted that television's realism is constructed through the devices of spoken discourse fused with visual images. This combination of speech and moving human figures creates a kind of ontological realism. Fiske believes such realism to be "a socially convincing sense of the real" that does not reflect reality but, instead, produces "the dominant sense of reality" (p. 21). He points out that form is also an important element of realism and notes that the realist narrative follows the basic laws of cause and effect, that everything is in the program for a reason, and that the relationships of all the elements in a realistic text are logical and clear (pp. 21-36). The program appears to have a smooth continuous flow as if it had not been edited. In addition, the camera positioning, lighting, music, casting, setting, action, and dialogue are all manipulated to make the program appear realistic (p. 8). In contrast, the postmodern text contains the formal qualities noted by Collins as signs of the postmodern, which are similar to channel surfing but in this case can be found within a single program, that is, *Twin Peaks.* These qualities can be directly related to disruptions in subjectivity as opposed to the realistic text that struggles to produce a *unified* subject.

Twin Peaks

Twin Peaks is known for its innovations, not only in program content but also in the area of publicity and promotion. Because of sophisticated promotion, *Twin Peaks* began with reasonably high ratings (21.7/33), which consistently *declined* over a two-year period to 6.7/12 in its final episode. Ultimately, most audiences rejected the program, a fact that did not prevent the show from becoming one of the most talked about series on television in 1990 and 1991. Despite its ratings failure, *Twin Peaks* has had an influence that belies its short television run. The involvement of a major filmmaker in television has led to other "quality" products such as George Lucas's *The Young Indiana Jones Chronicles* and Oliver Stone's *Wild Palms*. Two popular series—*Northern Exposure* and *Picket Fences*—have benefited from the public's appreciation of *Twin Peaks'* "quirkiness," the unpredictability and playfulness of its narrative ruptures, and the genial eccentricity of its characters.

The style of *Twin Peaks* is often described as "cinematic" rather than "televisual." While David Lynch, an acknowledged film *auteur,* as director of the series confounded expectations in terms of the usual concept of television as a group production, he also brought with him a film style that is clearly postmodern. His filmic style has as one of its elements a system of representation that makes use of surrealist elements such as distorted voices, giants, midgets, dream images, and dream logic. It requires that the reader let go of realistic expectations and pay attention to surface qualities. The level of attention required of the viewer is much closer to that traditionally ascribed to film rather than to television (Ellis, 1992).

One of the main differences between *Twin Peaks* and many other television narratives lies in the types of elements selected to delay the moment of disclosure. Previously, shows such as *Hill Street Blues* and *L.A. Law* used their large ensemble casts to present several related stories at once, intertwining them in ways that entertain viewers as they wait for the denouement. *Twin Peaks,* on the other hand, pretends to be telling one story—the search for the murderer of Laura Palmer. According to Barthes (1974, 1975) and others (Silverman, 1983), the nature of the closure grants meaning to the narrative. The tactic adopted by *Twin Peaks* to postpone the moment of revelation for ever longer periods—the abrupt and unmotivated intrusion of hermeneutically irrelevant events—becomes its primary identifying characteristic. Thus, closure either never comes or is ultimately irrelevant. In addition, the relationship between events on *Twin Peaks,* in most cases, is sequential and not consequential. *Twin Peaks,* like its cousin the daytime soap opera, breaks the primary rule of narrative construction beyond mending.

Reading Strategies and the Postmodern Audience

If we consider television a postmodern apparatus because of its decentered address and its ability to flatten things into systems or networks (Kaplan, 1988, p. 154), and *Twin Peaks* a postmodern text because of its excess of surface and its refusal to generate the meanings expected in a "hot" universe of investment, desire, passion, and seduction (Baudrillard, 1985), then we propose to call fans of *Twin Peaks* a postmodern audience. The group of *Twin Peaks* fans we interviewed was gathered by placing an ad in three alternative newspapers in a northeastern U.S. city for fans of *Twin Peaks* who wanted to talk about it.[3] We asked respondents if they would also bring to the interview gatherings others with whom they had watched or discussed *Twin Peaks*. At these gatherings of 10 to 15 people, we broke into small groups for discussions of the program, which were audiotaped. Although the participants sometimes talked of their own life experiences, our aim was not so much to delineate the background of the participants but to determine how people who liked this text interacted with it—what we are here calling reading strategies.

In relation to constructing a notion of self, the reading strategies that became apparent in analyzing the interviews were five, as follows:

1. Being fooled—joy in unpredictability, humor: This is what we earlier called a surface strategy.
2. Meaninglessness—a nonjudgmental acceptance of the program without having to establish a coherent meaning: This we also called a surface strategy.
3. Aesthetic/technical—seeing the text as a text or an object, seeing the text as commenting on its own conventions: This was a previously mentioned "art" strategy.
4. Intellectualization—an us/them mentality recognizing a high-art/low-art distinction, which includes Lynch as *auteur* or artist and thus makes *Twin Peaks* unlike other U.S. commercial TV: This was previously descried as a *group* identification strategy.
5. Identification—seeing the characters or events as if they might have taken place in the world as we know it: This is what we called a "That's me!" strategy.

We collapsed numbers 1 and 2 in our final analysis, calling both surface reading strategies. This is the type of reading strategy we expected to be most common because it matches the theoretical descriptions of postmodernism summarized earlier. Further analysis, however, revealed subtleties within these strategies.

We designated the first three strategies—surface (1 and 2 above), aesthetic/technical (3 above), and intellectualization (4 above)—as postmodern reading strategies. The identification category we called a realistic reading strategy. The first two are more stable than the last two categories, intellectualization and identification, because they are, to a large extent, text controlled. *Twin Peaks* encourages a surface reading at the same time that its artistic film production values encourage analysis that attends to precise visual aspects. The latter was so prevalent that fans would often tape the show as they watched it so that they could go back and freeze-frame and/or reanalyze what had happened. As we shall see, the last two reading strategies depend more clearly on the audience member for their application.

Among the fans in the first group, pleasure was associated with surprise. The suspense of wondering whether or not they were going to be fooled was what kept many hooked on the program. One viewer expressed it this way:

> [Lynch] did twist you around a lot. You really had to know what was going on to know how he was doing that to the audience. I kind of enjoy that, you know, when an author or an artist can do that to me, trick me.

Readers used this strategy in a gamelike, playful manner, trying to outthink the *auteur*.

Some viewers recognized that some portions of the text made little sense and were hard to follow. These viewers dealt with this possible source of frustration by deciding to "go along for the ride and just enjoy it." Viewers using this strategy had a tendency to mention the unpredictability of the program. It was obvious that, although they enjoyed it, they were not able to make as much sense out of it as they would have liked.

Other viewers using this reading strategy simply considered the oddities of the program to be meaningless, as if the director threw them in for no reason, reading around the things that did not make sense to them: "It's fun to sit there and sort of be serious about something for a while; yet, at the same time, knowing that it really doesn't mean anything." Another viewer suggested: "Maybe he doesn't even have an idea of what something meant, he just said, 'Hey, that'll be neat to put in there and let the viewer, the participant, finish the painting.' " This comment expresses the postmodern sentiment most exactly. The lack of meaning is not a problem when using this type of reading strategy.

Another reading strategy was an appreciation for individual creativity. Many responded that they watched the program for its directing, camera work, lighting, and script rather than for the actual plot. This strategy explored *Twin Peaks* from a technical and aesthetic point of view: "It had an incredible script. It was really well written and had great vocabulary, but also the cinematography was like a feature film. It had a feature film score, feature film cinematography, acting, writing. It was tremendous!" Another viewer noted: "I just love anything where there are really weird camera angles, and it's not just shooting from one angle all the time." In addition to the pleasure of analysis, viewers employing this strategy were able to gain distance, insulating themselves from content by concentrating on style.

Sometimes, however, viewers chose to make sense of the *Twin Peaks* text by using the strategy of intellectualism. These viewers felt that it takes a discerning, intelligent, television connoisseur to understand the show. Thus, they were not like that average viewer who "doesn't want to have to think" while watching a television program. The "average" viewer might choose sitcoms while the intellectual group chose to watch *Twin Peaks*. This seems to be a group reading strategy in that it separated the insiders—those who understood the show—from the outsiders—those who presumably did not.

> I felt the show aimed for bright people, and I felt privileged to understand it. That I was one of the people that was hip to the show. You know, he [Lynch] was not going after typical people, the masses that can't, that have to be spoon-fed simple messages in order to understand anything.

Those who chose this strategy rarely mentioned the unconventionality of the show. And in the few instances when they did, the bizarreness was not viewed as a hindrance but as something to intellectualize about: "Most people who watched it [regularly] probably can intellectualize about it and not take it all at face value. You wouldn't stick to it if you just took it at face value." Up until this point, the majority of reading strategies required the viewer to remain on the surface of the text; for them, going deeper would mean losing the entertainment aspect of the program, but the intellectualizing reading strategy suggests that the postmodern text may yield more than surface pleasure.

Finally, the reading strategy that was most frequently used, either in conjunction with others or by itself, was to view the show as if it were similar to real life, the "That's me!" type of reading strategy. By identifying with the characters, their problems and their relationships, the viewers compared them with real life and often spoke about them as if they were real people with real problems. Although these same viewers described the program as strange, weird, and bizarre, they also found ways to incorporate what they saw into a realistic reading.

Identification is the primary way that audiences are thought to relate to the realistic text. In this process, audiences put themselves into the places of particular characters, usually main characters. Because the setting and all other elements are thought to be universally real or truthful, the audience members judge the text by its closeness to, or deviation from, their notions of reality. Many interviewees, when asked about the characters, spoke about them as if they were thinking and feeling people. They also made comments such as "I guess she had a conscience," "She deserved it," or "She was into it by choice," as though it never occurred to them in this reading mode that the characters were created and did not really exist. They often referred to sources outside of the text, such as *The Diary of Laura Palmer,* to justify their interpretations. Because, at this point, the audience is looking for a character with whom to identify, the nature of the character's existence is never in question. The audience members, attempting to identify with the characteristics of a fictional character, create an existence for that character. In this way, the audience is able to say, "That's me!"

In addition, when the laws of cause and effect *were* implemented in *Twin Peaks,* the audience had a tendency to label these occasions "realistic." Even if an event did not make sense according to the viewers' own lives, as long as it was logical in terms of the plot, it was labeled realistic. When the characters acted "in a skewed manner" or when events that were "out of the ordinary" took place, the audiences who at the time saw realism in the text wrote it off as being, for example, "usual for small town life": "Small towns are, on the surface, normal, beautiful, quaint; and underneath they are all nuts."

Another area *Twin Peaks* viewers labeled realistic consisted of the types of problems the character encountered. "They all worked for a living, they all did things. They had kind of human problems, whether it was having a baby or something, you know, just human problems, I thought." The problems that fans of the program considered the most realistic were relationship problems, violence against women, and family problems.

Finally, these *Twin Peaks* viewers revealed that they had more success finding the program's more realistic points when they could relate to the characters. About half of those interviewed found one or more characters they could identify with, in one way or another, and thus felt that a particular character was realistic. Audience reliance on character was perhaps greater in the case of *Twin Peaks* than with a conventional program in which a more classically organized plot serves to orient the viewers. For example, in commenting on a scene that opened implausibly with the closeup of a stuffed deer head lying on a conference room table, one person said: "Cooper just sort of glanced at it and the sheriff is like, you know, this happens all the time."

Unfortunately, for those viewers who depended on the characters' reactions as a guide for their own reactions to the odd behavior presented in the program, *Twin Peaks* held relentlessly to its logic as a postmodern text and disrupted character consistency just as it did away with narrative continuity as an organizing principle for the creation of meaning.

Conclusion

Viewers will go to great lengths to find a way to organize a text in their own way, but they do have limits. A major distinction that our interviewees made was judging the plot by different standards than the characters. Where plot digressions, ruptures, and loose ends were greeted with pleasure, playing fast and loose with character integrity was not. For example, many people considered whatever long-term plotting *Twin Peaks* exhibited as simply the result of accident and serendipity.

Reading the show required a great deal of attention, but these fans usually felt that the unpredictability was a source of pleasure rather than frustration. One audience member commented: "I just wanted to see what was going to happen. I didn't want to get ahead of it and guess what was going to happen." Another had a similar view: "Don't try to figure out the whole thing or try to explain it or really to understand it. Just enjoy it." Yet another generalized to the whole program: "Anyone that tried to predict anything on *Twin Peaks* was usually wrong." The show's unpredictability, which was a result of its narrative ruptures and absent character motivations, was often cited as a major distinction between *Twin Peaks* and the rest of television programming.

Audiences seemed aware that the plot of *Twin Peaks* was playing with established narrative conventions, and they enjoyed making fun of those conventions. Realist cinema, like history, is built on the convention that sequence equals consequence. Because narrative segments on network television are more widely separated by commercials, promotional announcements for other programs, and news breaks, applying this principle to television narrative is more problematic. The organization of television narrative is much more sequential and much less consequential than film narrative. Because *Twin Peaks* represents an exaggeration of existing television conventions, audiences can enjoy its excesses as a kind of parody or even conventionalized pastiche. Those plot events that were recognized as annoying and irrelevant (for example, the drawn-out series of conversations between the seriously wounded Cooper and a senile waiter) were ultimately approved of as part of the show's "quirkiness" and originality. This comfort with the lack of relationship between narrative events is a highly postmodern attitude and has complex ramifications. As the fictitious character, Ian Malcolm, puts it:

Chaos theory teaches us that straight linearity, which we have come to take for granted in everything from physics to fiction, simply does not exist. Linearity is an artificial way of viewing the world. Real life isn't a series of interconnected events occurring one after another like beads strung on a necklace. Life is actually a series of encounters in which one event may change those that follow in a wholly unpredictable, even devastating way. That's a deep truth about the structure of our universe. (Crichton, 1991, p. 171)

This same level of acceptance for a text that foregrounds the lack of relationship between the past and the present at the level of the narrative, however, is not transferred to the construction of the characters who live in the chaotic world of *Twin Peaks.*

Experienced viewers of film and television narrative are very familiar with the conventional ways in which information about character psychology is disclosed. These interviewees seemed to enjoy the playfulness of the program's narrative construction, but they became quite annoyed when the program broke the rules of character construction, particularly those requiring the clear motivation of behavioral changes. They absolutely refused to make the next step in the logic of postmodernism to say that ruptured discourses mean ruptured identities, and that disintegrated plots mean unintegrated selves.

Readers struggle with texts because, in effect, we convert our lives to realist texts. When faced with a postmodern text like *Twin Peaks,* viewers can make increasingly desperate gestures to ground the work's excesses in some stable external reality, by citing David Lynch as an *auteur,* by referring to information reported in the press about the program and its cast, and, finally, by reading characters in the classic realist fashion, inventing psychological reasons so as to identify with a character's otherwise inexplicable behavior. These gestures become striking when compared with the shrug and smile with which these viewers responded to the free-form structure of the plot. At this juncture, for these subjects, reading the postmodern may mean incorporating only part of the instability implied in postmodern theory. The vectors that cross individual subjects in their nomadic wandering incorporate elements of postmodernism, modernism, and realism in approaching reading strategies. If we look at audiences not as specifically rooted in a period or position but as responding to diverse influences—grazing, if you will—we can see how conceptualizing reading strategies instead of audiences may give us further insights into the possibilities of postmodern selves or subjectivities.

Notes

1. *Twin Peaks,* as a television show, begins with the discovery of the body of Laura Palmer (Sheryl Lee), the 17-year-old high school homecoming queen. The body is discovered on the rocky beach of a nearby lake by Pete Martell (Jack Nance), the easygoing foreman of the Packard Sawmill and husband to Catherine (Piper Laurie). Sheriff Harry S. Truman (Michael Ontkean) begins his investigation and notifies Laura's father, Leland Palmer (Ray Wise). The subsequent discovery across the state line of Ronette Pulaski (Phoebe Augustine), alive but viciously tortured, justifies the entrance of FBI agent Dale Cooper (Kyle MacLachlan) to conduct the investigation. A close look at Laura's last few days casts suspicion on many of the citizens of Twin Peaks. Her relationship with Bobby Briggs (Dana Ashbrook), the local football hero and drug dealer, reveals a darker side of both Laura

and the town. Laura's look-alike cousin Madeline (Sheryl Lee) arrives, only to be killed also. Cooper and Truman explore Twin Peaks' intricate web of affairs, plots, and eccentrics, ultimately revealing that Laura's father, Leland, was secretly possessed by the evil entity, Bob (Frank Silva). Subplots also included Catherine Martell and Ben Horne's (Richard Beymar) attempt to steal the Packard Mill, the town's largest industry, away from Josie (Joan Chen), Catherine's supposedly widowed sister-in-law; the triangle of Shelly Johnson (Madchen Amick), Bobby Briggs, and Shelly's husband, Leo (Eric Da Re); and the triangle of Norma (Peggy Lipton), Big Ed (Everett McGill), and Ed's wife Nadine (Wendy Robie). After Laura's murder is solved, Cooper stays on to solve other murders by his former FBI partner Windom Earle (Kenneth Welsh). Earle kills people every time he takes a chess piece in a game played in the newspaper with Cooper. Cooper is finally drawn into the "Black Lodge," where he confronts Earle and loses his soul to Bob.

2. This is only part of Foucault's discursive formation. See Foucault (1972).

3. Of these participants, 3 were working class, 1 lower middle, 18 middle, 2 upper middle (class was self-designated). In addition, there were three individual interviews (2 males, 1 female) and one family interviewed (5 people; male, female, and 13-year-old male were fans), all middle class. In all, 33 fans were interviewed. In the group interviews, there were 25 people: 13 women and 12 men. Ages were as follows:

Age	F	M	Total
10-20	1	2	3
20-30	5	2	7
30-40	6	5	11
40-50	1	3	4

These fans were gathered by advertising for fans of *Twin Peaks* in three newspapers in a northeastern city of 300,000. The newspapers were all alternative newspapers—one black, one Hispanic, and one aimed at upper-middle-class people of all races. Only the latter one brought responses. The interviews were conducted at *Twin Peaks* parties where coffee, donuts, and cherry pie were served and where people who dressed as various characters from the series made appearances. Parts of an early episode were watched to set the stage and then groups of two and three were interviewed in separate rooms. The series of gatherings lasted 3 hours, 1½ hours of which was interview time. Focus groups were chosen as an interviewing tactic because we were interested in the process of being a fan as well as in how people who viewed the show talked with each other and fellow fans about the show.

References

Barthes, R. (1974). *S/Z* (R. Miller, Trans.). New York: Noonday.

Barthes, R. (1975). *The pleasure of the text* (R. Miller, Trans.). New York: Hill and Wang.

Baudrillard, J. (1983). *Simulations* (P. Foss, P. Patton, & P. Beitchman, Trans.). New York: Semiotext(e).

Baudrillard, J. (1985). The ecstasy of communication. In H. Foster (Ed.), *Postmodern culture* (pp. 126-134). London: Pluto.

Collins, J. (1992). Postmodernism and television. In R. Allen (Ed.), *Channels of discourse, reassembled* (pp. 327-353). Chapel Hill: University of North Carolina Press.

Crichton, M. (1991). *Jurassic Park*. New York: Bantam.

de Certeau, M. (1986). *The practice of everyday life* (S. F. Rendall, Trans.). Berkeley: University of California Press.

Ellis, J. (1992). *Visible fictions* (rev. ed.). New York: Routledge.

Fiske, J. (1987). *Television culture*. London: Methuen.

Fiske, J. (1991). Postmodernism and television. In J. Curran & M. Gurevitch (Eds.), *Mass media and society* (pp. 55-67). London: Edward Arnold.

Foucault, M. (1970). *The order of things*. New York: Vintage.

Foucault, M. (1972). *The archaeology of knowledge* (R. Sawyer, Trans.). New York: Pantheon.

Grossberg, L. (1988). Wandering audiences, nomadic critics. *Cultural Studies, 2,* 377-391.

Grossberg, L. (1992). *We gotta get out of this place*. New York: Routledge.

Jameson, F. (1985). Postmodernism and consumer society. In H. Foster (Ed.), *Postmodern culture* (pp. 111-125). London: Pluto.

Kaplan, E. (1988). Who's imaginary? The television apparatus, the female body and textual strategies in select rock videos on MTV. In E. Pribram (Ed.), *Female spectators: Looking at film and television* (pp. 132-165). London: Verso.

Kellner, D. (1992). Popular culture and the construction of postmodern identities. In S. Lash & J. Friedman (Eds.), *Modernity and identity* (pp. 141-177). Oxford: Basil Blackwell.

Morris, M. (1988). At Henry Parks Motel. *Cultural Studies, 2,* 1-46.

Nietzsche, F. (1964). *Human, all too human* (P. Cohn, Trans.). New York: Russell & Russell.

Radway, J. (1988). Reception study: Ethnography and the problems of dispersed audiences and nomadic subjects. *Cultural Studies, 2,* 359-376.

Silverman, K. (1983). *The subject of semiotics.* Oxford: Oxford University Press.

5

"Gilt by Association"[1]: Talk Show Participants' Televisually Enhanced Status and Self-Esteem

Patricia J. Priest

Although mass communication scholars have carried out countless studies of television audiences, few have examined the view from the other side of the screen. Star biographies and scattered, anecdotal evidence provide only glimpses into the effects of basking in the national spotlight. In this chapter, I describe the fallout that occurs when talk show participants trade intimate and potentially discrediting information about themselves to gain access to this preeminent medium. Situating inquiry about television from this vantage point increases understanding about a slippery new idea put forth by Ewen (1988), Tichi (1991), and others that stepping inside the set, getting in, represents access to a better-than-real "reality." Of particular interest are participants' feelings about themselves after they have been "there" and have pulled aside the curtain, revealing Oz at work.

To investigate the consequences of participation in a television forum many consider base and tawdry, I interviewed 43 people who had disclosed topics on television talk shows that ranged from the mundane to the profane.[2] I used a variety of sleuthing techniques[3] to track down guests who had appeared on *Donahue* and other daytime talk programs.[4] Informants were incredibly diverse, mirroring the range of subjects discussed on the genre. Roughly one third stepped into the national arena from the distant margins of society to speak about highly intimate and stigmatizing topics; these included, among others, a "sex priestess" who had had sex with more than 2,000 partners, a "transsexual lesbian," "swingers," prostitutes, and a self-proclaimed preacher who espouses drug use as the route to salvation and revolution.

Most of the others were more firmly situated toward the "center" in terms of their lived experiences (for example, a middle-class child with AIDS, a flight attendant who is a rape survivor, or a plastic surgeon's wife who has undergone about a dozen cosmetic surgeries) but had self-disclosed about a stigmatizing feature that marked them as outside the boundaries of "normalcy" on that one characteristic. At the other end of the continuum were a few who had discussed topics that carried no stigma, such as an organ donor and a married couple who were finalists in a *Donahue* contest celebrating exemplary husbands.

AUTHOR'S NOTE: Copyright to the work this chapter is drawn from is held by Patricia J. Priest.

In previous work, I discuss participants' rationale for appearing on talk shows and the role of television in their lives prior to disclosure (see Priest, 1995). In brief, I found that participants accepted the chance to sketch themselves into the television landscape because they passionately believed the public needed to hear their stories. Most of the panelists used self-disclosures during the show tapings as a stigma management tactic (Goffman, 1963) in their efforts to normalize images of their out-groups. They were fully aware of the freak show characteristics of the genre but agreed to step up to the forum nonetheless because of the potential to educate the public about topics generally neglected, bungled, or vilified by the press.

In this chapter, I describe the powerful and unexpected outcomes experienced by talk show participants willing to run the televised gauntlet of derision to "come out" on television as members of marginalized groups. I explore the shifting self-conceptions triggered partly by public reactions and partly by seeing one's reflected image emanating from the set. This work is the first to situate inquiry from the perspective of talk show participants. I render the data in some detail because they provide rare empirical evidence to support Baudrillard's (1988) and other writers' claims that members of postmodern societies now accord a higher value to televisual images than to offscreen, lived realities. I argue below that this ontological shift has important ramifications for the self-concepts of those chosen to appear on television. First, however, I summarize the critical work pertaining to television talk shows.

The Talk Show Literature

The talk show genre is surely an odd amalgam. The shows, peopled with drag queens, presidential candidates, and children with AIDS, veer daily from inane to somber discussions. Munson (1993) notes that the juxtapositions are inherent in the form, which he describes as quintessentially postmodern: "Like the term itself, the 'talk show' fuses and seems to reconcile two different, even contradictory, rhetorics. It links conversation, the interpersonal—the premodern oral tradition—with the mass-mediated spectacle born of modernity" (p. 6).

Although viewers may sometimes feel squeamish to hear panelists tell all on television, Carbaugh (1989) notes that *Donahue*'s underlying motifs (which he identifies as the rights of individuals to speak their opinions and to make choices for their lives) are long-standing themes valued in American culture. Carbaugh argues that talk show panelists are rewarded by tolerant listening and praise for their honesty because disclosures serve society's need for a wide range of information: "A speaker can reveal information that may seem untoward and thus bring discredit to one's self, community or country, yet do so in a way that is redeemable socially" (p. 137).

Many who critique talk shows generally assume that participants use the genre as a confessional or as a therapy session. Crow's (1986) and Banks's (1990) studies of Dr. Ruth Westheimer's *Good Sex* television show point out that the show's dynamics mimic therapeutic encounters. Banks speculates that "Westheimer may have taken the place of an earlier confessor, even to the granting of absolution" (p. 85). Conrad (1982) suggests that Donahue's appearance and his Catholic upbringing make him well suited for this role as father confessor.

White (1992) contends that therapeutic patterns of discourse permeate television programming. She notes the similarities between participants involved in such diverse programs as the *Love Connection,* Dr. Ruth's *Good Sex,* and *The 700 Club*: "These are all subjects who are set into televisual representation (sound and/or image) in direct proportion to their willingness to participate in a therapeutic transaction through confession, in a context wherein representation is always commodified, one way or another" (p. 137).

Masciarotte (1991), however, compares the disclosures on talk shows to the "Protestant activity of testimony or witnessing before the group" (pp. 84-85) rather than to confession or therapy. Alcoff and Gray (1993), in their work on rape and incest survivors' discourse on the media, also eschew the label of confession: "A witness is not someone who confesses, but someone who knows the truth and has the courage to tell it" (pp. 287-288). I agree with the authors of these two works that the disclosures on TV talk shows are generally not guilt-ridden but are instead powerful declarations of identity. I will return again to this issue of the assumption of "guilt."

Much of the research cited above grapples with the genre's paradoxical workings: Participation is potentially empowering and transgressive—while the risks of containment and trivialization are great. Several authors refer to Foucault's (1978) work concerning the power imbalances inherent in confessional practices. Foucault argued that those hearing confessions during psychiatric sessions or religious ceremonies have the power to exonerate, punish, or normalize the speakers' behaviors. The manifest power differentials on most talk shows, in which hosts rarely disclose and the audience demands answers to the most intimate of questions, have prompted several writers to voice their concerns about the damaging or limiting potential of the genre when participants attempt to force societal change through public speaking about private issues.

White (1992) and Alcoff and Gray (1993), for example, note that producers, hosts, and audience members channel participants' stories in various ways that strip them of control over how they tell and defend their life stories. Knapp (1988) contends that the structure and sensational tenor of episodes of *The Oprah Winfrey Show* that pertain to gay issues "insidiously undermine any possibility of a positive response to their lesbian guests" (p. 4).

None of these writers, however, actually questioned participants about outcomes that occurred within or beyond the studio.[5] A smattering of writings on television's potential to boost the status of those who appear on the medium indicate that researchers must address the broadcast nature of the experience. Over 45 years ago, Lazarsfeld and Merton (1948) noted a media function they called *status conferral:*

> The mass media bestow prestige and enhance the authority of individuals and groups by legitimizing their status. Recognition by the press . . . testifies that one has arrived, that one is important enough to have been singled out from the large anonymous masses, that one's behavior and opinions are significant enough to require public notice. (p. 101)

This work investigates whether television's imprimatur of a larger-than-life status extends even to those who essentially discredit themselves during their brief 15 minutes of fame.

Finally, critics' recurring notes of concern about the commodification of talk show panelists also warrant closer attention. Although Knapp (1988), Rapping (1991), and Steenland (1990) decry the shows' exploitation of participants for spectacle, White (1992) cautions: "It is important to remember that there is little in contemporary American culture that escapes commodification. This cannot be, in itself, automatic terms for absolute critique: the issue instead is negotiating one's position within this context" (p. 80). Indeed, the postmodern clutch of consumerism works in certain unexpected ways to participants' advantage; the peculiar results of the struggle for self-inscription on TV talk shows are the focus of this chapter.

A Brief Case History

Before I describe the public responses and the reported surge in self-esteem, I offer a case study that illustrates some of the unusual consequences of public disclosure. Michael Elmeer,[6] a very personable 27-year-old who works at a design firm in Florida, has been on *Donahue* twice. Michael, who has AIDS, wrote to the handful of daytime talk shows on the air in 1989 to ask for the opportunity to talk about how his former partner had knowingly deceived him about his HIV status. To tantalize producers, Michael mentioned some particularly intimate information in the letter. He revealed that he had worked for an escort service for three weeks after learning of his own HIV status and, in what he calls his "broken state of mind," had not protected his "clients." He says he also disclosed this to demonstrate the utter degradation he felt after being rejected and put at risk by his partner.

Michael wanted to appear on TV to warn viewers that they should protect themselves, even in relationships they presume are monogamous. He also stepped forward as a plaintiff to argue his case that he had been wronged by his lover. At the time Michael first appeared on *Donahue,* only his parents and his former partner knew he was HIV positive. He was aware of the risk of ostracism by those who fear people with AIDS.

Producers at *Donahue* put Michael right on the air. They ran with the prostitution angle, and Donahue intimated that Michael might have put 100 or so people at risk for AIDS. Members of the studio audience were sharply critical, and Michael felt the show had been disastrous. He left the taping with great trepidation, feeling he "had been branded this horrible thing" on *Donahue.* In one fell swoop, he came out as a gay male with AIDS who had briefly worked as a prostitute. He said he had been willing "to admit what I had to admit to," but was mortified by the show's myopic focus on that three-week stint of his life.

After the show aired, however, he was greeted with excitement—so much so that he was rather puzzled by the degree and nature of the responses. He noted the reaction of a friend he had known in high school who ran into him in a store:

> He almost was more impressed with the getting on *Donahue* than saying, "I'm sorry you are HIV positive." I think because it's something that most people can't even believe that—I guess average America doesn't think they could ever get on a talk show.

People congratulated him wherever he went. Furthermore, Michael found he was able to use his *Donahue* credentials as a "calling card" in diverse situations from contacting Ryan White's mother to calling up the actor Dack Rambo (whom he had also seen on *Donahue*) to securing additional media coverage for his AIDS awareness crusade.

Although the responses from people everywhere were very supportive and upbeat, Michael still seemed to be struggling to make sense of that brief period in his life as well as the resulting depiction on *Donahue*. Nevertheless, he said he would appear again, because of the high-profile status he had achieved among AIDS activists and in the larger community. Michael said, "I don't want to use the word *celebrity,* but, in the eyes of people who know you, you are a celebrity. Because you've done something that they can't do, and that you have put yourself before the public."

Public Responses

Michael is actually an unusual case in that the label affixed—"former prosti-tute"—was not the one he expected. More commonly, panelists shouldered the often pejorative labels so as to squarely address stereotypes and circulate new meanings about the topic—whether it was swinging, stepparenting, or surviving rape. Many expected to face a negative backlash after their television appear-ances because of the transgressive nature of the disclosures. Although they steeled themselves for harsh repercussions, they were pleasantly surprised and somewhat baffled by highly favorable public responses when they returned to their communities.

An electrified reaction was quite common. Sherrol Miller, once married to a gay, con-man, bigamist, was very popular with viewers. She said, "Oh, they just kiss me and hug me and carry on. I'm thinking, 'What would it be like to be a real celebrity?' " She has received thousands of letters and more than two dozen plane tickets from viewers around the country who have invited her to visit their towns.

Every single informant described enthusiastic responses from the general public. A woman who appeared on a *Sally Jessy Raphael* episode about sexy moms and jealous daughters spoke of the small town atmosphere in her commu-nity: "There's not a whole lot that goes on, so when this happened, it just sort of shot us to celebrity status." She noted that the delighted recognition of "I saw you on *Sally Jessy!* " was still happening a couple years after their appearance. She added, "It was like rooting for a football team, the same kind of enthusiasm."

Only rarely did participants relate unpleasant repercussions. Patrick Gill, an advocate of gay marriage rights, described a frightening incident on the metro:

> A group of youths, black youths, were looking at me. . . . They went, "That fag on *Oprah!*" or something like that and they all ran over to the door of the train . . . but the doors shut on them and then the others were banging on the windows and glass and no one else on the train understood why.

On the other hand, however, Patrick's partner Craig Dean felt that the media exposure often protected them:

We've been treated worse as anonymous gay people. . . . People see Craig, us, as a gay couple, they don't know who we are on the streets, you know, we receive abuse, you know, harassment, they'll yell, "Faggot!" at us. One time someone tried to shoot us as we were leaving the club. Uh, if . . . when people know us as Craig and Patrick, if they're anti-gay, they aren't anti-Craig and Patrick.

Participants reported that the overwhelming majority of the feedback was limited to brief, friendly exchanges. Significantly, responses were often merely the simple but excited recognition: "I saw you on TV!" Kate Bornstein, a transsexual lesbian, said:

When people come up and say those kinds of things like, "Oh, I saw you on *Donahue*." But then they don't go and try to engage in conversation, like, you know, "What you said about this, I would really like to talk." There's nothing to do with that. [Instead,] with "You, it's you!"

Ken Henningson, married to his ex-wife's sister, said, "A lot of people talk to you that didn't talk to you before: 'Hey, I saw you on TV.' " "Renee," who had appeared on a *Ricki Lake* episode that blasted men as "dogs," said that people enthused over the fact that she was going to be on national television, but "they didn't even want to hear what the topic was."

Many noted they were more popular with friends and associates after their appearances. "Doris," who exhibited graphic photographs on *Donahue* of how she looked prior to liposuction surgery, said, "It's very interesting how some people really really really think that's a big deal; I mean, like it influences their being with you, which blows my mind." Joy Schulenburg, a lesbian who shares parenting responsibilities with two gay friends, commented, "There are some people, yeah, like casual friends, I guess, um, that did treat me kind of different. They'd somehow act like my opinion is more valuable than it used to be."

An appearance on a daytime television talk show also generated an outpouring of support from similarly marginalized others via calls and letters, what several called "fan mail." Everyone seemed slightly flattered but also somewhat un-nerved by those infatuated responses. Formerly invisible out-group members revealed themselves to them and were especially warm in their congratulations. Talk show guests often quickly came to be seen as leaders within their social circle. Patrick and Craig, for example, were asked to be the grand marshals at a gay parade. Joy, a gay parent, said, "It has, within my own [lesbian] community, given me somewhat, again, of that celebrity status." This was due in large measure to the activism that originally generated the publicity, but their willing-ness to speak in the contested space of the TV talk show about issues confronting their stigmatized groups accelerated their ascendancy to leadership.

Changes in Self-Esteem

Their sojourn in the television landscape bolstered participants' self-esteem in a variety of ways. Many felt they were special because producers had selected them as participants. Dale Potruski, who appeared on *Donahue* with his wife to discuss his low sex drive remarked, "We got this like awesome compliment that for some reason we're like, you know, invited in to appear." Another participant, a devout Christian who discussed his former lifestyle as a homosexual on *Donahue,* felt that God had chosen him and his wife to be on the program. He said:

> We felt special in our relationship to God, because both my wife and I have in those—some areas of low self-esteem because we weren't valued, you know, a lot by our parents and uh, it feels special in God's eyes—that was very encouraging.

Each was aware that there were others who were similarly situated (for example, other transsexual lesbians or other prostitutes—other "others"), and they were pleased that they had essentially won the casting call to represent their groups.

Many felt their life stories were certified as true and worthy because producers had chosen them over others. Lorretta Woodbury, an incest survivor, said, "It goes back to being validated. Uh, and people knowing that—I hadn't made this up all these years." Later, she continued: "It's a relief. 'Cause I know that there's people over the years that I worked with who thought I was a little odd. . . . [They] can sit there now and go, 'Well, I'll be. There was a reason.' " Michael, who asserted that his former partner had carelessly exposed him to the AIDS virus but was uncertain whether mutual friends believed his claim, said:

> I think my going on the show was my way of proving some credibility to my story. Because I thought if—if a talk show is willing to talk about it, then they must be willing to—or at least there's some credibility there.

Informants often described long years of struggle to come to terms with their difference in society, a period during which they had been buffeted by low self-esteem. Leanne Dees, serving prison time for adoption fraud, said of her appearance on *Donahue*: "It gave me—I realized that I didn't have low self-esteem, I had no self-esteem. And now I've managed to get it up to low self-esteem."

Many felt that weathering the sometimes heated exchanges on the show was a thrilling accomplishment. Participants were buoyed by newfound feelings of self-efficacy. Heather Wright, the target of sexual harassment at her Iowa high school, said, "It made me a lot more stronger than I was, that I was able to stand up for myself. I had more self-confidence—by doing this." Lorretta, an incest survivor, said:

> I like myself, and I think that may even have intensified it, that uh, I really know that I'm OK. After that show, people came up and were putting their arms around me and just very—guys too, very nurturing, very caring . . . and so I just really felt like what I had done was really OK. I felt like I had contributed something, uh, to society.

Bert, part of a gay parenting trio, described similar feelings: "In my down times, and when I think I'm useless or something like that, I think, 'But, wait, I have touched these people.' . . . It makes me feel good about myself." After the public repeatedly conveyed its respect to them, participants felt brave for taking up the banner for their group and serving in the vanguard.

Several described the delight they felt when they watched the program and saw how composed they appeared or how well they were able to stand up to the negative members of the crowd. Catherine Harrison, the lesbian partner of a transsexual, said:

It gave me a lot of confidence that I didn't know before that I could be articulate. . . . I could actually acknowledge that about myself and [say], "Oh. I sound intelligent, or I actually have something to say that—" and, you know, "I can look good on camera."

Significantly, informants often referenced their screen images as the trigger of these feelings of self-worth. The Christian man who appeared on *Donahue* with his wife to talk about his former gay identity said:

Having been on the show and then watching ourselves on the show—I mean it's not often that you get to watch yourself on TV and how you really come across to people. And I really liked myself. I mean, it was like, it really improved my self-image.

Bert said, "I was happy with how I looked because I thought I was horrible, you know, and I thought, 'No, you're not bad at all,' you know, 'You look all right.' And the makeup helps too." Kate, a transsexual lesbian, explained how she felt when she glimpsed herself in the monitor: "That was really nice, it was so nice, because I felt, fine, OK, I don't look like, you know, a complete jerk. I don't look like a travesty, and I'm OK." This verification of being "OK" and "not bad" was particularly important for those who had stepped in from the farthest margins of society.

Television seemed to serve as the quintessential "looking-glass self" for those who appeared on the medium. Cooley (1902) wrote: "The thing that moves us to pride or shame is not the mere mechanical reflection of ourselves, but an imputed sentiment, the imagined effect of this reflection upon another's mind" (p. 152). The "imputed sentiment" of the televised reflection may be one of specialness, being chosen and certified worthy of joining the ranks of those whose images have been broadcast on television. "Doris," whose body and face had been recast by thousands of dollars of surgery, said of her appearance on *Donahue*: "So it's given me permission, it's almost like it's given me permission that I'm really OK."

Carl Blandino, engaged to a woman 40 years his junior, said that it felt wonderful to see himself on the monitor: "Here I am, a little boy from a little town in Pennsylvania, on TV!" "Doris," too, marveled at how far she had come, saying:

You're meeting a star [Donahue], you know—he's famous. You know, I mean, I'm from, you know, originally, Norton, Mass. You know, I'm a little kid from a small town, and I'm thinking, Does he really know who he has here?

Pete and Charlotte Lumpkins, a married couple struggling to accommodate her newfound lesbian identity, also stressed their humble beginnings. Charlotte said, "Now you understand, Pat? We are nobodies, come from nowhere." Pete reminded me that they returned to "no-man's-land," a city housing project in Sacramento, after the show taping. Sherrol, once married to a bigamist, spoke of the people waiting in line after the show to get her autograph, "And I tell 'em, I say, 'Honey, my hand to God, I'm telling you, I am nobody special. You know, I empty bed pans and give pain shots for a living. I'm nobody.' "

A former exotic dancer who calls herself Rocki Mountains was pleased to be singled out for recognition when producers invited her as a guest on an episode of *Sally Jessy Raphael* featuring big-busted women:

I went to a rural school, you know, graduated in a class of 70 kids, and went through the routine that most everybody did around here, and . . . I just never expected to even be called to do anything like that. I didn't expect anything in my life to happen that was important enough for anybody to want to hear about.

The transition from "nobodies, come from nowhere" to people whose stories are worth hearing in a national forum (or whose bodies are deemed worthy of display) happened in a single catapulting leap when producers plucked them from obscurity.

A woman who appeared with her daughter on two shows about sexy moms expressed a feeling of disbelief at seeing herself framed there, on TV:

Here we are, nobodies, and we're on this show, and it's just hard to believe, really hard to believe. I mean, we watch all these stars and, you know, all these famous people, and suddenly there *you* are? You know—most assuredly not a star! It's like, "Gosh!"

Several believed that being singled out by Donahue and his staff was an achievement of the highest order. "Doris," whose body had been reshaped by numerous plastic surgeries, said, "If you're on the *Donahue* show, you've made it. There's nothing else other than maybe we could be invited to President Bush's for dinner." Bert said passionately,

And that show [*Donahue*] was sort of like, I want to say a second honeymoon, but that's not quite it. It was like a toast from the country that we were doing OK, that's how I felt . . . being asked on to do it and also to get the feedback that we got from that show.

Later, Bert added, "It was nice to be able to ah, be presented by him or something."

Participants were keenly aware of the national reach of the program. Several stressed the word when discussing their appearances. Carl, for example, said that his former wife had always held him back from the fame he felt was his due as a dancer. He said of his young fiancée, "I give Michelle a lot of credit. For going on television. *National* television." Many amended their comments about TV in this way. Marty Crossman, whose son has AIDS, extended the geographic coverage to the show further still. She said, "Is it a big deal? Yeah, cause it's national. International!" Susen Henningson, married to her sister's ex-husband, expressed the same theme: "It aired all over the world, you know."

The actual experience of the show taping was described as somewhat unimpressive. Participants were treated well and appreciated the first-class accommodations, but they seemed to find their moments on TV rather lackluster. The disappointment they described reminded me of Dorothy's dismay in *The Wizard of Oz* when she discovered the grandeur was faked. Dale, who talked about his sex life on *Donahue,* compared the sensation to the slight letdown he experienced when he lost his virginity. Their impressions reversed, however, when they began to receive positive responses from strangers who had seen them on television, and when they saw themselves situated onscreen. Only then did they seem to be aware of the impact of the medium, and did the cycle of positive effects truly kick in.

The status accorded those who had appeared on television occasionally worked to the panelists' disadvantage. For example, Jim Lightner, a swinger, when asked whether his appearance had attracted sexual partners, replied:

Actually, in some ways, I think it's had some of the opposite effect. In some ways, I think, with a few people that we've ended up encountering in the past months, it's been a bit of an intimidating effect on them because we're, quote, too well known. . . . Well, some of the people we know that we meet haven't been involved in this for quite some time, so, I guess, they may end up thinking we're a little more hardcore about this than they are . . . and they may think that we're just a little too fast for them, if you want to use that term—which isn't the case, but I think the aspect of being on television magnifies that a bit.

A related drawback was that some participants felt they had to match the image they were representing. Craig, an advocate for gay marriage rights, said, "People see us as an ideal couple, and that's the hardest thing to live up to." Bert and Joy, gay parents, related how they found it very stressful to play the perfect family on TV talk shows and return home to bicker about working out their complex parenting arrangement. Generally, however, disclosers found this newfound status useful as well as affirming.

As predicted by Lazarsfeld and Merton (1948), media attention for talk show participants accelerated in a spiraling fashion. For many, a talk show appearance led to other offers. Catherine, who was later interviewed for a feature story in a lesbian magazine and asked to appear on a local talk show, said, "I'm sort of looked at differently in that, 'Oh, I guess she has something to say.' " Sabrina Aset, head priestess of the Church of the Most High Goddess, said:

The more people that know about you, the more will listen to what you have to say. And that's great. So I have enjoyed being like at that rally against police brutality and having a—one of the channel people come up an' say, "Oh, hi, Sabrina; I recognize you. What do you think of this?" And say, "Hey, someone wants to listen to me." I can say something and the people out there watching TV will take my opinion and maybe think about things.

The combined effect of the quickened pace of press attention, positive public responses, and a sense of mastery over the rather daunting experiences left participants with feelings of generalized empowerment. Susen, married to her sister's former husband, commented:

Well, I think it's a kick, cause if you can go on national television, and sit in front of those people, what can't you do? I mean, it's like college, I keep thinking I'm never going to make it. . . . But if I've been on television, and I've got this far in my life, why can't I finish that?

Wendy KruppDespain, a rape survivor, said, "I think it was probably a major stepping stone in giving me a boost of confidence to go out there and do public speaking seriously." "Doris" began to take a more active role in animal rights causes after her appearances on *Donahue* and *The Oprah Winfrey Show* that centered on her many cosmetic surgeries. She said, "I don't want to make a difference anymore, I mean, I want to make a *huge* difference. . . . It has empowered me . . . that people really want to listen to me, like I'm interesting, My God!"

Although many hoped their visibility would precipitate a simple normalizing effect, gains exceeded expectations as participants found themselves enveloped in a mantle of distinction. Monaco (1978) calls the perception of worthiness that emanates from a television appearance "gilt by association" (p. 6), a phrase that aptly summarizes the effects experienced even by those whose participation entailed disclosure of information that would have in former times warranted community censure. The process of status conferral is triggered in a rather content-neutral way, transferred regardless of the topics brought forward. In the next section, I explore the cultural underpinnings for these perplexing outcomes, in which televised declarations of norm-breaking behavior that disavow guilt earn transgressors a gilt veneer.

Margin to Center, Outside In

Baudrillard (1988) contends that members of postmodern societies prefer simulated hyperrealities over a nonmediated reality that seems pallid by comparison. He asserts: "The cinema and TV are America's reality!" (p. 104). Schickel (1985) writes: "What matters is that if we do not somehow insert ourselves into this reality, we run the danger of being, in our own eyes, unpersons" (p. 263). The corollary to the status conferral function discussed previously in which individuals are singled out as worthy of attention, then, concerns the impact of omissions. Many participants felt unworthy, marginalized, until they were allowed to represent themselves and their issues in the hyperspace of television.

Ewen (1988) argues that this yearning for inclusion in the televisual realm can be traced to pervasive feelings of anomie and dislocation that characterize postmodern life:

> In a society where conditions of anonymity fertilize the desire to "become somebody," the *dream of identity,* the *dream of wholeness,* is intimately woven together with the desire to be known; to be visible; to be documented, for all to see . . . when "being no one" is the norm. . . . Becoming "someone" is a gift bestowed upon people by the image machine. (pp. 94-95, italics in the original)

The chance to ride the nationally broadcast airwaves was especially valuable to people who felt their out-groups were invisible on television.

The role of the television personality is one of many "possible selves" (Markus & Nurius, 1986) that audience members can slip into with ease because of countless years of watching the role enacted. A handful of respondents clearly articulated a desire to play the role within the set and described daydreams that expressed these yearnings. Bert said:

> I used to fantasize when I was 12 or 13 watching *Donahue* how I would love to be on that show and be such an individual that people would, you know, clamor, you know, hang on my every word. . . . It was in those dreams of being a movie star. You know, and then my life progressed, then I wasn't that movie star, but was just ultimately myself. And people were interested in me.

Joy said of her many talk show appearances, "It fulfills, in some ways, a fantasy. I used to listen to the late night radio talk shows and imagine what I would say." When asked to elaborate, Joy replied:

> You know, kids have fantasies. I know more people who have fantasies [about] being on the Johnny Carson show. . . . Whether it's playing the spoons or, you know, bringing

their 18-foot python or something on. We grew up with it, it's part of our American culture, um, and I think everybody who dreams of being famous . . . [thinks], "I'll be so famous, Johnny Carson will invite me on his show."

Although the on-air experience itself had been somewhat disappointing, the red carpet treatment they received before and after the taping made them feel like stars. Dale, who discussed his sex life on *Donahue*, conveyed his excitement:

It's very cool like you know, they send the limo and you ride over in a limo and pull up to the 30 Rock, and you walk beneath the canvas . . . like in the old days, you know. . . . Then they ah make mention to the guard and these people are waiting in line to be audience participants, the lengthy lines, and somebody comes out of the elevator and greets you . . . and you're just really glad that you got this really fancy Swiss hotel and we go back and jump on the bed, yell out the window.

The exclusivity, being one of few to cross the boundaries beyond the people waiting in long lines, made the experience all the more valuable to Bert, a gay parent, who said:

Before the *Donahue* show, uh, I was unemployed, looking for work, and after I was on that, and realized that me, Bert Lacquement, was on this and these people that I was interviewing on had never reached that fame and it was sort of like a status, in like the world: This is my perception of it, that I could indeed do anything and have anything I wanted. And uh, so just that self-worth of knowing that I had been on TV. You know, in front of millions. And ah, I carried it off, didn't make a complete idiot of myself, that um, I could find something other than a minimum wage job. And I did.

The limited potential for access to television allows participants to join an elite community of those who have appeared onscreen.

Meyrowitz (1985) contends that narrow parameters of information shared across groups in the era prior to television "distinguished insiders from outsiders" (p. 131).[7] On talk shows, participants become "insiders" alongside celebrities and politicians—other groups allowed access to this hallowed place. Participants' membership shifted from an outcast status to celebrity, from margin to center, outside in.

Ewen (1988) writes of the media's power to bestow significance to individuals: "In their ability to magnify, and to create near universal recognition, the mass media are able to invest the everyday lives of formerly everyday people with a magical sense of value, a secularized imprint of the sacred" (p. 93). Informant reports occasionally alluded to television's hyperreality as a sacred cultural space. Kate, an insightful and witty transsexual lesbian who had appeared on numerous shows, was cognizant of television's magical ability to grant celebrity status. She mentioned Joseph Campbell's work on myths:

I think our myths, or gods and goddesses or demons or demi-gods and goddesses, are our celebrities. The myths are their stories, and—and in a way, I think that by appearing on there—that kind of elevated you into this, kind of like, hierarchy of a myth maker, and it does.

A young man who appeared on a *Donahue* show that highlighted past guests spoke during the program about the response from the public after the earlier broadcast:

I felt like Bo Jackson. It's like, "I know you!" . . . We were walking around the Village about a week after the show. It was a couple from Philly. They stopped like they seen God.[8]

Marty, whose son has AIDS, said acquaintances often exclaimed, "You've met him!" when they learned she had been on *Donahue*. A common question asked of participants after their experience was, "What's Donahue like?" Talk show panelists had gained access to an inner sanctum populated largely by deities viewers feel they know intimately but are separated from by the glass wall of the set. People responded effusively when they recognized participants, marveling at their success at reaching the mystical-but-real ground zero of television transmission.

In our postmodern era marked by a profusion of and fascination with simulated images, participants took their places on the set to have their images—constructed but real—floated. As Michaels (1987) noted: "In postmodernist space, the activity of the audience is self-inscription. One is invited to create meaning in the text by writing oneself there. . . . Within the text, we displace the star" (p. 91). I believe this rare opportunity for active and actual displacement is part of what causes the public commotion[9] and the boost to self-esteem.

The star mapping that Seigworth (1993) describes, using Jameson's (1988) ideas about cognitive mapping, allows individuals to position themselves after their appearances closer to the stars than to the commonplace and commoners. Viewers who recognize participants "hail" them (to use Althusser's, 1971, term) or "position" them (Davies & Harré's, 1990, concept) not as "deviant"—as many feared—but as someone "seen on TV."

Tichi (1991) describes the influence of the "as seen on TV" label used for 50 years by advertisers to connote distinction:

> The slogan points further, toward the cultural change wrought by television in the introduction of a new set of cognitive and perceptual categories in which what is real or unreal is superseded by what is televised and what is not. . . . To be transposed onto television is to be elevated out of the banal realm of the off-screen and repositioned in the privileged on-screen world. (pp. 138-140)

Panelists and viewers alike reveled in each participant's new status as commodity. In this era of image, commodification is highly valued when the stamp of "as seen on TV" is affixed. Those chosen to participate earn the favored role identity of "as seen on TV"—an ace among what Gergen (1991) called the shuffled "cards of identity" (p. 176).

Goffman (1959) notes the range of props that individuals use to telescope status. Apparently, appearing framed in a 19-inch television set is a prop that prompts extravagant, unstudied respect from others. Dale, a part-time disc jockey who spoke on *Donahue* about his sex life, pointed this out. He said of the "big deal" acquaintances made of his appearance: "It's context. People get to see you framed at that 21-inch electronic —-."

Williams's (1974) concept of television's undifferentiated flow and McLuhan's (1964) claim that "the medium is the message" (p. 7) reverberate in these findings, as specificities of content are largely washed out by powerful effects of the medium. This engulfment over even discrediting content suggests that "as seen on TV" constitutes a new and powerful "master status determining trait." Becker (1963) describes the term:[10]

Some statuses, in our society as in others, override all other statuses and have a certain priority. Race is one of these. Membership in the Negro race, as socially defined, will override most other status considerations in most other situations; the fact that one is a physician or middle class or female will not protect one from being treated as a Negro first and one of these other things second. (p. 33)

Garnering an appearance on television—for whatever reason—similarly subsumes other attributes of the individual. The important role television plays in modern life and the relative exclusivity of the experience have fueled this creation of a fairly new master status trait.

The exclusivity fuels the afterglow of participation longer than one might expect. Participants have succeeded in "stepping in" to a valued place, and, rather like the limited number of men and women who have orbited the earth, one only has to get there once to have that lasting credit. I have kept in touch with many of my informants, who report that strangers continue to recognize and greet them with infatuated responses two to three years after the shows originally aired.

The positive public reactions surprised many participants; gains exceeded expectations. Some of the more savvy participants, however, remained uneasy with these outcomes. What hooks (1989) calls "naming the self as a site for politicization" (p. 106) spun into something grand yet, paradoxically, blunted, because of the undifferentiated nature of the acclaim accorded to everyone who shared the panel. For example, a "vigilante dad" ready to avenge his daughter's rape was frustrated that the audience was equally receptive to a woman who had become a prostitute to support her children. When transsexualism equals vigilantism equals infantilism, participants were rightfully worried that viewers were not sifting their rhetorical claims. This blurring resulted in mixed gains for participants who were earnestly trying to effect social change.

There were other ways that efforts toward social activism were neutralized. Some participants seemed to languish at this stage, riding the carousel of talk show appearances as a vehicle to get their word out. Few seemed to apply energy toward more conventional methods for effecting political change. Bud Green, for example, who repeatedly insisted that he is a radical and touted drug use as a way to foster revolution, bemoaned the time-consuming nature of drumming up talk show appearances. He routinely called producers, angling for more publicity for his cause. This, then, may be how participants are co-opted; they get caught up in the attention, paralyzed in the floodlights, and cease their efforts on other fronts.

hooks (1989) cautions that speaking of one's experience "is only part of the process of politicization, one which must be linked to education for critical consciousness that teaches about structures of domination and how they function" (p. 108). Many participants had hoped to provide information to the mainstream about essential similarities that warrant equal treatment. Televised self-disclosures seem particularly useful as a starting point, both as a call for solidarity and as an outcry that signals visibility. Importantly, more research is needed both to determine the extent of the information audiences glean from the unfolding discourses on talk shows and to examine whether gains made by individuals extend to the out-groups they represent.[11]

Overall, participants were delighted by the positive responses garnered from the public and felt these reactions signaled hope for wider social acceptance of their out-groups. Although participants were often seeking merely to be included within the boundaries of normalcy, the power of the medium instead conferred a larger-than-life status that boosted their self-esteem enormously. Talk show panelists who self-disclosed about intimate areas of their lives on TV felt empowered, chosen, and worthy after years of languishing on society's periphery when producers provided them the chance to speak for themselves via the central medium of culture.

Notes

1. Monaco (1978, p. 60) coined the phrase.

2. Participants were eager to talk about outcomes and peppered the conversations with examples of the enthusiastic responses they had received. In addition to these profuse and ad hoc comments by informants, the data reported here are culled from answers to the following two questions that generally addressed issues of self-concept and responses from the public: "Did you feel differently about yourself after being on a talk show?" and "What has happened as a result of being on the show?" The status conferral processes operating were a rather accidental finding in a larger study about what the opportunity to participate meant to talk show guests.

3. I detail my methods and analytic stages in Priest (1995). To briefly summarize, I was occasionally able to establish contact using directory assistance when a panelist's full name and hometown were mentioned on a program. I contacted others through the therapists they had appeared with or via letters addressed to them in care of the show. I used other investigative techniques as well.

4. All but six appeared on *Donahue*. Most had appeared on several shows.

5. Only a single, small unpublished study has used interviews with talk show guests to provide insight into outcomes experienced. Feder (1993) explored the genre's frequent coverage of white supremacists and found that members of hate groups drew new converts to their organizations as a result of the publicity. These interviews were not the focus of her study.

6. Of the 43 informants, 35 asked to have their real names used in published works.

7. I am taking his terms *insiders* and *outsiders* to underline my idea that stepping inside television reality provides a new social distinction for participants. His ideas about blurring apply in the sense that access enables marginalized group members to garner a measure of acclaim granted previously to a much narrower group.

8. This episode of *Donahue* aired on April 29, 1991.

9. Alternately, the expressions of support from strangers may simply mirror findings in the self-disclosure literature of increased liking for disclosers who discuss intimate topics (see Archer, Berg, & Runge, 1980; Worthy, Gary, & Kahn, 1969). Liking may have resulted from the extended opportunity afforded the discloser to disavow stigma.

10. Becker borrowed this phrase from Hughes (1945).

11. Another issue that needs addressing is whether these public responses are somewhat illusory. Members of the public may not know what else to say when they recognize participants in what they may perceive as an awkward situation, or they may keep negative comments to themselves. Nevertheless, participants interpreted the public's reaction favorably, and this imputed sentiment (Cooley, 1902) then favorably affected their self-esteem.

References

Alcoff, L., & Gray, L. (1993). Survivor discourse: Transgression or recuperation? *Signs, 18*(2), 260-290.

Althusser, L. (1971). *Lenin and philosophy and other essays.* London: New Left.

Archer, R. L., Berg, J. H., & Runge, T. E. (1980). Active and passive observers' attraction to a self-disclosing other. *Journal of Experimental Social Psychology, 16*, 130-145.

Banks, J. (1990). Listening to Dr. Ruth: The new sexual primer. In G. Gumpert & S. L. Fish (Eds.), *Talking to strangers: Mediated therapeutic communication* (pp. 73-86). Norwood, NJ: Ablex.

Baudrillard, J. (1988). *America.* London: Verso.

Becker, H. S. (1963). *Outsiders.* New York: Macmillan.

Carbaugh, D. (1989). *Talking American: Cultural discourses on Donahue.* Norwood, NJ: Ablex.

Conrad, P. (1982). *Television: The medium and its manners.* Boston: Routledge & Kegan Paul.

Cooley, C. H. (1902). *Human nature and the social order.* New York: Scribner.

Crow, B. K. (1986). Conversational pragmatics in television talk: The discourse of "Good Sex." *Media, Culture and Society, 8,* 457-484.

Davies, B., & Harré, R. (1990). Positioning: The discursive production of selves. *Journal for the Theory of Social Behavior, 20*(1), 43-64.

Ewen, S. (1988). *All-consuming images: The politics of style in contemporary culture.* New York: Basic Books.

Feder, R. (1993). *A qualitative study of white supremacists on daytime television talk shows: Is it hate TV?* Unpublished master's thesis, Boston University.

Foucault, M. (1978). *The history of sexuality: Vol. 1. An introduction* (R. Hurley, Trans.). New York: Pantheon.

Gergen, K. J. (1991). *The saturated self: Dilemmas of identity in contemporary life.* New York: Basic Books.

Goffman, E. (1959). *Presentation of self in everyday life.* New York: Doubleday/Anchor.

Goffman, E. (1963). *Stigma, notes on the management of a spoiled identity.* Englewood Cliffs, NJ: Prentice Hall.

hooks, b. (1989). *Talking back: Thinking feminist, thinking black.* Boston: South End.

Hughes, E. C. (1945). Dilemmas and contradictions of status. *American Journal of Sociology, 50,* 353-359.

Jameson, F. (1988). Cognitive mapping. In C. Nelson & L. Grossberg (Eds.), *Marxism and the interpretation of culture* (pp. 347-360). Urbana: University of Illinois Press.

Knapp, L. (1988). Oprah Winfrey presents: The lesbian as spectacle. *Feminisms, 2*(2), 4-7.

Lazarsfeld, P. F., & Merton, R. (1948). Mass communication, popular taste and organized social action. In L. Bryson (Ed.), *The communication of ideas* (pp. 95-118). New York: Harper.

Markus, H., & Nurius, P. (1986). Possible selves. *American Psychologist, 41,* 954-969.

Masciarotte, G. (1991). C'mon, girl: Oprah Winfrey and the discourse of feminine talk. *Genders, 11,* 81-110.

McLuhan, M. (1964). *Understanding media: The extensions of man.* New York: McGraw-Hill.

Meyrowitz, J. (1985). *No sense of place: The impact of electronic media on social behavior.* New York: Oxford University Press.

Michaels, E. (1987). My essay on postmodernity. *Art and Text, 25,* 86-91.

Monaco, J. (1978). Celebration. In J. Monaco (Ed.), *Celebrity* (pp. 3-14). New York: Dell.

Munson, W. (1993). *All talk: The talkshow in media culture.* Philadelphia: Temple University Press.

Priest, P. J. (1995). *Public intimacies: Talk show participants and tell-all TV.* Cresskill, NJ: Hampton.

Rapping, E. (1991, October). Daytime inquiries. *The Progressive,* pp. 36-38.

Schickel, R. (1985). *Intimate strangers: The culture of celebrity.* Garden City, NJ: Doubleday.

Seigworth, G. (1993). The distance between me and you. In C. Schwichtenberg (Ed.), *The Madonna connection* (pp. 291-318). Boulder, CO: Westview.

Steenland, S. (1990). Those daytime talk shows. *Television Quarterly, 24*(4), 5-12.

Tichi, C. (1991). *Electronic hearth.* New York: Oxford University Press.

White, M. (1992). *Tele-advising: Therapeutic discourse in American television.* Chapel Hill: University of North Carolina Press.

Williams, R. (1974). *Television: Technology and cultural form.* London: Fontana.

Worthy, M., Gary, A. L., & Kahn, G. M. (1969). Self-disclosure as an exchange process. *Journal of Personality and Social Psychology, 13,* 59-63.

6

Mediating Cultural Selves:
Soviet and American Cultures
in a Televised "Spacebridge"

Donal Carbaugh

Talk Shows, Selves, and Cultures

The idea of a "talk show," if not exclusively American, has been cultivated in a distinctively American way for at least three decades. The current plethora of offerings in this televised genre is truly mind-boggling. Part of the intrigue, I think, is that these programs showcase the audience and are thus built, largely, upon the performance of audience members. In the 1960s, the first popular show in the genre, *Donahue*, seized the day by placing a segment of the audience typically deemed unworthy of airtime (i.e., housewives and the unemployed who were home watching at 9:00 a.m.) right in front of the cameras, and thus gave them the opportunity to speak about the issues of their day. Although the topics being addressed over the years have changed, one fact has not: Whatever topic is addressed (from foreign policy to male born-again go-go dancers), it is the audience's reaction to the topic, as much as it is the topic itself or the scheduled guests, that makes the "talk show" what it is. Without this audience participation, this display of the folk's sayings, there would be no "talk show" as it has come to be known in America today.

This wide-scale display of participation in televised talk has captivated a huge public and cultivated certain beliefs and values. Chief among these are particular *beliefs about a kind of public discourse*. The "talk" that is being "shown," that unwieldy discursive formation, has itself assumed a life of its own. Typically, with this public discourse, it has become rather common for people to stand before millions and freely speak their minds (or "share their feelings"), for others

AUTHOR'S NOTE: Parts of this chapter were originally published in the *Quarterly Journal of Speech, 79*, 182-200 (1993); used by permission. Earlier versions of this chapter were presented as a Public Lecture at the New University, Lisbon, Portugal (December 1990); at the Social Psychology Forum of Linacre College, Oxford, England (November 1990); at the conference sponsored by the State University of New York, Albany (February 1990); at colloquia at the Department of Communication, Arizona State University (December 1989 and April 1990); as a Public Lecture at the University of Tampere, Finland (November 1992); at the inaugural Communication Colloquium at the University of Haifa, Israel (May 1993); and at Hebrew University, Israel (May 1993). I would like to thank Nelson Traquina, Rom Harré, Robert Sanders, Charles Bantz, Liisa Lofman, Tamar Katriel, and Shoshana Blum-Kulka, among many others, for opportunities to discuss these ideas.

to grant them the "right" to do this, and for many to believe that this is something important to do (to "talk it out"). That this discursive production is a rather recent accomplishment, that it is the particular workings of a particular American culture, that it is prominent in televised conduct, and that its enactment displays particular beliefs and values about public discourse (and proper uses of television), all of this warrants our vigilant attention.

In the process of "showing" this kind of "talk," and through the participation of the common folk in it, the "talk show" also has cultivated certain cultural *beliefs about the person.* Some of these beliefs about the person can be summarized in this way: As one believes that speaking up—or speaking out—is important and valued, one also believes that being one who so speaks is important and valued. As earlier studies have shown (Carbaugh, 1988), implicated in this televised discourse is a message: One should "be honest" and "share feelings" in public, and these acts should foreground the seemingly endless flaws of society (or its oppressive institutions or corrupt corporations). In the process of televising this kind of talk, the "talk show" has thus also cultivated certain beliefs about the person, or self.

The media of communication can be conceptualized, similarly, as operating fundamentally on the bases of the particular beliefs of particular social and cultural communities. If beliefs about public discourse and persons vary by community and scene, so the argument would go, then so too do *beliefs about the media of communication.* The media, however, do not just vary in how they are used but more fundamentally in their very nature—what, indeed, different people believe the "media" are (can and should be). For example, whether television (or a genre of it, or a particular program) is conceived as a conduit to a real world, as an instrument of a corporation or a nation-state, or as a window into the spiritual (and all of these hold considerable weight somewhere), this makes a radical difference. Cultural beliefs about the media thus establish a complex frame for what is shown (what it "is" one believes one is seeing-hearing) and for how that "show" should be interpreted (seen and heard). In other words, the media (and selves) play upon social and cultural foundations. To take this seriously, then, we must treat the media not just as a constant core en masse that is multilayered and laminated with various cultural features, but as an organic plant whose very fruit may shift contingent upon the cultural soil in which it gains root. From this angle, as the distinctive cultural foundations of the media (and selves) shift, so does their very fundamental nature in social life.

Starting here, and granting that there are many other places to start, and by focusing on a "Spacebridge" that is rooted in Soviet and American soils, I explore how different beliefs about persons, public discourse, and the media get woven into a single televised episode. Demonstrated, I hope, are some of the sociocultural variations that make public communication, and thus televised communication (and selves), fundamentally different in different cultural scenes (Carbaugh, 1996). Reflecting these commitments, the analyses presented here explore "media and selves," not unlike the "talk show" itself, through an intensive involvement in a kind of audience participation.

Ethnography and Audiences as Cultural Communities

Justin Lewis (1991) summarizes a recent review of audience research with this basic finding: "We now know that the power to produce meanings lies neither within the TV message nor within the viewer, but in the active engagement between the two" (p. 58). He elaborates: "Television's power lies in the specificities of its encounter with the audience. One cannot exist without the other" (p. 61). Lewis then goes on to discuss various social meanings of various television texts. Foregrounded here is the problem of interpreting viewers' meanings of texts, and relations among those various meanings whether uniform, oppositional, or resistant. Lewis addresses this problem with an interview-based methodology that he subsequently applies.

The ethnographic approach taken in this chapter also addresses the problem of linking viewers and particular TV messages. As Lewis puts it, it addresses "the specificities of [TV's] encounter with the audience" (p. 61). This study does so, however, by treating particular television texts not as something sui generis but as part of a larger expressive system that a group or community interprets (with) and uses. By exploring that expressive system, one gains a particular perspective from which to interpret the (sometimes various) ways **that** community views television's messages. The approach suggests a shifting of focal concerns, then, from "viewers" to cultural communities, and from "TV messages" to the cultural messages (beliefs and values) they bring to, or "see" or hear on, the TV. By foregrounding cultural communities and their messages, their own beliefs about communication, and using those beliefs to interpret mediated messages (and selves), one can conduct a kind of audience research that is anchored, conceptually and methodologically, not in one televised "text" but in a community's communication system (including television). The conceptual shifts—from viewer to community, from text to expressive system—carry with them certain methodological consequences. How does one design and execute this type of audience research?

Given the aims of this study, the following procedures were employed. A first phase of analysis was fairly open and exploratory and involved these various tasks: detailed *readings* about each culture, its customs, beliefs, and ways of living; various *observations* of, in this case, Soviet (Russian, and others from the former Soviet state) speakers, Soviet students, various Soviet interactions with Americans, Soviets' stories about contacts with Americans, Americans' stories about contacts with Soviets; *recording* on video, creating, and procuring verbal transcripts of several hours of Soviet and American exchanges that were televised; and a first phase of *interviewing* that explored some of the above observations, focusing at times upon moments of asynchrony or confusion between the two so as to understand what was common and different about each community's expressive systems. This procedure created some sense of the general discursive terrain that each group traveled.

A second phase of analysis was very focused. For this phase, I selected specific televised texts that exhibited some of the general cultural dynamics formulated above. Each was transcribed and then analyzed, first, by me alone, extending the preliminary analyses developed above. Next, I arranged for Soviet consultants (alone), then American consultants (alone), to watch these segments with me. I recorded these viewings on audiotape, then we listened to ourselves watching, so to speak, as another source of data. This proved to be extremely valuable for our reactions were always keyed directly to specific moments in the televised texts. Finally, I selected one televised text—the one my coinvestigators and I came to understand as most "rich" or culturally dense from the vantage point of both systems (a transcript of this text appears on pp. 90-93). As a final procedure, I conducted focused interviews based on a detailed transcript of this text, its viewing by Soviets and Americans, and the audio recordings of these coviewings. The focused analyses of this second phase were linked consistently (by myself and the consultants) to the general themes, dynamics, and difficulties formulated in phase one.

Following this process produced an interpretation of Soviet and American conversational rituals, and meaning systems, as these interpenetrate a particular "Spacebridge" text. The resulting analyses, then, focus not so much on television and viewers as they do upon communal conversations and cultural selves, that is, upon the social and cultural resources that viewers use to render television texts meaningful, in their own way. I hope this way of approaching the matter demonstrates some of the potential for an ethnographic understanding of "selves in a mediated world."

Conversation and Cultural Selves

> The general capacity to be bound by moral rules may well belong to the individual, but the particular set of rules which transforms him into a human being derives from requirements established in the ritual organization of social encounters. (Goffman, 1967, p. 45)

Conversation, from one view, is everywhere a culturally situated accomplishment, shaped as it is by local codes, local expressions of what persons and social relations are (and should be), what persons can (and should) do, and what, if anything, can (and should) be felt. But nowhere do participants invoke the same codes, the same currents of culture, on all conversational occasions. Nor anywhere do these necessarily situate all participants in the same way. This latter dynamic—of crosscurrents in talk—is especially pronounced on intercultural and multicultural occasions when various communication codes—various beliefs about persons, actions, and feelings—become deeply perplexing one to the other.[1]

As mentioned above, this chapter explores one such conversational occasion, a televised "Spacebridge," in which two different cultural currents are flowing— one Soviet, the other American.[2] The general theoretical approach informing the study of this occasion is elaborated elsewhere.[3] The analytical problem is one of hearing cultural systems in televised conversation, with the general response being one of treating seriously participants' own terms, the dimensions and domains of meaning they invoke, their cultural forms of expression, indigenous conversational rules (or structuring norms), and the meanings about persons, actions, and feelings implicated in these. These concepts, together, provide a general lens with which to view (or hear) culturally communicated meaning systems, with each separately bringing into focus a more specific theoretical concern with regard to particular televised moments. Through the application of the general framework, distinctive cultural currents in this conversation are discovered, with each being a local theory for conducting and interpreting this particular communicative action. The case thus demonstrates the workings of a general theoretical approach, the fruits of which unveil culturally situated communication systems, as these appear in a segment of television.

The title of the chapter invites reflection upon the concept of culture while suggesting that, whatever culture is, indeed for the title to make full sense, it is something that is implicated, employed, or creatively invoked in conversation. Treated this way, conversation is at times a cultural accomplishment and, in turn, culture at such times animates, lives in, or provides tangible resources for conversation. From this view, then, culture is not a physical place, a social group of people, or a whole way of living, although it does create, when used, mutually intelligible senses of place, persons, and patterns of living. What culture is, from this view, is a system of expressive practices fraught with feeling, a system of beliefs about persons, places, and patterns of living. When culture is creatively invoked in conversation, whether on television, in talk about television, or in other scenes of social life—with convergences among these suggesting rich cultural themes—it alerts interlocutors to their common life, its particularities of place, people, and patterns of life, whether these exist in conflict or harmony.

Ethnographic studies of communication—like the kind being done here—have examined the cultural patterning of communicative activity within specific social situations and communities.[4] As some investigators have pointed out, no ethnographic work has yet been done that involves a cultural interpretation of face-to-face, or televised, intercultural interaction.[5] The current study is warranted, then, because it explores (a) a televised, conversational segment, (b) in which different cultural systems come into contact, which yields (c) initial interpretations of Soviet public communication (and the Russian self), with further attention to American patterns of communication (and self), and reveals (d) some deep sources of difference in the television medium.

The segment examined in this chapter[6] appeared as part of a weeklong series titled "Donahue in Russia." The series was taped in Moscow and broadcast in the United States during the week of February 9, 1987. The particular segment of concern to us here consists of the first 3 minutes and 40 seconds of the second program in the series.[7] Other than a brief "talk-over" by Phil Donahue (that lasted 16.8 seconds), the segment—following Donahue's normal production format—underwent no postproduction editing. Because this segment displays a generic form of ritualized face-work, it is ideally suited for interactional analysis.[8] Because it involves different cultures being creatively employed to guide, evaluate, and justify actions, it is ideally suited for ethnographic study. Because it was seen by Soviets and Americans to be a televised expression both troubling and rich, it is ideally suited for a kind of media study. If the following analyses attain some degree of success, that is, if different cultural features are unveiled, readers should be better positioned to hear and see how cultural selves have shaped this conversation and better positioned to understand why, as one Soviet (bilingual in Russian and English) put it, "They think they're talking about the same thing, but they're not." What, in this televised conversation, has led this person to this conclusion? How could she hear in this encounter (as did others who are members of both communities) not just one but two very different systems operating? How does one hear in this, and other mediated conversations, culture(s) and self at work?

Ritual and Cultural Discourses

Some conversational episodes foreground a particular interactional goal: the remedy of improprieties. More than anyone, Goffman (1967) has drawn our attention to the ritualized form of this type of corrective process:

> When the participants in an undertaking or encounter fail to prevent the occurrence of an event that is expressively incompatible with the judgments of social worth that are being maintained, and when the event is of the kind that is difficult to overlook, then the participants are likely to give it accredited status as an incident—to ratify it as a threat that deserves direct official attention—and to proceed to try to correct for its effects. At this point one or more participants find themselves in an established state of ritual disequilibrium or disgrace, and an attempt must be made to reestablish a satisfactory ritual state for them. (p. 19)

Typically, claims Goffman, such corrective processes follow a rather loosely bounded generic sequence, such that an exigence is created through an impropriety; it is socially identified, then further publicized; the publicity precipitates an offering of corrections by the violator(s); which is subsequently accepted (or not), leading to the reestablishment of what Goffman calls "the expressive order" (or its continuing negotiation, or disruption) (Goffman, 1967, pp. 5-45; also see Bitzer, 1968).

Let us look briefly at the ritual Donahue invokes here, then at the Soviet one that engulfs him.[9] It is no surprise that Donahue, in his opening segment, initiates discussion with a version of the ritual form that is familiar to him and his American audience. In his first utterances on lines 1-2, 4, 6-7, 11-12, and 24-25, Donahue inquires about sex, contraceptive use, pregnancy, and virginity. Topics such as these, Donahue presumes, provide an exigence for public discourse, just as similar topics do in his homeland, erected on the communal assumption, in Bitzer's (1968) terms, that there is an "imperfection marked by urgency" (p. 10). In this case, presumably, the imperfection consists of unwanted pregnancies and perhaps irresponsible premarital sex.[10] The scene is a rhetorical one in that Donahue presumes it can be positively modified, with a partial remedy possibly created through the means of public discourse. Donahue presumes his interlocutors can be influenced by televised discourse and thus can subsequently become "mediators of change" (Bitzer, 1968, p. 11) better equipped (or informed?) to redress these presumed imperfections. Donahue, then, attempts to co-create with

(text continued on page 94)

TRANSCRIPT

1a) DONAHUE: Would you kindly stand for one second, please?

2a) You had sex, when you were 18 years old?

3a) SOVIET MALE A (trans.): Yes, that's when I started.
  b) (.........................)
  c) (.........................)

4a) D: Did you use contraceptive when you practiced sex at age 18?
    [Audience laughter]

5a) SMA (trans.): Yes.
  b) Yes.
  c) Да.

6a) D: Did you take care of this matter yourself or did the girl insist that
7a)   you do it?

8a) SMA (trans.): Yeah, I knew about it before.
  b) Well (.) I knew it before that (.)
  c) Ну я до этого знал

9a) Before that I knew quite a bit.
  b) I knew a lot before that (.)
  c) Я до того знал уже многое
     [PAN TO AUDIENCE LAUGHTER, SMILES]

10a) I knew how, when, what, etc. I was well prepared.
  b) Well before I knew how, what, why (.) I was well prepared.
  c) Ну до этого знал и как, что, чего... Был хорошо подготовлен.

11a) D: Are most Soviet boys conscientious, like you, in protecting the
12a)   girl from pregnancy?

13a) SMA (trans.): Basically, yes. Why don't you ask the others?
  b) Yes (.) basically, yes (.) But actually ask the people themselves.
  c) Да, в основном да. А вообще-то спросите у ребят самих
     [PAN TO AUDIENCE SMILES]

14a) D: Yes?

15a) Sov. Female A (trans.): You talk as though everybody here was
  b) # You talk as if everyone present here is
  c) Вы так говорите как будто бы вот каждый из пресутствующих

16a) already involved in that . I think when most of my girlfriends had
  b) doing it. I don't know about that, most of my girlfriends
  c) этим занимается. Я не знаю , большенство моих подруг

17a) gotten married at 18 or 20, they were virgins,
    b) got married when they were 18 and 20, and they all were virgins. # (.)
    c) вышли замуж в 18 и 20 они были девушками.

18a) and before marriage they did not engage in sex.
    b) # Before marriage did not even plan on having sex or sexual life.
    c) До брака и вообще не собирались заниматься сексом и сексуальной жизнью.

19a) They were waiting for that one special man, for that one special
    b) They were waiting for their one # (.) and only (.)
    c) Они ждали своего одного единственного

20a) person, and they found that one special person.
    b) #marriage with one person # (.) and they found it.
    c) брака с одним человеком, и они его нашли.

21a) And most of their husbands also, for most of them their wife
    b) And for the majority of their husbands (.)
    c) И для большенства их мужей

22a) also was the first woman with whom they had ever had sexual relations.
    b) as well (.) for them their wife was their first girl. (.)
    c) тоже для них их жена была первая девушка.

23a)·
    b) Woman that they liked.
    c) Женщина которая понравилась.

24a) D: Is it true with most girls, most young women are virgins when
25a)   they get married in the Soviet Union?

26a) SFA (trans.): Well, a great number of girls are virgins until marriage.
    b) Well, (.) in general, (.) the larger part of girls are virgins before marriage. They just start leading that type of life after marriage.
    c) Ну, ну в общем большая часть девушек является девушками до замужества. Они начинают только жить такой жизнью только после замужества.

27a) I don't really know, maybe not everybody.
    b) Well, I don't know, maybe not (all/quite).
    c) Ну я не знаю может быть не (все/совсем)

28a) Sov. Female B (trans.): You know, I just want to say
    b) #I want to say
    c) Я хочу сказать,

29a) that I think it's quite the opposite. You can't really say that it's
    b) on the contrary# well in my opinion if not to say that it is
    c) что наоборот, ну по-моему если не

30a) very good if a girl when she gets married is still a virgin, because
  b) negative (.) you definitely cannot say that it is very good, if the girl when getting married is still a virgin (.)
  c) отрицательное , то нельзя сказать что это очень хорошо если девушка выходя замуж еще девушка.

31a) I think quite the opposite. She should be quite sure
  b) #Because I think that by that time, she basically should be sure
  c) Потому что я считаю, тогда она вообщем-то уже должна быть уверенна

32a) of what her husband is as a man, that he'll be a real partner
  b) of her husband as a man # (.)
  c) в своем муже как мужчине

33a) for her, otherwise it could be a real tragedy.
  b) because otherwise it could be a tragedy. #(.....................) #
  c) а иначе же может быть трагедия а иначе может быть трагедия (........)

34a) And sex for a married couple is extremely important.
  b) It is very important # (.....................) #
  c) Это очень важно(...............)

35a) After all, sex is 80% of happiness for a married couple
  b) Practically (.) makes up, #well, 80% of happiness.
  c) Практически, ну 80 % счастья занимает.

36a) but, of course, that depends on each individual woman.
  b) Of course it depends on every individual woman #
  c) **Естественно это зависит от каждой женщины**

37a) But for me I think that's very important.
  b) (.....................)
  c) (.....................)

38a) Sov. Female C : I think it is necessary to change the subject
39a) of conversation, because these questions are very deep
40a) to be concerned by us.

[AUDIENCE APPLAUSE]

41a) D (speaking over tape): This is day two of our visit to the Soviet
42a) Union. In this hour Soviet teens give a powerful exchange on
43a) everything from religion to war. But unlike American teenagers,
44a) areas they were reluctant to discuss included dating,
45a) school and sexuality.

46a) Sov. Male B (trans.) (in response to an inaudible question by Donahue): It's not a surprise that American students can't
  b) (.....................)

c) (.........................)

47a) understand us, because they have many more problems
  b) Much more serious problems than (.) ours because (....................)
  c) На много серьезнее проблемы чем у нас потому что (............)

48a) than we have, the criminality, drugs, etc. Secondly,
  b) (....................) Secondly (.)
  c) (............) во вторых

49a) all boys and girls here are in somewhat different surroundings.
  b) all the young people here (.) found themselves (.) well, in (....................)
  c) все ребята сидящие здесь попали ну в (............)

50a) This is new to them. They've never been on television
  b) (....................) situation. (....................)
  c) (............) ситуации (............)

51a) and this is the reason why they can't immediately talk to you
  b) (....................)
  c) (............)

52a) as they do in America, where they are probably more easy going,
  b) We are not used to (*hanging out*) more uptight (....................) not
  c) Мы не привыкли (*шататься*) скованней (............) не вероятно,

53a) and when they may even have experience of being on television.
  b) that they (*have ever been on television*).
  c) что они (*когда-нибудь были на телевиденье*)

54a) Sov. Male C (trans.): What can we do if everything is all right here?
  b) Well, what can we do if everything is all right? (.)
  c) Ну что мы можем сделать если все в порядке?

55a) Should we create problems?
  b) Should we think up a problem?
  c) Что, проблему придумать?

56a) Sov. Male D (trans.): We don't want to invent problems. Why?
  b) We don't want to invent ourselves the problems. Why?
  c) Мы не хотим придумывать себе проблем. Зачем?

  [LAUGHTER AND APPLAUSE]

57a) Sov. Male E: School is likewise, sometimes you are happy
58a) and sometimes you express just no particular emotions,
59a) and that's all.

60a) D: All right, I will listen to your advice and I will change the
61a) subject.

his audience a kind of ritualized and rhetorical action, to display what he considers to be "a fitting response to a situation which needs and invites it" (Bitzer, 1968, p. 2). The exigence (e.g., the unwanted pregnancies), the means of responding (e.g., public discourse, confessions, truth-sayings), and its meanings (e.g., the remedy of a societal impropriety through public participation) all cohere from this view. Together, they provide a common and productive way to address social problems through open, public discussion, that is, by engaging in an American communication ritual. Donahue's interrogative utterances, as such, are not just journalistic questions or directives, they are moves in a culturally expressive—albeit ritually performed—game.[11]

The ritualized speech that Donahue presumes and initiates, however, from the standpoint of the Soviet expressive order, is inappropriate, even incoherent. Immediately at lines 2-4, Donahue's interlocutor is taken aback (i.e., literally steps back from Donahue) while others laugh out loud, smile broadly, and whisper in each other's ears. The exigence Donahue invites his audience to address (e.g., the unwanted pregnancies) becomes immediately supplanted by another of their own (i.e., the foreign talk show host's unusual conduct). This imperfection grows with mounting urgency until finally, on lines 38-40, a woman speaks in English, the first Soviet to do so, and tells Donahue, to the delighted applause of her "contemporaries,"[12] that "it is necessary to change the subject," which Donahue eventually, on lines 60-61, agrees to do.

An American Voice

Note the question by Donahue on line 2: "You had sex when you were 18 years old?" He probes the issue by asking further about "contraceptive use" (line 4) and who took "care of this matter" (6), "protecting the girl from pregnancy" (11-12). What exotic American tree is planted here, but later uprooted from Soviet soil? What must be presumed for these comments indeed to be intelligible?

Donahue's speech characterizes a kind of human activity, presumably coitus, as "had sex" and "practiced sex"; he refers to it as an activity that is "practiced," then associates this "practice" with a technique, the "use" [of] a "contraceptive"; probes which individual was responsible for its "use"; and mentions a biological motive for contraception ("protection from pregnancy"). Human procreative activity is communicated here, then, as "sex," as an experience one "has" or "practices" in a particular way, which involves as part of the practice the possibility of contraceptive use, with this use being a primary responsibility of one of the involved individuals, because "protection" from deleterious biological consequences is desirable or necessary. The symbolic structuring of the topic invoked by Donahue thus draws attention—and directs subsequent discussion— to at least three prominent American cultural domains: physical facts (who did this activity, at what age, with what biological consequences), technical utilities (what techniques or technologies were used), and individual actions (did *you* do it—who is responsible). The tone used for the discussion could be characterized as a "serious rationality" that foregrounds not the passionate bonds among persons, or their moral status, but "sex" as a factual, technical, "practice" among individuals.[13]

Note further the sequence of symbols used, from "sex" (2, 4) to protection from "pregnancy" (11-12). The symbolic sequence takes "sex" in the direction of a problem of unwanted pregnancy and brings closer to the interactional surface other projectable problems that are culturally associated with this, problems such as premarital sex, irresponsible sexual practices, single-parent families, abortion, venereal diseases, AIDS, issues of morality, welfare systems, the population explosion, and so on. To an American ear, exposed to such a system, all of this could come to pass rather naturally. One can hear, without too much strain or reflection, even if angered by this line of questioning, the kind of thing Donahue is "getting at."

This line of questioning demonstrates a kind of "problem talk," or self-help dialogue, that functions—in part—to foreground various imperfections and thus to motivate subsequent utterances. The communicative form, a round-the-rally of problems-responses, involves a three-part spiraling sequence that introduces a topic, renders it problematic, precipitating responses that redress or further elaborate the problems.[14] Note how the form takes a topic in the direction of problems, thus creating an exigence for various additional responses. The form—when animating American public discourse—creates outcomes in two directions: Concerning the topics of discussion, it problematizes them, directing interlocutors along a plaintive conversation of flaws; concerning the form of public discussion, it motivates a spiraling of utterances that legitimate lengthy public discussion of the topic at hand. The form underlies much American public "discussion," from talk shows to self-help groups to faculty meetings, leading those familiar with it to identify in it a kind of integrative communal action in which problems are discussed (not solved) and present relationships supported (or perhaps even strained). In popular American terms: "Here's the topic, it's problematic, we need to talk." On some occasions, this is a ritualized way of being American together.

Hearing Donahue as one engaged in this culturally expressive practice, then, leads us to hear that one might discuss this topic (i.e., coitus) in public, that it might be called "sex," that it might be symbolically constituted as a physical, technical, individual activity, that facts about it might be discussed rationally and seriously, that it is discussed and discussable as problematic. All of this is at least intelligible (if not entirely acceptable) to an American audience. The cultural game Donahue plays implicates a belief about "problem" talk: It is a potent social activity, an efficacious remedy for important social problems (which motivates a communally sensed urgency to the whole performance, once again).

The presupposed sequence—topic initiation, problematizing, response cycle—as a general cultural form, invokes four common ground rules for speaking, with each containing culturally loaded symbols (in quotes): (a) In some American conversations, the presentation of "self" is a preferred communication activity, with statements of personal experiences, thoughts, and feelings counting as proper "self" presentations; (b) interlocutors must grant speakers the moral "right" to present "self" through personal statements; (c) the presentation of "self" should be "respected," that is, tolerated as a rightful expression; (d) corporate and global (i.e., collective) standards are dispreferred because they unduly constrain "self," infringe upon "rights," and violate a code of personal "respect." These rules enable a public sense of free expression, a sacred grounding of the communal identity, "self," but they also create—necessarily—dissonance on topics and systematic refracting of such things as consensual truths, or collective standards of and for public judgment.[15] The above "expressive order," the form and rules, implicates and affirms a model of and for being a person: The person is deemed, first and foremost, "an individual" with a "self." As when one asks about "sex," or who is "responsible for contraceptive use," a belief is displayed about persons such that experiences and feelings are deemed unique, and culpability of agency is located with each. Affirmed in such a system is a powerful equivocal balancing, an affirmation of both the separateness of a person (each person is a unique individual with freedoms and rights) and the common humanity for all (every person is at base an individual). Each and every "individual" can and must make "choices" such as whether to "have sex" or "use a contraceptive." Using these symbols in this way creates a cultural person that has (or should have) "power" and "control" over the (societal/personal) "environment," but also, because of this, the "individual" is the locus of responsibility and bears the greatest burden of and articulation in social life (Carbaugh, 1988, pp. 21-86; also see Carbaugh, 1988-1989).

These beliefs about the person are associated with the beliefs about talk and implicate a system of cultural premises:

The person has two main parts:
   the physical (body) and, within it,
   the nonmaterial (thought and feeling).
The nonmaterial cannot be seen.
It is a part of an inner world.
Things are not part of that world.
Other people can't know what things happen in that part.
Speaking makes these things known to others
and is a preferred action.

These premises create a cultural notion of person that includes a body and its "mindful" part, the nonmaterial seat of personal being, which becomes the cultural site of discursive action and feeling.[16]

Turning back to our utterance, then, by Donahue on line 2, he is asking for a factual disclosure (confession?) about a Soviet male's "individual self" (not the public's collective morality), about his physical experiences on an issue deemed publicly important and problematic. In so asking, he creates a cultural discursive space into which he expects his interlocutor to move. His hope is to create, with his Soviet interlocutors, a ritualized—albeit American—public discussion. So designed, it is presumed that each person—"self"—can (and should) rationally discuss his or her own experience, thoughts, and feelings, display a serious rationality about "sex," thereby help to remedy the difficult exigence, the presumed "problems" with the Soviet person and "society." These meanings, or something like them, must be hearable for his speech to make sense. With them, we hear a culture at work, upon a televised, intercultural occasion.

A Soviet Reply

Immediately upon hearing Donahue's first question, the Soviet audience is aroused. Eyebrows are raised, laughter ensues, torsoes wave back and forth, and startled glances are exchanged. At one level, and following the corrective action taken by the Soviet woman on lines 38-40, we might explain much by positing the Soviet rule: In public discussions, especially with outsiders, it is not preferable (even though possible) to discuss sexual matters. It is this moral proscription, evidently, that Donahue has violated with his line of questioning (1-2, 6-7, 11-12), thus precipitating the above reactions. The rule also accounts for some of the expressed embarrassment and reserve by the two Soviet women who spoke. As Donahue notes in his talk-over (line 44), "They were reluctant to discuss." For an American ear, we hear through this phrasing an implication that "something fishy is going on," perhaps more evidence of a "closed society"—people unable, perhaps even constrained by the state, to speak their mind. But, as stated, we have a negative, a general moral proscription, a how not to speak. What, then, is affirmed? What communication, from the standpoint of the Soviet expressive order, should be forthcoming? And what does it instantiate that is cultural? What does it say about persons, social relations, talk, and feeling?

At this point, the justifications offered by the Soviet males on lines 46-59 help orient our interpretation. Note that the utterances take on an agonistic form, a contrasting of "your" ways with "ours." A comment made consistently and recurrently throughout the dialogues appears on lines 46-47: You Americans "can't understand us." Although several reasons are given elsewhere by the Soviets for this (e.g., a biased and uninformed American media, poorly educated about Soviet culture and history), the reasons that express the difference here are that you "have many more problems than we have, the criminality, drugs, etc." and Americans are accustomed to "being on television" and talking a certain way, but we (the Soviets) are not. What is amplified and applauded, to the delight of the audience, is this: "What can we do if everything is all right here? Should we create problems? We don't want to invent problems. Why?"

These Soviets have heard Donahue plodding down a problem-strewn path that to them is incoherent—thus laughable—in this public context. "Should we create problems" just so we have something to talk with you about? There are at least two premises supporting the Soviets' question. First, we do not have these problems of premarital sex, drugs, and criminality. They are not parts of our lives. Indeed, during some interviewing, this position was asserted as an actual truth. Such things are said not to be part of some Soviet lives: "We don't hear about these things in our press, and we don't live with these kinds of people [drug users, criminals]. Sure, it might exist somewhere, but it's not part of my life, in my community." Given this as an uncontested discursive fact, then indeed "problems" such as these—at least for the immediate interactional moment—are ruled out of social existence.

Placing this Soviet social fact alongside the American premise of "problems" precipitates replies by Americans of disbelief and skepticism. Thus, Donahue's talk-over mentions a "reluctance to discuss" (44), "reluctance" implying that "they" are holding back the presumed truth about their problems, rather than "coming out" and stating it. Again, "reluctance" here becomes an American code word that simply reasserts the Americanized "problem" focus and preferences for publicly personal self-talk about facts, translating the matter again into American terms and premises.

A second premise for the Soviet line, "everything is all right here . . . we don't want to invent problems" (54, 56), orients less to facts and truth than to a proper stance for public conduct. The stance introduces the affirmative side of a Soviet rule system, a norm for proper comportment: In public discussion, especially with outsiders, it is preferable to speak in a unified, corporate voice with statements of common morals and shared virtues counting as unifying. Given this rule, it becomes easier to hear how the first 37 lines of the segment are highly unusual for the Soviets. Why would anyone come here and start talking, first of all, about private matters like "sex" and further, if pursuing that topic, about *problems* like premarital pregnancies?[17]

The Soviet form for proper discussion, then, does not follow an American sequence of topic initiation, problem statement, and response but another in which a public topic, when socially ratified, is predicated to a collective agent through common virtues. Looking back to our segment from the standpoint of this Soviet form, we can now hear, from the first speaker (3, 5, 8-10, 13) to the second (15-23), how discussion moved from the less virtuous, personalized, and factual, "I started [sex at 18]," to the more virtuous, collectivized, and moral "most/they/the majority were virgins before marriage." We also have an account for how the second Soviet female speaker (28-37) (called "courageous" by one Soviet informant, a "bimbo" by another) dared reveal an individualized (Westernized?) moral, "[Before marrying him] a woman should be quite sure of what her husband is as a man." In so doing, she contributed to a sense of violation of the above Soviet rule because her statement was an individual opinion about a moral issue rather than a collective belief about shared virtues. This intensified the mounting sense of imperfection and urgency (i.e., more personal and public talk about sex), which immediately precipitated the corrective action on the next lines (38-40).

Soviet dimensions of meaning ground the above rules and form, and need to be highlighted. Note the rules require a clear division between public and private life, and distinguish the kind of talk proper in private among "insiders" from that which is proper in public for the sake of "outsiders," especially for "outsiders" who are sensed to be "officials of the [Soviet and American] state," as Donahue was keenly sensed to be.[18] This became quite pronounced when Donahue tried to interview Refuseniks, who would not talk with Donahue because they believed he was "cavorting" (*blat*, or connection) with the "state." Donahue, being the freestanding individual he sensed himself to be, kept expressing utter bewilderment: "You appear to be upset with me, and I don't understand why." His reply, to "being a puppet in the state's hands," was, "I'm controlling this!"[19] For our purposes, we simply use the moment to demonstrate how the Soviet conversation, when deemed *public* or for *outsiders,* expresses a virtuous, connected collective. When matters turn *private,* for *insiders,* more individualized themes can prevail.

Listening with these Soviet rules, the form, and dimensions, one begins to hear in this talk a Soviet sense and, with it, to discover the various interactional sources of Donahue's breach. Here he brings to a public, collective forum, where shared virtues guide discussion, a private matter that he explores through personal, individual, and scientific or factual terms. The exigence he creates, or the "precipitating event" as Goffman called it, includes a configuration of at least these features: An improper topic (sex rather than the common morality of public life) is brought to a setting and discussed in an improper way (scientifically rational, technical, and individual rather than moral, passionate, and corporate) through an improper form (foregrounding societal problems rather than shared virtues). That Soviets should act according to their own cultural forms and norms was made even more apparent to me during a meeting with a Soviet student in my office. While discussing the public-private distinction in Soviet life, and seeing pictures of my children and wife rather hidden behind books and papers, I was asked: "Why make your family pictures available? You devalue your family and experiences and memories by doing this." And further, with regard to the topic of "sex" and related matters: "We don't discuss our personal experiences whatever they are [in public], love, sex, relations with God. We cannot express these in words. You make it shallow if you speak it in public." As one underground artist put it: "The most interesting things are going on in private where you can't see them." Here, then, we hear elaborated another feature: Public expression involves collective sayings that, relative to the individual/private, are shallow.[20] Private expression involves more intensely passionate sayings that are, as the woman in lines 30-40 put it, "very deep to be concerned by us." Private discourse among insiders runs deeper and involves greater volubility. Soviet beliefs about public talk, then, orient to shared moral bases of life and distinguish a kind of *reserve* in *public* with *outsiders* from a greater *expressiveness* in *private* among *insiders.*

Our interpretation here can be extended by recourse to a central Russian cultural symbol, *dusa* (roughly, "soul"), which the Soviet woman's phrase, "very deep," and the above dimensions culturally invoke. The beliefs about the person associated with this cultural symbol and elaborated with this expressive system create, like the American system, a *persona* of two parts, but the deeply felt, focal symbolic site of being differs:[21]

The person has two main parts:
    the body and the soul.
One cannot see but one can feel the soul.
Because of the soul, things can happen in and among persons that cannot happen
    in anything other than persons.
These things can be good or bad.
Because of this part, a person can feel things
that nothing other than persons can feel.

This symbolically constructed notion of the Soviet person identifies a dynamic integrative world that is "above all, emotional" and morally colored, *and* that holds strong transcendental overtones (Wierzbicka, 1989, p. 52). *Dusa* not only symbolizes a model person as a distinct physical body with a rational and mindful self within, but further contrasts this organismic entity with a kind of cosmological connectedness, with a transcendent moral (good or bad), deeply feeling, and distinctly interhuman realm. The desired locus of discourse, when forthcoming in public or in private, is not so much a rational, scientifically technical, individual utility as it is a passionate, morally connected, shared feeling.[22] As Pasternak put it in *Doctor Zhivago,* "You in others, that's what your soul [dusa] is."[23] Preferred Soviet sayings usher forth, at least generally and characteristically, as soul-felt and relational expressions more than individually mindful and factual disclosures.

The Soviet form for public discussion, conversational rules, and premises of personhood thus place us in a better position to hear this intercultural segment, especially the topic of "sex." Note that, for Soviets, the concept "sex" entitles an activity that is more in the animalistic domain than it is in the distinctively human. As such, it violates the Russian sense of "soul," for the deeper soul of the person can and should involve only those things that can happen in persons. As one Soviet woman put it: "Sex is something animals do." To discuss this topic in a factual, rational, scientific way, with regard to contraceptive techniques and "practices," in public terms of "animalistic mechanics," rather than in a proper moral tone of deep feeling that weds it with a common morality and with uniquely human sensual passion, all of this is rather incoherent, thus laughable to Soviets. It is easier to see, then, how a Soviet female, upon viewing the segment, discussed how the first male speaker was *put in the position* of being a "fool and jerk," for he was swept into more rational/factual disclosures of individual, personally problematic, and animalistic experiences with "sex." The proper tone, form, and meanings, matters of the soul, virtuous positions, and unified themes were being wholly supplanted and elided.

Soul, Self as Mediated Conversation

Russian conversation, as Russian life generally, is conducted through three fundamental cultural dimensions. The primary one is the keenly sensed difference between public/private contexts, with two respective others: shallow/deep and taciturn/voluble. With these axes, discourse becomes public when outsiders or an outside influence is deemed present, precipitating rather taciturn sayings of relatively shallow, if collective, virtues. Created in the process is the rather famous Soviet public "front," the requisite "official Russia," *Pravda*'s Russia, a conversational *pokazukha,* or show.[24] Private contexts, on the other hand, are created primarily with insiders (e.g., kin and like ethnicity), framing speech as possibly going much deeper, as a context into which the passionate and sentimental dimensions of lives are given a voice through what is called a "broad-spirited" *(shirokaya dusha),* heart-to-heart or soul-to-soul *(po dusham)* kind of exchange.[25] The intensity, frequency, and durability of this relatively deep privatized expressiveness led one student of Soviet culture to write of a "nation of incurable romantics" but also to contrast this with the cold, stuffy, pompous persona performed in public (Smith, 1976, pp. 135-148 ff.). Conversational and cultural life in Russia apparently revolves around such axes, contrasting a publicly shallow and taciturn discourse for outsiders with another more private, deep, and voluble one for insiders. As a public medium, television assumes these cultural bases for conduct and interpretation in Russia.

This cultural framing of televised talk-in-action reflexively constructs a dual quality in the Russian person. As a prominent observer of Soviet life, Hedrick Smith (1976), put it:

> From childhood onward, Russians acquire an acute sense of place and propriety. . . . They divide their existence into their public lives and their private lives, and distinguish between "official" relationships and personal relationships. . . . They adopt two very different codes of behavior for their two lives—in one, they are taciturn, hypocritical, careful, cagey, passive; in the other, they are voluble, honest, direct, open, passionate. In one, thoughts and feelings are held in check. . . . In the other, emotions flow warmly, without moderation. (pp. 139-140)

The "soul" (dusa) of the Russian person, as a passionate, morally committed, distinctly human agent, and as the shared locus of communal symbolic life, is presupposed for each discursive performance, but is more happily and intensely elaborated in private. Given these beliefs about the medium, about conversation and the person, one can hear in such conversation its prominent symbolic motive and meanings: Express the "soul" of persons, human passion and morality, the good and the bad, in its dually distinctive, ritually performed, public and private ways.

American conversation, at least that part of it initiated by Donahue in this segment, is prominently motivated on the basis of an alternate view: Express your "self" honestly, with private experiences and personal opinions becoming easily elaborated as the context for public discussion. "Self," as something uniquely within, as something communally valued, and as something implicating the dignity both of that individual and implicitly of the person so conceived, becomes a public symbolic scene. Who is this particular person? What does one, as such, have to say, to contribute? Informing others of one's own experiences, thoughts, and feelings, one's true and authentic self, the personal facts of the matter, becomes a prominent motive and context for public discursive action.

The above interpretations offer several initial substantive findings with regard to Soviet and American patterns of televised communication, with each distinctive in its ritualized form. We find, on the one hand, a soulful collective conversing on the basis of morality, orienting to the possible virtues of societal life. On the other hand, we find mindful individuals conversing on the basis of factual information, disclosing their real personal experiences in response to societal problems and issues. The former might sense the latter, at times, as soulless (lacking morality, commitment, and loyalty to the common good), just as the latter might sense the former as mindless (lacking factual information and analytic abilities). These statements are, of course, generalities, characterizations of two distinctive discursive styles, but they capture some of the conversational and cultural bases in this mediated conduct, and they identify some of the sources whereby each conceives of and evaluates the other. This general reading, built as it is around the cultural selves of each, is erected on the particular televised dynamics detailed above (see Carbaugh, 1993b, pp. 195-196).[26]

I hope that beyond these substantive findings, the chapter demonstrates how a kind of media theory and audience analysis can be erected upon the social and cultural foundations that people presume about communication. In this case, what is suggested is that the Soviets see and hear this television text as a channel through which only certain things can (or should) be accomplished. Because it is a public text, conducted with and shown for "outsiders," it is a place for themes that are, relative to Americans, shallow and reserved. That Soviet themes of morality and propriety are countered by American themes of efficiency, openness, and freedom for the "same" mediated text should not escape our notice— nor should all such cultural variations in the nature and social uses of the various media. Further, I hope these analyses suggest and entice others to an ethnographic or cultural pragmatic version of audience research. Erecting media theory on social and cultural foundations, and conducting our studies in this general way, should lead to some productive insights into the media, the messages of TV, and the cultural communities in which they have their basic, practical residence.

The chapter demonstrates some of the possibilities of communication and culture theory for studying selves, cultural scenes, and the media (Carbaugh, 1996).[27] By drawing attention to an intercultural moment of self-presentations, I have brought to the fore culturally diverse, mediated dynamics that are dense with meaning.[28] Exploring this moment has suggested certain modifications to the general theory of ritual and social drama through which cultural selves are being expressed, and viewed here.[29] In this conversational segment, we have heard how the sacred symbols of "soul" and "self" are active. Summarizing cultural beliefs about the person and mediated communication through such key sacred symbols as these is risky, however. This might suggest a singular entity, a reified "thing," or unitary whole, a central or core symbol standing alone, somehow above or apart from a cultural communication system. But can one sever a part from the whole? I think not. Instead, one begins hearing distinctive cultural systems at work in singular scenes of television. One travels through the local discursive terrain to know each verbal ecosystem and the species of symbol that sets it apart. So, in the above, we come to see, and hear, in the ritualized and dramatic sequences, cultural systems being asserted and reasserted, and symbolic meanings being acted. The eventual outcome is the replacement of an American "self" with a Russian "soul," a symbolic shift from the unique and honest one to the collectively compassionate moral locus of all. But the cultural force of this symbolic transformation can be fully displayed (if this is at all possible) only by tracing the relevant radiants of meaning throughout each expressive system. In so doing, we find the ritualized drama motivated by such things as cultural dimensions (private/public, shallow/deep, taciturn/voluble), cultural forms for expression (proper topic, moral comment), and conversational rules (disprefer-ring bestial topics and preferring public displays of a moral voice), that is, the mediated coding of a cultural identity (an emotional, morally colored, and transcendent person). In this sense, the ritualized renewal of the Soviet expressive order reinstitutes a core and sacred symbol, as it also supplants an American one. This happens, however, rather metonymically, making a change of topic, a shift in the cultural frame for the mediated discussion. And thus cultural selves view and verbalize the life of television, sometimes in distinctively ritualized forms, such that, within this single televised event, one seeks facts while another speaks morality. To know how this is so, we must hear in televised conversation not only generic forms and channels but with them cultural beliefs about selves and media.

Notes

1. For a treatment of televised discourse as culturally coded, see Donal Carbaugh (1988, 1990b).

2. Throughout the chapter, I use the term *Soviet* because that was the main term used by my informants and because the patterns I report were produced by speakers from various ethnic groups within the now dismantled "Soviet Union." The term is, of course, not without its difficulties. I switch to the term *Russian* when the analysis suggests a distinctly Russian feature. Following standard usage, *American* refers to patterns prominent and distinctive within the United States.

3. The ethnographic approach derives from Dell Hymes (1972), with recent formulations in Gerry Philipsen (1987, 1990) and Carbaugh (1990a, 1990b, 1991, 1995).

4. See, for example, Richard Bauman (1970), Jack L. Daniel and Geneva Smitherman (1976), Kristine Fitch (1991), Yousuf Griefat and Tamar Katriel (1989), Tamar Katriel and Aliza Shenhar (1990), Gerry Philipsen (1992), and Ronald Scollon and Suzanne Scollon (1981).

5. See William Gudykunst and Stella Ting-Toomey (1988, p. 231) and Wendy Leeds-Hurwitz (1990). But also see Carbaugh (1990a, 1990b, 1990c).

6. For uses of exemplars or instances in communication studies, see Robert Hopper (1988) and Scott Jacobs (1988).

7. The transcript consists of numbered lines and three tiers, a, b, and c. The text spoken in English appears as line a. When tier a is an untranslated utterance in English, it is unmarked (e.g., 2a). When tier a is a translation into English (provided by an on-air network translator) of an utterance spoken originally in Russian, it is marked (e.g., 5a: [trans]). The b tier of a line provides, whenever possible, a second English translation (by an independent Russian speaker) of utterances spoken originally in Russian. This provides readers with a kind of cross-check between the translation provided by a television network and that provided by a relatively independent Russian-speaking viewer. This translation (on tier b) was, of course, not broadcast. Tier c provides, as far as was possible, transcriptions of the Russian that was spoken on this occasion. This was very difficult to retrieve because the spoken Russian was often inaudible "behind" the on-air English translation. More details about how this kind of transcribing was done appear elsewhere (Carbaugh, 1993b, note 8, pp. 198-199).

8. The ritual interchange is a kind of "aligning action," a practice that invokes culture in conduct. See Randall Stokes and John Hewitt (1976) and Brad Hall (1991).

9. The interpretations of the Soviet communication system were produced in collaboration with Olga Beloded, Diane Chornenkaya, Lazlo Dienes, Joseph Lake, and Vicki Rubinshteyn, among others.

10. As Donahue might know, part of the unspoken consensus in urban Soviet common culture is that many women have multiple abortions, with numbers in the twenties and thirties not uncommon. See Hedrick Smith (1976, pp. 187-191).

11. See Tamar Katriel and Gerry Philipsen (1981) and Carbaugh (1988, pp. 153-176).

12. See Clifford Geertz (1973, pp. 365-366).

13. A similar introduction to the topic of "sex" was made by an American medical doctor on a college campus who was conducting a "workshop on sex education and birth control." He began with, "Tonight we're going to talk about sex. We're here to talk about social things, not moral issues.

Whether it's right or wrong, good or bad, you'll have to decide for yourself. We're just going to talk about sex" (reported in "Condoms, Spermicides?" 1991, p. 3).

14. See Carbaugh (1988, pp. 127-166).

15. This summary is based on Carbaugh (1987).

16. This is adapted from Anna Wierzbicka (1989). For a related discussion of the person, see Rom Harré (1984).

17. Extremely important to note is that the Soviets in this segment almost never use the term *sex* alone. Their discussion of this topic occurs in a rather veiled style. The four veiled references to the topic are as "it" (8), "that" (16), "that" (37), and "the subject" (38). At two points, the Soviet translators supply differing terms. At line 34, the network translator (34a) supplies "sex," while the independent translator (34b) supplies "it"; at 35, the network translator (35a) supplies "sex" while the independent shows no translation of the term. Similarly, the veiled predications (with implications) about the topic are as follows: "I started" [sexual life at age 18] (3); "I was well prepared" [for sexual life] (10); "sure of what her husband is as a man, that he'll be a real partner" (31a-32a) or "be sure of her husband as a man" [adequate partner for sexual life] (31b-32b). One difference between translators occurs with regard to the relevant predications: "the first woman with whom they had ever had sexual relations" (22a) or "their wife was their first girl (.) woman that they liked" (22b-23b). Reference to the topic is thus relatively veiled, oblique, or indirect (e.g., "it" or "that"), as are predications about the topic (e.g., "be a real partner" or "woman that they liked").

18. See Smith (1976, pp. 6-7, 137-140).

19. See Smith (1976, p. 18) for the cultural (more than the political) roots that highlight the connected agent over "the individual." As one informant put it: "In the Russian culture it is common to address issues of life from a global and moral perspective. Personal beliefs about social practices are presented as exercised patterns of behavior. They might be heard as more or less typical, but they are usually predicated to a collective agent. The speaker's views are supposed to be shared by a collective beneficent." The importance of designing speech with a collective and connected voice is evident also in a common Russian proverb told to schoolchildren: "I is the last letter in the alphabet," which means, according to one informant, "put yourself after the others on your list of priorities." The same cultural principle creates the Soviet form of postal address, beginning at the *top* with the country of the addressee, under which comes their city name, then their street name, with the individual's name at the *bottom*, last name first.

20. See Smith (1976, p. 21).

21. The following formulation is adapted from Wierzbicka (1989).

22. Realizing this helped me reflect upon what had been a very puzzling situation. A Russian student had called me at home one evening and asked, with no explanation, the date of my birth. Later, I realized the student was making decisions about advisory committees and wanted to know my astrological sign as a way of interpreting the nature of our connection within a transcendentally connective, feeling-full domain. The inference I draw from this exchange is not, of course, that all Russians are astrologers or actors on cosmic feeling. What the exchange displays, I think, is a communicative instance of a cultural orientation that itself coheres activities in terms more passionate, transcendentally connected, and feeling-full than does the American, centered as it is in terms of scientific rationality, expressive technicality, and individual utility.

23. The quotation is taken from the Russian version; see Wierzbicka (1989, p. 54).

24. Analyses based on other data corroborate and extend the claims developed here. See Carbaugh (1993a, 1990b, pp. 159-160).

25. The precise ways the public/private dimension becomes interactionally operative are unclear, although "public" is apparently cued not solely on the basis of outside participants (like Donahue) but outside influences generally, including jazz. Hedrick Smith (1976) described how Moscow audiences responded with heightened intensity, great amounts of sobbing and laughing, to Russian ballet, but when viewing American ballet, or jazz, were much more restrained and reserved.

26. The primary data for this report were gathered in 1987-1990, prior to the dismantling of the Soviet Union. What effects these recent political developments may have on the patterns described here are currently unknown. For some informants, the patterns described here are very durable, even in the face of pressures to change. As one informant put it, "We don't know how to do it any other way," with "it" referring to their habitual patterns of expressive life. For the robustness and pervasiveness of traditional

Russian styles, see Jane Kramer (1990). Whether these cultural dynamics apply more generally cannot be firmly asserted on the basis of this report. I can, however, add that I have witnessed the Soviet-Russian pattern identified here in many contexts in the United States, in Europe, and in Russia. Various readers of this report assure me they have observed these patterns in various places including in Israel among Russian immigrants. Perhaps most gratifying have been reactions by Russians, various scholars of Russian culture and history, and Russian scholars themselves, the latter soliciting this chapter for publication in a Russian journal. I mention this not to claim any final word in the matter—in fact, I see what is here as only a beginning—but to suggest that this report, whatever its flaws, has struck at least some cultural chord. How broadly the Soviet and American patterns apply and, if so, how intercultural encounters between them display these patterns, and to what extent these apply to various contexts and media of communication—all of this warrants further study.

27. See Michael Moerman (1988, pp. 104-107).

28. For the social drama frame, see Victor Turner (1980).

29. See Victor Turner (1980), Gerry Philipsen (1987), and my related studies (Carbaugh, 1993a, 1993b, 1996).

References

Bauman, R. (1970). Aspects of 17th century Quaker rhetoric. *Quarterly Journal of Speech, 56*, 67-74.

Bitzer, L. (1968). The rhetorical situation. *Philosophy and Rhetoric, 1*, 1-14.

Carbaugh, D. (1987). Communication rules in Donahue discourse. *Research on Language and Social Interaction, 21*, 31-62.

Carbaugh, D. (1988). *Talking American: Cultural discourses on Donahue.* Norwood, NJ: Ablex.

Carbaugh, D. (1988/1989). Deep agony: "Self" vs. "society" in Donahue discourse. *Research on Language and Social Interaction, 22*, 179-212.

Carbaugh, D. (Ed.). (1990a). *Cultural communication and intercultural contact.* Hillsdale, NJ: Lawrence Erlbaum.

Carbaugh, D. (1990b). Intercultural communication. In D. Carbaugh (Ed.), *Cultural communication and intercultural contact* (pp. 151-175). Hillsdale, NJ: Lawrence Erlbaum.

Carbaugh, D. (1990c). Toward a perspective on cultural communication and intercultural contact. *Semiotica, 80*, 15-35.

Carbaugh, D. (1991). Communication and cultural interpretation. *Quarterly Journal of Speech, 77*, 336-342.

Carbaugh, D. (1993a). Communication competence and cultural pragmatics: Reflections on Soviet and American encounters. *International and Intercultural Communication Annual, 17*, 168-183.

Carbaugh, D. (1993b). "Soul" and "self": Soviet and American cultures in conversation. *Quarterly Journal of Speech, 79*, 182-200.

Carbaugh, D. (1995). An ethnographic theory of communication. In D. Cushman & B. Kovacic (Eds.), *Watershed theories of human communication.* Albany: State University of New York Press.

Carbaugh, D. (1996). *Situating selves: The communication of social identities in American scenes.* Albany: State University of New York Press.

Condoms, spermicides? Dr. Abel doesn't blush. (1991, May 13). *Collegian*, p. 3.

Daniel, J., & Smitherman, G. (1976). "How I got over": Communication dynamics in the black community. *Quarterly Journal of Speech, 62*, 26-39.

Fitch, K. (1991). The interplay of linguistic universals and cultural knowledge in personal address: Colombian *madre* terms. *Communication Monographs, 58*, 254-272.

Geertz, C. (1973). *The interpretation of cultures.* New York: Basic Books.

Goffman, E. (1967). *Interaction ritual: Essays on face-to-face behavior.* New York: Pantheon.

Griefat, Y., & Katriel, T. (1989). Life demands *musayra*: Communication and culture among Arabs in Israel. *International and Intercultural Communication Annual, 13*, 121-138.

Gudykunst, W., & Ting-Toomey, S. (1988). *Culture and interpersonal communication.* Newbury Park, CA: Sage.

Hall, B. (1991). An elaboration of the structural possibilities for engaging in alignment episodes. *Communication Monographs, 58*, 79-100.

Harré, R. (1984). *Personal being*. Cambridge, MA: Harvard University Press.

Hopper, R. (1988). Speech, for instance: The exemplar in studies of conversation. *Journal of Language and Social Psychology, 7*, 137-153.

Hymes, D. (1972). Models of the interaction of language and social life. In J. Gumperz & D. Hymes (Eds.), *Directions in sociolinguistics: The ethnography of communication* (pp. 35-71). New York: Holt, Rinehart & Winston.

Jacobs, S. (1988). Evidence and inference in conversation analysis. In J. Anderson (Ed.), *Communication yearbook 11* (pp. 433-443). Newbury Park, CA: Sage.

Katriel, T., & Philipsen, G. (1981). "What we need is communication": "Communication" as a cultural category in some American speech. *Communication Monographs, 48*, 301-317.

Katriel, T., & Shenhar, A. (1990). Tower and stockade: Dialogic narration in Israeli settlement ethos. *Quarterly Journal of Speech, 76*, 359-380.

Kramer, J. (1990, March 12). Letter from Europe. *New Yorker, 74*, 76-90.

Leeds-Hurwitz, W. (1990). Culture and communication: A review essay. *Quarterly Journal of Speech, 76*, 85-116.

Lewis, J. (1991). *The ideological octopus: An exploration of television and its audience*. New York: Routledge.

Moerman, M. (1988). *Talking culture*. Philadelphia: University of Pennsylvania Press.

Philipsen, G. (1987). The prospect for cultural communication. In L. Kincaid (Ed.), *Communication theory: Eastern and Western perspectives* (pp. 245-254). New York: Academic Press.

Philipsen, G. (1990). An ethnographic approach to communication studies. In B. Dervin, L. Grossberg, B. O'Keefe, & E. Wartella (Eds.), *Rethinking communication: Vol. 2. Paradigm exemplars* (pp. 258-268). Newbury Park, CA: Sage.

Philipsen, G. (1992). *Speaking culturally*. Albany: State University of New York Press.

Scollon, R., & Scollon, S. (1981). *Narrative, literacy and face in interethnic communication*. Norwood, NJ: Ablex.

Smith, H. (1976). *The Russians*. New York: Ballantine.

Stokes, R., & Hewitt, J. (1976). Aligning actions. *American Sociological Review, 41*, 838-849.

Turner, V. (1980). Social dramas and stories about them. *Critical Inquiry, 7*, 141-168.

Wierzbicka, A. (1989). Soul and mind: Linguistic evidence for ethnopsychology and cultural history. *American Anthropologist, 91*, 41-58.

7

Constructions of Self and Other in the Experience of Rap Music

Timothy A. Simpson

In recent years, rap music has become a cultural staple of American society. Rap tops record charts and booms loudly from jeeps rolling through urban streets and suburban strip mall parking lots; it pops up in movie soundtracks and out of the mouth of the Pillsbury Dough Boy; it gains money and prestige for some of the artists who make it; and it shouts an anger and hopelessness that many people would like to forget exist. Rap speaks loudly and incisively, softly and offensively, ambiguously and clearly, but most of all it speaks, and it has become increasingly difficult to ignore.

As rap has become a more popular and influential form of music, it has also become an intensely political site for contemporary skirmishes over racism, marginalization, public values, and freedom of expression. Rap constitutes a contemporary media forum where dominant and marginalized views come together and continuously negotiate the borders that separate them.

I was interested in rap long before I came to see it as a serious subject for scholarly research. Rap called out to me, tapped into my interests in popular music, technology, and politics, articulated my own feelings of ambiguity and resistance toward mainstream society. When Chuck D of Public Enemy—over frantic beats, blaring horns, staccato record scratches—warned his listeners to watch out for the "Prophets of Rage," I knew I was a follower. But I also recognized the ironic nature of my relation to rap—a middle-class, suburban, white male rapping along to the tune of underclass, urban, revolutionary black nationalism.

Although I acknowledged some skepticism about my study of rap music and hip-hop culture, and in part because of this skepticism, I wanted to explore my experience of rap music, the ways it forms up in my life. It is my hope not to solve some "problem" about rap, or to affix some final meaning to it, but to meditate on the reflexive relationship between the model of "self" offered by rap and the ways I find and explore my own selves within that model. In this chapter, I suggest that rap music offers up a particular structure of time, space, and the material world—repetitive time, authentic space, appropriated material—that come together to form the self-referential landscape of rap. It's difficult, however, to map such a landscape. The ways we hear the territory depend a great deal on where we've come from and where we are now. This is true of listening to all music. For me, rap finds its meaning in the constellation of my autobiography; memories of experiences, relationships, and insecurities all seem present in the echo of rap. Because of this, the roles I play as writer, researcher, and fan fold back into the kind of assumptions I make about rap. My interest in rap music, in turn, informs the ways I perform those roles. So this chapter, much like the relationship between rap and the self, is inherently *reflexive*; it folds back on itself (Steier, 1991).

Rap Redemption and Resistance

Music has always offered me solace from life's tensions, creating a space for me to find both myself and a sense of belonging with others—listeners I knew must be "out there" somewhere. I had looked to punk and hard-core music for these same reasons, to indie rock, ska, and heavy metal. In my own way, I became a student of the music before I thought about my involvement in those terms. In fact, it was the realization that I could study popular music and style in the academy that led me to graduate school. It was rap that I played on my car stereo as I drove to the university.

But I also found that obstacles stood in the way of my study of rap. I entered the conversation as debates about multiculturalism were prevalent. I learned about margins and borders, presences and absences, canon and colonization. I became increasingly conscious of my relation to rap, wary about pursuing it as a site for study. Russell Ferguson (1990) notes:

> In our society dominant discourse never tries to speak its own name. Its authority is based on absence. The absence is not just that of the various groups classified as "other," although members of these groups are routinely denied power. It is also the lack of any overt acknowledgement of the specificity of the dominant culture, which is simply assumed to be the all-encompassing norm. This is the basis of its power. (p. 11)

I became confused about exactly where I stood. Although in one sense located at the "invisible center," I felt alienated from that center and sought alignment with the "margins," where again I encountered my self as an other. I also became conscious of the ways that those in positions of power are able to reproduce dominant definitions of cultural forms, and I began to see people who write about rap in the popular media as dominant voices exercising their power. For example, Princeton University Mellon Fellow David Samuels (1991), in an article in the *New Republic,* calls rap, "The 'black music' that isn't either"; neither "music," according to Samuels, nor authentically "black" (p. 24). I recognize the serious problems that arise in such accounts of rap, and I fear my own perpetuation of this kind of subjugation.

As I continued my studies, my whole notion of subculture began to slip away. I came to see subcultures as constructions that defied clearly demarcated boundaries, that did not so much exist in the real world as they did in the minds and discourse of the people who wrote about them (Clifford, 1992). As I ventured out to study the hip-hop subculture that produced rap, I realized that there was not some specific place where I could go to find it. In contemporary America, subcultures aren't generally tied to geography. Rap music comes to me on television, on records, in clothing styles and slang, on tapes I play in my car as I drive around the city. It travels through spaces, over borders, into experiences and memories.

Rap music speaks to me and in some ways it speaks me. Rap's voices both invite me in and tell me I am not at home when I check myself into a room at the hip-hop hotel. And the voices are right. I came uninvited. I am essentially a tourist. I survey the shifting scenes of rap, picking up a souvenir here, taking a snapshot there, trying to piece together what it means—and my understanding can at best be incomplete. In their song "For the Funk of It," one of the members of Above the Law suggests that to tell him "where I'm at" you must have been where he's been. Chuck D of Public Enemy is a bit more direct: "Take somebody white, they start reading Malcolm and everybody to the T, then all of a sudden they think they're black, and then they start criticizing *you*" (D & Allen, 1990, p. 68, used by permission).

Multicultural theory not only helped me problematize my relation to rap culture and my understanding of culture itself but also allowed me to enter the conversation again, but this time in a different position. Henry Giroux (1992) notes that scholars

> need to move their analysis and pedagogical practices away from an exotic or allegedly objective encounter with marginal groups and raise more questions with respect to how their own subjectivities and practices are present in the construction of the margins. (p. 15)

We need to examine our research practices to understand how *we* construct our subjects, how our relationships with our subject matter, our research practices, and reporting procedures create the cultures we purport to study and, perhaps, how those cultures create us (Jackson, 1989). In this vein, I looked to the music for some answers. The form and structure I heard in rap—"the mix"—provided me with a metaphor to help explain not only how it worked but how I might write about it as well.

Writing and Mixing

The metaphor of the mix is a useful one for writing about culture. It encourages a constantly shifting, open-ended, multivocal discourse, one that evokes the ambiguity of experience rather than obscures it. The *mix* refers to the common contemporary recording industry practice of releasing various *mixes* of rap songs (and pop songs in general) (Tankel, 1990). The song is mixed and remixed into sometimes radically different versions; the mixer might add different instruments or sounds (more bass for dancing, for example), extend certain sections of the song, add background vocals, delete profanity to allow for radio play, or delete the vocals altogether and make an instrumental track. Record companies benefit from multiple mixes by encouraging consumers to buy more than one version of the song. Artists and producers are afforded new, potentially creative technology with which they effectively eradicate the notion of an "original" work of art. Each mix deconstructs the others as it reconstructs itself, illuminating the general constructedness of the musical product. As audience members, we get a back-stage look into how music is assembled, how elements of the mix get combined in ways that privilege some voices and interpretations over others. For example, Public Enemy released a mix of the song "Louder Than a Bomb" on their album *It Takes a Nation of Millions to Hold Us Back.* The musical track that the words are rapped over angrily confronts me, providing an aural environment that positions me as the recipient of a verbal assault from which Chuck D emerges as the clear victor. A later version of the same song—the "JMJ Telephone Tap Groove Mix"—has a slower, melancholy, less frenzied musical track, changing the context of the rapper's voice, bringing him into the passive position that I had occupied in the other mix.

Dick Hebdige (1987) uses the "mix" metaphor in his book *Cut 'n' Mix* to explore the histories of Caribbean music and its relation to culture. I want to use it to explore the experiential qualities of rap music and to reflect on how different conceptions of my own self—"critic" versus "fan," for example—lead me to think and write about rap in different ways. So two mixes follow. The first, an interpretive textual reading of rap, unravels the music into the components of appropriation, repetition, and authenticity. The second, a fan's account of adventure, escape, and discovery at an Ice-T concert, weaves those same components back together within the context of my own life, for, as Karl Schiebe (1986) suggests, we need adventures to satisfactorily construct and maintain our own narratives of self.

Rap Experience: The Critical Mix

Sample One: Appropriation

"Incident at 66.6 FM," a song on Public Enemy's controversial album *Fear of a Black Planet,* consists of snippets of dialogue from a radio call-in talk show on which group members were guests. Many of the callers, whose voices are laid over a musical track, articulate hostile and racist sentiments. One caller recalls—in a high-pitched nasal voice—seeing Public Enemy in concert and thinking they were "appalling," adding, "when I see someone wearing one of their T-shirts, I think they're scum too." "Go back to Africa," exclaims another caller, while a third asks the show's host, "Why do you pay homage to these people by putting these monkeys on?" Interspersed with these voices are callers who speak on Public Enemy's behalf. One merely yells the name of Public Enemy's DJ—"Ter-minator X!"—while another argues with the show's host: "I think that white liberals like yourself have difficulty understanding that Chuck's views represent the frustrations of the majority of black youth out there today." Throughout the song, the empty sound of a telephone dial tone punctuates the callers' voices. The members of Public Enemy are strangely silent, but that doesn't mean their feelings aren't present on the track. The song doesn't merely document the radio show; by cutting up the voices and recontextualizing them, it comments on the callers and on the attitudes they represent. The irony of hearing this exchange in the context of the album turns criticisms of the band into critiques of the callers. "It was real live from a radio station," Chuck D (quoted in Wetherbee, 1990, p. 12) said of the song in a magazine interview. "I'm not getting permission for it—I'll probably get sued for it, but it's worth it."

Public Enemy appropriated the voices on the radio show for their own use. Rap music is built around an aesthetic of appropriation. "Artistic appropriation is the historical source of hip-hop music," notes philosopher Richard Shusterman (1991), "and still remains the core of its technique and a central feature of its aesthetic form and message" (p. 614). The act of appropriation entails both an active political and physical encounter with history and a poetic of recreation. Appropriation provides the material stuff of rap, the basic beat and the noise that adorns it. The vinyl record disc acts as a storehouse of static cultural information, and it also evokes a particular time and place; traces of history reside within the sounds. The rap DJ is able to bring the past into the present and comment on it by recontextualizing the captured experiences.

We can better understand the emergence of appropriation in its connection to rap by tracing the music's historical development. "There is no such thing as a point of origin, least of all in something as slippery as music," writes Hebdige (1987), "but that doesn't mean there isn't history" (p. 10). Rap music as it is generally thought of today was born in the early 1970s, when house- and street-party DJs in New York played music for dance parties. They found that there were certain parts of songs—a particular bass riff or drum sequence, for instance—that initiated especially responsive reactions from dancers. DJs wanted to extend these bits of songs into longer "breaks," and by electronically connecting two turntables, they created a new type of musical instrument. They put copies of the same record on each turntable, and played the same bits of music over and over again, recuing one record while the other played and vice versa. Eventually, as the music and mixing became more complex, the DJs employed MCs: people who would talk, or rap, over the beats to entertain the audience while the DJs were spinning records. DJs began experimenting with the musical creation by alternating different types of music, so that songs were created solely by mixing together pieces of other songs. They would combine bits of rock, funk, calypso, classical, themes from television shows—any kind of music that might be interesting (Toop, 1984).

Hebdige calls this "cut 'n' mix" music, and he recounts historically how this aesthetic has fed into and out of Caribbean-based music. As the cut 'n' mix aesthetic has become popular, it has moved into the studio. This has made possible even more experimentation with the mix. DJs and producers use electronic equipment to "sample" or borrow not only music but bits of speeches, radio talk shows, film dialogue—basically any sound that is interesting—and add them to the mix. This mixing of sounds has been brought to the forefront of the production. It has made possible the physical mixing of different bits of history, the literal reinscribing of the past into the present.

According to Shusterman (1991), this appropriative aesthetic of rap music "challenges the traditional ideal of originality and uniqueness that has long enslaved our conception of art" (p. 617). Although artists have always borrowed from each other's works, they have usually obscured this fact and promoted an ideology of uniqueness. Rap, on the other hand, consciously promotes derivative borrowing, changing the meaning of *originality.* "Originality thus loses its absolute originary status and is reconceived to include the transfiguring reappropriation and recycling of the old" (Shusterman, 1991, p. 617).

Rap DJs are *bricoleurs,* thinkers, mulling over the bits at hand, teasing out ways to use them in the ongoing process of work and creation, and defining and extending themselves through the process of narrative de- and reconstruction. The DJ brings time and space together in the physical control over matter, the cultural artifact, found buried in an old record collection or hidden among the racks in a store, worked and reworked over the stylus, mining the grooves for traces of culture. DJs can even literally transform the record turntable into a percussive instrument by "scratching" the record, or quickly moving it back and forth while the stylus stays in the record groove. DJ Premier of the rap group Gang Starr says,

> I like dirty samples, static-y records, with a real trash sound on there. A real funky street sound. I loop the samples and then put a drum track over it. From there I'll add other elements, a hi-hat, horns, piano, funny sounds, whatever it takes to make that track build. (quoted in McElfresh, 1991, p. 59)

KRS-One of Boogie Down Productions makes a similar point in the song "Ya Slippin," where he says that he composes music "piece by piece," combining base lines, snare drums, and record cuts and then adding his name to make the music "fresh." The end result for KRS-One is what he calls "original art."

KRS-One's allusion to "original art" suggests that although rappers openly employ the appropriative aesthetic, value comes from *creating* rather than merely *copying.* The idea is not to imitate, or "bite," a song that has come before, but to use some bit or piece of the song to make something new. Whether a particular artist's music is original or not is a subject of constant discussion and debate. For example, a fan complains in a letter to a rap magazine:

> It's a shame that we allow rappers nowadays to not only sample the beat of a James Brown, Parliament, or whomever—but it seems that many artists are getting paid from straight up ripping an entire song off of another MC. Case in point being Naughty By Nature's "O.P.P.," which obviously ripped off Tony D's track, or the most recent MC Breed's "Just Kickin It," which many know he ripped off of Mob Style's "Street Wise." This industry's no longer creating music, but in-fro-tratin' music. Yet we want to be accepted as artists creating art; this sham discredits those true artists. (Producer X, 1992, p. 11, used by permission)

Similarly, a record reviewer complains about a recent release from the rap group X-Clan that, "lyrically and topic-wise, X-Clan remains on point, but production-wise, they sometimes opt for already proven grooves rather than breaking new musical ground. Be ready to play a few rounds of 'who used that beat before?' " (L. R., 1992, p. 36, used by permission). And perhaps the best way for rappers to prove the originality of their beats is by contrasting themselves with other artists. In his song "My Bad Side," Sir Mix-a-Lot disses Biz Markie's classic "old-school" song "Vapors." Mix-a-Lot objects to Biz's tendency to rely on what he thinks are unimaginative loops and beats in his song:

I've never been a fan of yours, "Vapors" ain't my thing, slick
You bite something then you hide it with a drum trick
Takin' apart every rap that's on the charts
Mix theirs with yours, spin it back—it ain't hard
Please! Get off the James Brown tip . . .
Your producers are bitin', you're gettin' paid but you're lame
And no two songs of mine sound the same. (Rhyme Cartel Records, Inc./Sir
Mix-a-Lot; used by permission)

Sample Two: Repetition

In the studio banter that introduces his instrumental song "Just a Beat," Rakim
calls himself a "true black man" and then instructs his listeners to check out "the
beat." His DJ, Eric B, samples Rakim's words—"the beat"—and they repeat over
and over again until "the beat" forms the actual beat of the song. Drums kick into
the track, and snippets of dreamy music swirl up and fall away, but "the beat"
remains at the heart of the mix.

"Just a Beat" is the simplest track on Eric B and Rakim's classic album *Follow
the Leader,* and it's also the most direct. The voice and the beat are central to rap
music—Hebdige calls them the "vital mix"—and by collapsing them together
and connecting them so literally with identity, Eric B and Rakim provide their
listeners with a crash course in rap aesthetics.

Rappers bring the cultural capital claimed through the appropriative act
together to construct a temporality of repetition. The repetitive beat is at the heart
of rap music, and DJs weave loops of appropriated noise into and around those
beats. Repetition is key to understanding rap because it is a temporal construct
that allows for cultural identification through enactment and display of common
cultural memory, memory that never passes away and is always there to be
retrieved and reexperienced. Repetition provides a platform in time, a place to
go to isolate and grasp a moment, a place from which to speak.

Repetition resides at the borders of Western culture, always present but dismissed,
masked, and marginalized. "The world is not inexhaustible in its combinations,"
notes James Snead (1990, p. 213), and therefore repetition is a necessary condition
of culture. For Snead, one function culture serves is self-perpetuation, maintenance
of cultural identity and continuity, "coverage" against internal and external threats;
repetition aids in this objective. Snead (1990) maintains that the West tends to view
culture as a series of progressions (or regressions), while non-Western cultures have
celebrated, even reveled in, repetition.

> Black culture highlights the observance of such repetition, often in homage to an original
> generative instance or act. Cosmogony, the origins and stability of things, hence prevails
> because it recurs, not because the world continues to develop from the archetypal
> moment. Periodic ceremonies are ways in which black culture comes to terms with its
> perception of repetition, precisely by highlighting that perception. (p. 218)

Snead (1990) explains how repetition is inscribed in African music in the form
of the "cut": "an abrupt, seemingly unmotivated break . . . with a series already
in progress and a willed return to a prior series" (p. 220). You can leave a beat

wherever you want, and then return to find it again. The idea is to emphasize continuity, "to confront accident and rupture not by covering them over but by making room for them inside the system itself." Repetition becomes key in generating a sustained sense of collective cultural identity and individual identity within the culture.

Rhythm is perhaps the most basic form of repetition, for it is possible only through the continual recurrence of discrete sound (or lack of sound). Nietzsche (1989) interprets the rhythmic nature of poetry as a site where humans attempt to escape material existence. He says,

> The magic in rhythm consists in a quite elementary symbolism by which the regular and the orderly imposes itself on our understanding as a higher realm, a life above and beyond this irregular life; that part of us which has the power to move with the same rhythm follows the urging of that symbolic feeling and moves in unison with it or at least feels a strong urge to do so. (p. 244)

Hebdige (1987) says it like this: "Repetition is the basis of all rhythm and rhythm is at the core of life" (p. 15).

Rhythm's ability to create such a unity is particularly important to oral cultures. Because oral cultures rely on the passing of cultural memory from one generation to another through oral narrative, it is essential that important details of that history be remembered; what is forgotten is lost forever. Therefore, a sense of rhythm is imposed on the message to aid in its memory.

Cultural memories are in a sense preserved in rhythms, Hebdige says, and rhythm is important in providing cultural continuity. He explains that African slaves expressed their anger and frustration through music. "Drumming was particularly important. By preserving African drumming traditions, by remembering African rhythms, the slaves could keep alive the memory of the freedom they had lost" (Hebdige, 1987, p. 26). There were different songs for different occasions and rituals—work, marriage, birth, death, battle. "Each event in the life of the tribe has a rhythm which can be immediately identified" (Hebdige, 1987, p. 30). Historical continuity is embedded (or at least implied) within the rhythm, within the repetition.

Musical tracks for rap songs, as well as the raps themselves, are built around rhythm and repetition; rap celebrates repetition as a condition of culture. Rap music calls up bits of history and the experiences that give it form and meaning, and it lets them unfold in a continual present, providing continuity through an eternally constructed site around which audience members can identify.

Sample Three: Authenticity

In 1986, MC Shan released a single called "The Bridge," arguing in the song that rap's origins could be traced back to New York's Queensbridge housing project, where he grew up. A newly formed group called Boogie Down Productions (BDP) launched their career with a response record in which they claimed the "South Bronx" area of New York as the progenitor of rap. MC Shan answered this record with "Kill That Noise," and BDP responded with "The Bridge Is Over." At issue in the exchange was "realness," authenticity. Both MC Shan and

BDP became legitimate rappers by arguing over the legitimacy of their versions of rap. Authenticity, however, lay not so much with who had the "correct" information about rap's beginnings, as with the fact of the claim itself.

When identity is constituted on the tenuous thread of appropriation, fixed by repetition, and tempered by marginalization, authenticity becomes paramount. Rap music unfolds in a space of negotiated authenticity. Rap songs cover any number of diverse subjects and constitute many different musical styles and genres, but proclamations of the rappers' originality and realness are perhaps rap music's most pervasive subject matter.

The tradition of proclaiming who you are and where you're from is as old as storytelling itself, and it is essential to rap. Whether it's Gang Starr beginning their album *Daily Operation* with a song that explains that Brooklyn is "The Place Where We Dwell," or N.W.A. dwelling on the fact that they come "Straight Outta' Compton," a now-notorious neighborhood in South Central Los Angeles, a connection to place is fundamental to rap identity, or the "real." A *Spin* magazine critic (Blackwell, 1991) notes that

> one of rap's main boasting and dissing points has always been whether or not each particular artist is truly "down" or "from the streets." From Eazy-E's somewhat convincing "gangsta" dissertations on his life in Compton to [white rapper] Vanilla Ice's "bullshit lies about his neighborhood" . . . rappers take glorious pride in their shady backgrounds. (pp. 14-15, used by permission)

"Authentic" selves emanate from "real" communities. Communities aren't just places, though; community exists within relationships between people. Evoking the names of the members of your "crew," or giving "props" to those artists who came before you, is a way of acknowledging the importance of the community from which you sprung, and of bestowing power and honor upon yourself. That is why BDP is able to demonstrate "We're Still #1" by simply naming all the people who are "down with us." Or why the Guru of Gang Starr begins his song "Soliloquy of Chaos"—a story about a violent incident that broke out before a Gang Starr concert—by naming 26 members of his crew who were present that night—and it is testament to his amazing verbal flow that he makes the names rhyme. This also explains what sometimes seem like overzealous "shout-outs," or thank yous, that rappers extend to friends and supporters. In the liner notes for *Fear of a Black Planet,* for example, Public Enemy thanks no fewer than 340 artists, groups, crews, political figures, disc jockeys, and athletes for their help and influence. Naming is a way to imagine, grasp, and express a sense of belonging and community, and to pay respect to the other members.

Although naming is sometimes an end in itself, it usually accompanies other rap subjects. Rappers expend the most effort on an exaggerated boasting about who they are, copping and proclaiming an identity that is overwhelmingly self-referencing. The proof of their words lies not so much in the ways they match up with some empirical reality as in the words themselves. You can refer to your possessions or past accomplishments, but the only way to prove that you are the best rapper is to *claim* it in the most creative, provocative, and interesting way—the moment of authentic presence. There is a quest to continually create new styles, new "flavors" (Public Enemy's rapper Flavor Flav's name is a claim to his ability to do just that), and to display the best rhyming skills.

Ultimately, rappers strive to constantly make something "new" in a genre organized around the acquisition and display of the music of others. Rap is caught within the tensions of moving forward creatively by looking backward—building repetition from appropriations, a repetition that allows rappers to ground themselves in the torrential movement of history, that allows them to connect past and future in an immediate authentic moment of creativity, a moment that was already gone before it existed.

The constant struggle for an authentic discourse is sometimes exhausting, requiring the text to muster all of its resources in pursuit of a construction that is always slipping away. A fan writes the following lament in a letter responding to a *Spin* story about rapper LL Cool J:

> Re: L.L. Cool J—"Real Rap's Real Superstar." Cool story by Poulson-Bryant, but what are y'all doin', running ads for Coke? I understand the authenticity issue here—yeah, L.L.'s back, he's dope, he's around-the-way. But in the age of the sound bite, "real"—as in "Real Thing"—don't count for shit, gang. Did "real" people die in the Middle East? The prowar sloganeers . . . probably don't think so. Nothing's "real" anymore, so we get "virtual" reality and lose ourselves even further. The word real is practically useless. (Woodlief, 1991, p. 16, used by permission)

The Loop: Appropriation, Repetition, Authenticity

I am reminded of Dick Hebdige's (1988) warning that lest we wander too far out into the field of theoretical thought, we should ground ourselves in the particular. An analysis of DAS EFX's song "They Want EFX" might be helpful in evoking how appropriation and repetition intersect in the negotiated space of authenticity, how the voices of popular culture speak a kind of cultural memory.

The song is, first of all, an amazing feat of verbal dexterity. The two rappers in DAS EFX trade off verses, and sometimes lines and words, in a lickety-split, tongue-twisting wordfest. They rap the words over a creepily mysterious rhythm track, and, at first listen, the rap seems to comprise a long series of nonsense syllables broken up by the chorus of the song: "They want effects," repeated several times.

The words seem like nonsense, but there's something familiar about them. That's what grabbed me when I first heard the song, and made me rush out and buy the album. As I began to concentrate on the words, I started to recognize bits and pieces, familiar pop culture references implanted far back in my memory and called forth by their surprising appearance in the text of the song. I think the first one I noticed was, "That's pretteee sneaky, sis," the catchphrase from a commercial for Connect Four, a vertical checkers game whose Saturday morning television advertisement I probably saw for the last time a decade ago. I began to identify more and more references until I finally realized the entire song is a constant stream of these bits—dialogue from old commercials, name-dropping from syndicated sitcoms, lines from forgotten songs—one tremendous pop-cultural regurgitation, the verbal manifestation of our televisual psyche. DAS EFX have turned our leftovers, our cultural refuse, into a defiantly produced piece of art.

"They Want EFX" is built around repetition. The different elements of repetition in the song do two things: First, they give the song a foreboding sense of sameness, making evident the pop-cultural rhythm embedded in our consciousness, suggesting that we have locked ourselves into a neurotic cage of disconnected, meaningless bits of discourse, and all we can do is babble it to ourselves. Second, they suggest a way out through our ability to identify with each other based on the common pop-cultural landscape we share.

The song is rapped over a tape loop of a bit of instrumental music sampled off of a record. The bit lasts about 3 seconds and is repeated over and over and over again throughout the duration of the song. Repetition also occurs in DAS EFX's rearticulation of our popular culture, holding it up for examination (and celebration). Further, they end each verse by vocalizing the last few bars of the *Beverly Hillbillies* theme—da da da dum dum, dum dum—adding a conclusion to the song that occurs throughout its duration, popping back up every time the song works it way back around to that position.

The chorus consists of DAS EFX repeating the title of the song, "They Want EFX," while a sample of a rapper answers, saying, "some live effects." The sampled rapper is a member of EPMD, who "discovered" DAS EFX and produced their album. So DAS EFX pay them homage by sampling their song, a bit of cultural exchange that allows EPMD to live on, to carry their legacy into the music of other groups, to survive the passage of time. DAS EFX authenticate EPMD, and EPMD return the favor. In Burkean terminology, we might characterize the relationship between the two groups as courtship, a rhetoric of exchange, trading authenticity hierarchically and sacredly—in other words, both as a cultural commodity and as a means to community.

But if we look at the conversation enacted between the two groups in the song, we see that it gets more complicated. DAS EFX says, "They want EFX," and EPMD answers "some live effects." The EPMD sample becomes the "live effects" that "they" want—"they" being the rest of us, the culture who wants both to revel in the special effects of the media and who wants to hear DAS EFX tell us about it. But the EPMD sample *isn't* live—it's recorded and resurrected. We struggle to deny the primacy of the spoken word—EPMD says it is "some live effects"; it becomes "live" because it is claimed to be so. But the fact that the phrase is repeated in exactly the same way so many times during the song points to the fact that it's not "live." Further, EPMD's "effects" become DAS EFX's "EFX." Would DAS EFX not be anything without EPMD's effect on the group? Or is it the other way around, with EPMD able only to muster some old "live effects" to match the EFX that everyone wants?

The elements of the song come together to articulate a story about the fragmented, neurotic sense of American popular culture, and provide a glimpse at the hold it has on us. The song demonstrates the technological simulacrum we have embedded ourselves in. It offers a tale of the mythic wonders of repetition—pop-cultural rituals that bind us together, technological rhythms that enclose us within ourselves, beats that imply opportunities for transgressing and escaping limits. It suggests that a sign can collapse into itself. It illuminates the nature of hierarchy and the symbolic exchange system that operates among the different levels, holding them together with its flexible bond, allowing each to authenticate the other. It encourages us to look into ourselves and the ways we place those selves within culture, avoiding potentially deadly cynicism by celebrating the wonder of our situation.

Although the foregoing discussion suggests some ways that self is contested, represented, and articulated within the medium of rap music, my personal response to "They Want EFX" points to a more reflexive relationship between my own sense of self and the model of self offered by rap. To investigate this latter subject further, let me relate another tale about my relationship with rap, how rap speaks to me and how I talk back.

Rap Experience: The Fan Mix

The Ticket

Ice-T is coming to Tampa with his hardcore band Body Count, and I'm hyped; I can hardly wait. I buy my $15 ticket several weeks before the show, in case they sell out. Although I have been a fan of rap for years, living in small college towns in Alabama and Arkansas has kept me from having access to rap shows. Now that I'm living in Tampa, this is my first opportunity to attend a major rap concert. I don't want to miss this.

The Drive-By

The day of the concert, I go to a record store near my house to see if a friend who works there is going to the show. "Aren't you scared there might be a drive-by shooting?" she asks. "Give me a break," I reply, laughing, thinking to myself that she has fallen victim to the media's constant portrayal of rap as dangerous and violent. I have a sudden image of my body being ripped apart by automatic weapons fire. I make a mental note to be sure not to hang around outside the concert hall.

Clothes Make the Human

I stare at my small collection of baseball caps. Should I wear a cap to the show, or not? If I wear a cap, will I look like a wanna-be, somebody trying too hard to fit in? But I like wearing caps. Does that make me a wanna-be, even if I don't mean to be one? Or maybe I am one. But if I wear a cap, and I admit that I am a wanna-be, then have I bypassed the whole wanna-be problem by being up front about it to myself?

OK, no cap.

But what clothes should I wear? How best to appear authentic in the field? I decide on baggy jeans, a black T-shirt, and a dark gray shirt, which I leave unbuttoned so as to look cool and casual. I am careful not to wear any red or bright blue—I don't want to be mistaken for a South Central Los Angeles crip or blood on a trip down to Tampa to do a little gang-banging.

The Body Search

I park my car and walk to the concert hall, keeping my eyes peeled for suspicious characters who look like they might be ready to perpetrate a little violence. I don't see anybody. They must be hiding.

I get to the hall. There are quite a few young, white teenagers hanging around outside. It doesn't look particularly dangerous; in fact, it doesn't look dangerous at all. A police officer is searching people as they enter. She gives me a cursory pat down. "Damn!" I think to myself. "I could have an Uzi stuck down my pants leg and she wouldn't even notice."

I enter the hall. Most everybody here is younger than I am, and they certainly aren't scary. I'm a bit disappointed. So much for the risk of venturing into unknown, alien, violent territory. I don't feel like I've crossed a border as much as I feel like I've walked back into my high school.

The Drive-Buy

The warm-up band is playing when I get there. They are an interracial rap/funk/rock band, and they're pretty good. The crowd is enjoying them. I stand around on the outskirts of the crowd and drink a beer. The band finishes.

The crowd waits anxiously. That sense of preconcert anticipation hangs over the hall. Suddenly the lights go down, and Ice-T takes the stage amid much music, whistles, sirens, and cheering. On stage with him are his DJ Evil-E and a couple of his homeboys. One of them is Sean E Sean, immortalized in Ice-T's song about gangster life, "6 in the Morning," as the guy who had a "beeper going off like a high school bell." The beeper has become a useful artifact and a potent symbol of hip-hop culture, a sign of affluence and a mysterious mediator between people who want to hook up but are separated by the space between them. The crowd wants to hook up with Ice-T, to experience the ease of connection supplied by electronic beeps. We cheer Ice-T as if we know him personally. Rap seems to have that power: It binds performer and audience in an intimate way that often seems missing from much commercial music—maybe because the rapper is essentially just talking, and we are caught up in the flow. Why do I feel like I know Ice-T? Is it something he does, or something I do? Or is it the magic of the corporate music industry, who can sell the thrills of gangster life to a middle-class white kid like me? $14.99 a pop. A real gangster would waste a sucker for $14.99. But I dutifully pay my money to hear someone else talk about it—a consumer drive-buy.

Ice-T's set includes a bunch of his songs, most of them in abbreviated form, so he can pack more in. He's giving us what we want. I push my way to the front of the stage, where to my surprise I encounter a mass of flailing bodies caught in a mosh pit, site of an alternative dance-floor ritual. Moshing is a form of dance, a seemingly chaotic display of a collective feeling of anger, energy, pleasure, and excitement. You throw yourself into the mosh as people circle among each other, spinning faster and faster, making physical contact with others, arms and legs flailing, constantly bumping into new people as the pit throws them and you from the periphery into the center and back out again. You can literally become, as the speed metal group Anthrax sings, "Caught in a Mosh." The mosh pit looks like chaos from the outside, but it is really a controlled, ordered ritual. Moshers lift others up on top of the pit, or people climb on stage and then dive back onto the pit, and those in the throes of the mosh pass them around over their heads. The risk of bodily injury is substantial due to the suspension of social norms concerning personal space and maximum energy exertion, but the interaction is generally conducted so that a relatively minimal amount of physical danger actually exists. One uncooperative person, however, can cause a quick change in the demeanor of the group.

I jump in the pit and start moshing myself. I haven't done this for several years. I forgot what a rush it is. Ice-T finishes his set and says he will be back in a few minutes with his new band, Body Count. I have heard of this band, but I'm not sure what to expect.

On Crossing a Border and Passing
Your Subject Going the Other Direction

About 20 minutes later, Body Count comes on stage. Ice-T is the singer, naturally. He's taken off his hat and shaken his hair out of its trademark ponytail. Clad in low-slung jeans and a white T-shirt, he looks like a genuine rocker.

Body Count is an all-black hardcore band. *Hardcore* is a genre of music that was born in the wake of punk, and it is a genre associated with a subculture I used to be very much a part of. Young white kids are the main consumers of hardcore—kids who often shave their heads, ride skateboards, and wear T-shirts that bear allegiance to bands like Crucial Youth and Minor Threat. A black hardcore band is an anomaly.

Body Count is rocking! "I wanna see some action," Ice yells, and we in the pit begin to mosh furiously. I am banging into people and they are bumping into me. I get knocked down, and immediately hands are all over me, helping me up. This is a rule of moshing—when someone hits the floor, those nearby pull them to their feet; otherwise, they will get trampled by the frantic dancers. Someone taps me on the shoulder, and I turn around. "I want up," he yells. I bend over and put my hands together, locking my fingers. He puts his foot in the makeshift stirrup and I boost him up on top of the crowd. Hands quickly go up and pass him around overhead. I feel like I'm 17 again. I'm back in touch with a part of myself I had almost forgotten about—I remember how many nights I spent moshing and thrashing to hardcore music when I was younger. A guy near me yells to one of his friends, "Isn't it great to be alive in the fucking 90s!"

Between songs, Ice-T talks to the crowd. "If you put kids of different races—white, black, oriental, Indian, Hawaiian—in a sand box together, they would grow up loving each other," he says. The crowd cheers. "Parents teach us to hate." Body Count breaks into a song called "Mama's Gonna Die Tonight" about a fed-up teenager who seeks revenge on his racist mother.

"The album is coming out on March 30th," Ice warns. "It'll be banned by March 31st." He was almost right. Several months later, controversy erupted around Body Count's song "Cop Killer." Ice-T eventually removed the song from the album in response to intense pressure inflicted on him and his record label by police departments and civic groups across the nation. Even George Bush made a point to speak out against the song.

Ice-T calls himself an "OG"—original gangster—a claim for authenticity that he breaks down for the crowd. " 'Original' means three things," Ice-T exclaims. "You aren't on anyone's dick; you listen to whatever you want to; and you do whatever you want to. As for 'gangster'; we're all gangsters. You have to be a little bit of a gangster to get by. Black people have to be gangsters to make it in America. White people have to be gangsters, too. When your friend called you up tonight and asked you to go out, and you said you couldn't because you were going to see Ice-T, they said, 'you don't want to listen to that rap shit.' And you said, 'Fuck you!' Then you're a gangster."

The crowd loves it. We long so desperately to be gangsters, whatever that means, and here's the real thing validating us. Ice-T is giving us what we want. I thought I was trying to cross some line into Ice-T's culture, to ford some gulf between us, but I think it's more accurate to say that he's taken up residence in mine. I question whether I can know the history he has lived, the community he claims, but he sure seems to know something about mine. Maybe it's all marketing. But Ice-T is somehow tapping into a part of me that I thought belonged to my past, and he is proving that it's still here, waiting for something to draw it out again.

This Is the End

The show is over, and I mill around dumbly as people file out of the hall. I don't want to leave. I want to remain in that moment that already escaped, in that ritual that ties me in the present to one of my past selves, that moment that gives me a sense of consistent identity, a fragment of my past I can connect with my future. I suddenly realize that I am exhausted and sweaty and sore. I'm getting old. I walk outside into the cold night. I don't hear any gunshots; nobody's getting beaten up. I sit down with my back against the wall of the building. A car rolls by, Ice-T's song "Rhyme Pays" pumping out of its stereo, the beat becoming increasingly distorted and eventually fading out as the car disappears down the road. A group of people are hanging around outside, sweaty, disheveled, talking excitedly. They all look so young. I long to be one of them, to feel the security of that group, to feel like I belong, to know that my doubts about myself and the world can be erased in a magical moment of moshing, of collective musical ritual. It seems so simple. Where did that go? How did I lose it? I feel old. I walk back to my car, alone. Ice-T pulled something out of me, or at least he gave me the opportunity to find it. The crowd accepted me. But they're all gone and I guess that part of me is too.

Back at Home

Tires screech. Gunfire rips through the night, claiming its victim. "Automatic Uzi mother-fucking gun blast," Ice-T says. I check myself for blood. I think I'm OK. I reach up and turn off the CD player.

Reviewing the Mixes

Appropriation, repetition, authenticity—not only the symbolic components of rap, these terms also suggest the shape and form of my own attempts to belong to rap, and hint at the strategies I adopt to write about it. Did I find these constructs in rap, did rap find them in me, or did they emerge somewhere between us, in my writing?

This chapter traces my relationship to rap in a neat line. My initial attraction to rap was a logical extension of my interest in music and youth cultures. That attraction gave way to a sense of unease, skepticism—even foolishness—as I encountered rap as a unified subculture where some people belong and some don't, where even the songs themselves articulate these divisions. My response was to turn the critical gaze onto rap and to generate some categories by which to organize my understanding of the music. By doing so, however, I lost that initial sense of participation I felt, so I attempted to belong again at the concert. Here I found that rap doesn't constitute a unified subculture, that I was encountering my own divisions, my own constructions of self and other, that I did belong and didn't belong, both at the same time. I learned that sometimes when we go looking for otherness, we are really trying to grasp a self. If life were only so tidy. . . .

Obviously, experiences don't unfold so neatly—we just collect them that way in retrospect. My senses of distance and belonging, of fandom and academics, of confidence and insecurity, all occurred—and continue to occur—simultaneously. Who I am and what rap is are always changing. If I've learned anything from rap, it's that the past isn't fixed. You can take a bit of history and change it by bringing it into the present. I'm not sure where fandom stops and academics begins, or if there is even a difference, or if the difference is merely one of style. I'm not even sure anymore whether this chapter is about rap, about me, or about my relation to rap.

Rap music offers up to me a model of self. Rappers are concerned with constituting and referencing an "authentic" self, and to do so they appropriate materials and memories from others to form, through repetition, a place from which to speak. My own attempt at gaining the authenticity to write about rap takes this same form. I appropriated the metaphor of the "mix" and used it to provide repetitions of the search for self (my two mixes) to create a place from which to claim my own self. Within my second mix, however, I found that rap brought me back full circle. Here, as I searched the "margins" for some sense of "realness" or authenticity I felt lacking in my own life, I found it by literally running head-on into my past in the mosh pit. The "past self" that the mosh pit referred me back to was itself initially constructed through the public discourses and styles of youth culture.

It is this reflexivity that defines the relationships between media and self, and I like the metaphor of the mix because it offers a strategy for writing about this reflexive relationship. I like the mix because it keeps things from being fixed. Just as the meaning of the words to a Public Enemy song change when they're mixed with a different musical track, changing the context of our meditations about a subject can lead us to find something different there. I like the thought that I could conceivably come back later and remix this whole thing: beat and voice—the vital mix.

I don't want to conclude this, to wrap it up, because it's not over. Tomorrow, rap will mean something different to me. Instead, I think I'll go pop in the new Gang Starr CD. There might be an old me in there somewhere.

References

Blackwell, M. (1991, May). Jail house rap. *Spin,* pp. 14-15.

Chuck D., & Allen, H. (1990, October). Black II black. *Spin,* p. 68.

Clifford, J. (1992). Traveling cultures. In L. Grossberg, C. Nelson, & P. Treichler (Eds.), *Cultural studies* (pp. 96-116). New York: Routledge.

Ferguson, R. (1990). Introduction: Invisible center. In R. Ferguson, M. Gever, T. T. Minh-ha, & C. West (Eds.), *Marginalization and contemporary cultures* (pp. 9-14). New York: New Museum of Contemporary Art.

Giroux, H. A. (1992). Post-colonial ruptures and democratic possibilities: Multiculturalism as anti-racist pedagogy. *Cultural Critique, 21,* 5-39.

Hebdige, D. (1987). *Cut 'n' mix: Culture, identity, and Caribbean music.* New York: Methuen.

Hebdige, D. (1988). *Hiding in the light: On images and things.* New York: Routledge.

Jackson, M. (1989). *Paths toward a clearing: Radical empiricism and ethnographic inquiry.* Bloomington: Indiana University Press.

L. R. (1992, May). [Review of X-Odus]. *The Source,* p. 36.

McElfresh, S. (1991, June-July). The clever art of sampling. *Creem,* p. 59.

Nietzsche, F. (1989). On rhythm. In S. L. Gilman, C. Blair, & D. J. Parent (Eds. and Trans.), *Fredrich Nietzsche on rhetoric and language.* Oxford: Oxford University Press.

Producer X. (1992, May). [Letter to the editor]. *The Source,* p. 11.

Samuels, D. (1991, November 11). The rap on rap. *New Republic,* pp. 24-29.

Schiebe, K. E. (1986). Self narratives and adventure. In T. R. Sarbin (Ed.), *Narrative psychology: The storied nature of human conduct* (pp. 129-151). New York: Praeger.

Shusterman, R. (1991). The fine art of rap. *New Literary History, 22,* 613-632.

Snead, J. A. (1990). Repetition as a figure of black culture. In R. Ferguson, M. Gever, T. T. Minh-ha, & C. West (Eds.), *Marginalization and contemporary cultures* (pp. 213-230). New York: New Museum of Contemporary Art.

Steier, F. (1991). Introduction: Research as self-reflexivity, self-reflexivity as social process. In F. Steier (Ed.), *Research and reflexivity* (pp. 1-11). Newbury Park, CA: Sage.

Tankel, J. D. (1990). The practice of recording music: Remixing as recoding. *Journal of Communication, 40,* 34-46.

Toop, D. (1984). *The rap attack: African jive to New York hip-hop.* Boston: South End.

Wetherbee, P. (1990, February). No easy thing. *Music Express,* p. 12.

Woodlief, M. (1991, September). [Letter to the editor]. *Spin,* p. 16.

Part IV

Relational Selves and the Mediated Context

8

Technology and the Self: From the Essential to the Sublime

Kenneth J. Gergen

Psychological essentialism—adherence to the view that individuals possess specifically mental processes or mechanisms—has long served as a pivotal feature of the Western cultural tradition. Already in Aristotelian philosophy there was an elaborate formulation of the workings of mental life. Platonic theory of knowledge, and its central concern with the reality of pure ideas, was also forged from a preliminary belief in the preeminence of the psychological interior. Such offerings from the Greek cultural world, when coupled with the Judeo-Christian conception of the soul, lent a solid palpability to the presumption of an inner world—identifiable, ever present, transparent, and central to the understanding of human action.

As variously elaborated over the centuries, such early speculations have undergone significant change. As medievalists such as Augustine and Aquinas expanded on the concepts of soul, sensation, and the emotions; as rationalist philosophers such as Descartes and Kant extolled the capacities of pure reason and a priori ideas; as empiricist philosophers such as Locke and Hobbes emphasized the significance of experience in the generation of ideas; and romanticist poets, novelists, and philosophers explored the mysterious terrain of the passions, creative urges, evil inclinations, genius and madness—so have we become a tradition in which the presumption of an inner life—as real and possibly more important than the external, material world—has become firmly fixed.

The discourse of the individual interior has also provided the major rationale for many of our central institutions. Religious institutions have long been devoted to educating and purifying the soul. Educational institutions are dedicated to the enhancement of individual mental functioning; families are centrally concerned with building the character of the young; democratic institutions are founded on the belief in independent judgment; and courts of law could scarcely operate without the concepts of intention, memory, and conscious knowledge firmly in place.

Placed in this light, we also find that one of the major effects of twentieth-century social science is the objectification of the psychological world. Whereas philosophers, priests, and poets of previous centuries were largely confined to a rhetoric of symbols—of written and spoken language—the social sciences were (and continue to be) additionally armed with a rhetoric of observation. That is, the social sciences—derived as they are from the combined logics of rationalist and empiricist philosophy—promised, at last, to ground theoretical speculation in the observable world. Whether in the introspective methods of the early mentalist psychologists, the experimental methods of the laboratory psychologist, the phenomenological methods of the humanist investigator, the attitude and opinion measures of the survey researcher, or the qualitative measures of the contemporary interpretativist, the promise has been to furnish empirical substantiation for propositions about psychological and social life. This has been strikingly clear in the science of psychology—from mentalism to present-day cognitivism, from Freud to the *DSM-IV*. It is also the prevailing tendency in communication theory and research—whether treating attitudes, intentions, or ideologies, or attraction, subjectivity, or self-reflexivity. In each case, the theoretical account bolsters presumptions of the reality of mental life. Through research practices, the array of mental predicates is subtly reified.[1]

It is this long tradition of psychological essentialism, supported by the major institutions and justified by a century of social science, that provides the basis for the day-to-day processes we index as self-understanding and self-realization—for the various ways we have of questioning, evaluating, and exploring the self ("I must be depressed." "Is this love or infatuation?"); for the manner in which we seek others' reactions, support, or nurturance for our interior being ("She misconstrues my intentions." "He doesn't appreciate my needs."); and for our modes of justifying and reasoning about our actions ("I thought it over, and decided . . ." "It would violate my moral values."). It is this same tradition that provides the individual with enormous and compelling reasons for treasuring personal identity. To have an identity is indeed to be capable of laying claim to an interior life: to one's *own* reasons and opinions, to existentially defining motives, personal passions, and core traits. To lack such psychological resources would be the equivalent of erasing one's identity. Failing to possess reason, emotion, morals, intentions, and the like would be an empty existence, without human significance and possibly lacking a rationale for continued life.

I shall propose in what follows that as we approach the twenty-first century, psychological essentialism is undergoing a subtle but increasingly discernible erosion. And, as beliefs in an identifiable, knowable, and significant world of the personal interior decay, so are we witnessing (and will continue to confront) a progressive emptying of the self—a loss in the credibility of subjectivity, agency, the "I" at the center of being. As I shall also propose, one of the chief forces at work in the dismantling of self is technological. With the profusion of technologies specifically designed to increase the presence of others—to foster and expand the degree of mediated communication—we obliterate the conditions necessary for sustaining belief in the obdurate interior. Although there is much to be said about the consequences of this obliteration, I shall touch only on the possibility of a single successor to psychological essentialism, that of relationalism. To illustrate its potentials, I shall attempt to make intelligible the contours of a "relational sublime."

Conditions for a Creditable Self

To appreciate the dynamics of self-deterioration in the current century, it is first essential to consider the conditions necessary to sustain the supposition of a palpable interior. That is, how have participants in Western culture managed to maintain their beliefs in a specifically psychological world? We cannot (with Descartes) justify the vocabulary of the inner world on the basis of its simply being there, transparent and self-evident. And to be sure, there are many other cultural beliefs that have waxed and waned in credibility over the centuries—for example, beliefs in Olympic deities, a Ptolemaic universe, ghostly presences, and the communion of souls. Although the durability of psychological essentialism poses a challenging and complex question, let me suggest that such essentialism—whether in the social sciences or the culture more generally—is importantly dependent on *forms of discursive homogeneity.* In effect, I am doing nothing more here than providing a sociolinguistic spin to the traditional view that opinion commitment is socially anchored. The greater the agreement among one's consociates—here within one's discursive ethos—the more intelligible, agreeable, and ontologically palpable the supposition. Given this general orientation, let us consider several forms of discursive homogeneity specifically relevant to sustaining commitments to an identifiable and pivotal psychological interior:

Ontological configuration. At the outset, the world of the interior acquires its creditability from ambient agreement in the categories of existence: the basic distinctions necessary for describing or explaining mental conditions. Without such a vocabulary, there simply is nothing to describe or explain. And without reasonably widespread agreement over the terms, ambiguity prevails and doubt is invited. Thus, for example, we can speak with some confidence about the emotions of *fear, anger,* and *sadness,* because these terms are constituents of a widely shared vocabulary (of approximately a dozen "emotion" terms) employed with a high degree of frequency within the culture. To admit ignorance of such feelings, or to declare them to be absent from one's makeup, would be to render doubt about one's membership in the human species. Would a person be altogether human if he or she could feel no anger or sadness? Other psychological predicates, shared by smaller and sometimes more marginal groups within the culture, fail to command such credibility. Such terms as *existential anxiety, post-traumatic stress disorder, spiritual awareness, flow,* and *channeling* command respect in various pockets of the culture but for vast numbers may be discounted as jargon or cult language. More extremely, to claim oneself to be overwhelmed with *acidae,* a term popular in medieval monasteries, suffering from a strong bout of *melancholy* (a term of great interest to nineteenth-century poets and novelists), or seized by *mal de siècle* (a term that moved many to suicide less than a century ago) would probably raise queried looks among one's companions. What precisely is the individual talking about—is he or she speaking metaphorically, is this a joke? In effect, without a chorus to render one's claims agreeable—to say, in effect, "yes, I know what you are feeling"—one can scarcely claim certitude of psychological existence.

Modes of expression. Confidence in a particular ontology of psychological states is further enhanced by homogeneity in accepted modes of expression. To the extent that there is broad agreement that certain actions are the outward manifestation of specific internal processes, mechanisms, traits, and the like, then we can continue securely in the belief that the vocabulary of the internal world is referential. One can be certain there is a process of rational thought, for example, when there is broad agreement that certain modes of speaking (e.g., using proper grammar, complex sentence structure, a rich vocabulary) are indicative of underlying intelligence, or that certain performances (e.g., in mathematics, chess playing, or engineering design) are obvious manifestations of superior cognitive functioning. Should we fail to agree on what constitutes a proper expression of a given process or state, we should become suspect of its underlying existence. It is an interesting fact that in most scientific accounts of human emotions the concept of "love" fails to appear. Among the dozen or so emotions about which scientific knowledge can be accumulated—emotions such as anger, fear, and sadness—love fails to be included.[2] This is largely so, I would suggest, because the term has been used to index so many different and varied actions over the century—from adoration to avoidance, suicide to homicide, the trivial to the profound—that it has lost candidacy for scientific respectability. If virtually any action—along with its opposite—can be an expression of love, there is no way to identify it or to test propositions about it. It may thus be discarded from the realm of "real knowledge" and dismissed as cultural mythology.

Context of expression. Mental predicates acquire further palpability by virtue of broad agreement in contexts of usage. This is to say that we identify mental states in part by the conditions in which their putative expressions are manifest. Tears shed at a funeral are indicative of sadness; we interpret the same tears at a wedding or the presentation of an award as indicators of joy. In effect, it is not the behavioral manifestation alone to which we attend but also the context of expression. And to the extent that there is homogeneity in the context of expression, belief in the underlying, psychological source is enhanced. Thus, for example, we may readily agree that anger exists, primarily because its "manifestations" are frequently found under conditions of conflict, frustration, and/or injustice. If relevant expressions were randomly distributed over contexts—occasionally bursting forth in the midst of quiet contemplation, a Brahms concerto, or a wedding ceremony—it would be difficult to interpret them. So extraordinary would they be to the circumstances that we might consider the actor as physically or mentally deranged. Our belief in the existence of anger as a psychological state, then, is significantly dependent on its expressions being circumscribed by a reliable set of contextual parameters.

Valued goals. Finally, a firm sense of psychological states is tied to homogeneity in views over the goals served by the ontology and the associated assumptions of expression. Our agreement over whether X exists is in part dependent on what we take to be the consequences of that presumption. If such agreement leads to bitter ends, we may wish to give up the presumption; if there is broad agreement that good outcomes result from the presumption, then we may continue in our confidence of its existence. To illustrate, if psychological powers of sorcery are used to justify burning individuals at the stake, whether I will accept powers of sorcery as truly existing will importantly depend on whether there is agreement that such executions are a social good. If we decry these methods, I will begin to cast aspersions on the ontology, raising questions about such capacities, and search for alternative explanations. I might ultimately fashion a vocabulary of "mental illness" because of the broad agreement that nurturant treatment is more humane than execution. Homogeneity in the language of value, then, buttresses commitment to a given ontology.

Technologies of Self-Expression

I propose that for the better part of the past three centuries—and owing importantly to the Enlightenment discourses of the seventeenth and eighteenth centuries—there has been substantial homogeneity in the discursive ecology—agreement concerning the primary ingredients of the psychological self, the modes of its expression, the contexts under which expression is appropriate, and the ends served by such expressions. The presumption that there are rational processes, for example, as opposed to emotions; that there are characteristics manifestations of these two modes of psychological activity; that there are conditions appropriate to their expression; and that certain cultural values are served by these "existents"—all have been supported by an enormous number of scholars, writers, poets, artists, politicians, clergymen, jurists, and so on. But what of the current century? Why should we begin to doubt these verities? In what respects is the culture changing that the conditions for continued belief are eroding? Although there are many possible answers to this question, I wish here to lay special emphasis on the technologies of human relatedness, those technologies that expose us to an ever broadening array of others, that expand exponentially our potentials for significant relationship, that bring others closer more often, and in greater numbers than ever before. Consider, for example, the following:

- A century ago, there were fewer than 100 automobiles in the United States. By the 1990s, there were over 123 million cars in use, with over 6 million new cars produced annually.
- At the turn of century, there was no radio; at the current time, 99% of the households in the United States have at least one radio, and more than 28 million new radios are sold each year.
- Air transportation was virtually unknown until the 1920s; there are now over 42 million passengers a year in the United States alone.
- Television was virtually unknown until the 1940s; at the current time, over 99% of American households have at least one TV set—a percentage that exceeds that of households with indoor plumbing.

- Personal computers were virtually unknown until the 1970s; there are now over 80 million in use.

Today, we find new technological "breakthroughs"—in microchip technology, computer software, telecommunication, image transmission, mobile computers, multiple channels, multimedia—almost daily occurrences. Certain effects of these technologies seem clear enough. In every way, we become increasingly engaged in a world *with* others—a socially saturated world (Gergen, 1991). We know more, see more, communicate more, and relate more than ever before. The more subtle issue, however—and that which most centrally concerns us here—is that of psychological essentialism. How does this confluence of developments affect our commitments to a specifically mental world, a world in which a viable self can (and should) be established, and that our cultural institutions should continue to support? To answer this question, we may return to the discursive conditions for sustaining belief, as previously outlined. For, in my view, these technologies operate as a group to undermine the conditions of homogeneity on which such commitments rest. Let us reconsider, then, the sustaining conditions for a belief in a psychological self as they are affected by the incremental consociation of the current century, as follows.

Multiple ontologies. With the proliferation of communication technologies, we are first exposed to an ever expanding vocabulary of being. No longer do we dwell within the boundaries of a single geographically contained community, a region, an ethnicity, or even a culture. We have not a single satisfying intelligibility within which to dwell, but through the process of social saturation, we are immersed in a plethora of understandings—the psychological ontologies of varying ethnicities, class strata, geographic sectors, racial and religious groupings, professional enclaves, and nationalities. We are exposed to the argots of the streets, the laboratories, the drawing rooms, the brothels, and so on, each with their particular and peculiar turns of self-expression. Further, because the technologies enable otherwise marginal groups to locate the like-minded—from across the country—and to articulate and publicize (if not proselytize) more broadly, one encounters well-articulated ontologies reinforced by large and determined numbers. Consider, for example, the proliferation of terminologies offered by the mental health professions alone. Prior to this century, one could not meaningfully experience a *nervous breakdown,* an *inferiority complex,* an *identity crisis,* an *authoritarian* personality tendency, *chronic depression, occupational burnout,* or *seasonal affective disorder.* Now, these and a virtual multitude of additional candidates are offered as candidates for ontological status. From the point of view of the mental health professional, the common psychological terms are mere folklore. As argued from lectern and scholarly text to pop magazine and television, the technical vocabulary of mental illness should replace such crude and naive terms as *the blues, infatuation,* and *rattled.* To this professional vernacular we must add the many terms resuscitated from our cultural history, for example, by religious groups describing various afflictions of the soul and states of grace, terms imported from other cultures (karma, no-mind), and additional terms invented by newly developing subcultures (consider the New Age vocabulary of *ecstasy, communion,* and *centeredness*). In effect, through the various technologies of social saturation, there is an explosion in the vocabulary of the interior. And this explosion brings to a virtual close an age of relative homogeneity. We slowly lose our sense of assuredness in "what there is"—for example, whether there is in fact any mental *disease,* any real creativity, free will, moral sentiment, superior aesthetic taste, and so on. As the candidates for the interior region continue to accumulate—spinning now into the several thousands—doubt is slowly cast on the referential base, the belief that there is indeed something special, palpable, and identifiable to which such terms refer.

Contested expressions. As we are immersed in multiplicitous modes of life, the relationship between expression and psychological origin also becomes increasingly blurred. Not only do differing groups claim that a given psychological condition is manifest in markedly different ways, but what stands as an expression of one state for certain people often indicates quite something else for another. Thus, in the first instance, a state of "love" may be properly expressed for many people by attentive and adoring actions: Can this be the same state that other groups find expressed in sadism, masochism, or self-destruction? And to these candidates for expression we must add the myriad attempts of television and moviemakers to locate nonhackneyed forms of expression, to press beyond the culturally acceptable expressions for dramatic purposes. Thus, we confront psychologists who despair of the existence of love, popular books that tell us in 50 different ways what love is, and the crooner who despairs that "you don't know what love is." In contrast, there are many actions, the psychological sources of which are variously contested. Criminal activity is of singular significance, but what is such activity an expression of? The technologies again furnish myriad answers: a manifestation of an underdeveloped conscious (psychopathy or sociopathy), greed, need, esteem seeking (among one's peers), achievement motivation, class hatred, racial revenge, and so on. At times, contested interpretations may be intense. For example, is performance on an intelligence test truly a sign of innate psychological capacities, as many psychologists maintain, or of cultural learning, as many sociologists are likely to argue? Is child molesting a product of depravity, psychological illness, or the child's imagination—each position championed by one or another highly vocal and articulate group within the culture? Again, as we fail to locate means of settling such issues, we slowly reach the brink of skepticism. If there is no means of determining what an action is an expression of, there comes a point at which we begin to doubt that actions are *expressions* ("outward pressings") at all.

Appropriated usage. Further breakdown in homogeneity stems from the deteriorating constraints on the contexts of expression. One is increasingly unable to identify the psychological source by virtue of its context of expression. This is largely so by virtue of a continuous tendency toward subcultural appropriation.[3] That is, as various groups are exposed to others' modes of life, they frequently locate forms of action that can be appropriated for local use. These patterns are ripped from their typical contexts of meaning and played out in conditions that ambiguate or destroy their traditional signification. Thus, for example, religious groups borrow romantic and rock idioms for expression in religious music, thus clouding the meaning of "religious expression" and, by implication, suggesting a resignification of both the romance and the rock idioms. Expressions of love are removed from intimate relations and placed on car bumpers to declare commitments to anything from modes of exercise to geographic locales. Spiritual expressions are extricated from the church, their religious connotations removed and then reconstituted in New Age rituals of communion with nature, sunsets, waves, and dolphins. Expressions appropriate to athletic events are replayed within political contexts; expressions typical of parent-child relations are recast in the confines of therapy. And as the technologies facilitate the continuous admixtures of expression and context, the context ceases to be a key to psychological condition. In effect, the expression becomes a free-floating signifier without a specifiable signified.

Controversial goals. Finally, confidence in the inner domain is challenged by the increasing controversy over the use to which such discourse is put, the values served by various assumptions of mental operation. As the technologies enable increasing numbers of people to communicate with each other, and to voice common cause (e.g., feminists, blacks, Asians, the elderly, the handicapped, homosexuals, Native Americans), such groups bring critical attention to the taken-for-granted vocabularies of the culture and their oppressive implications. In each case, their critiques begin to foreground the strategies, if not manipulative purposes, served by specifically mental predicates. In this vein, minority groups have raised significant questions with the presumption of general intelligence quotients; feminists have criticized the androcentric biases underlying the prevailing conception of rationality; ex-mental patients have banded together— joined by scores of family therapists and guidance counselors—to disclaim the existence of mental disease; and many scholars from non-Western cultures challenge the imperialistic ramifications of exporting the Western conception of psychological science and its particular vocabulary of mental functioning. As the mental terminologies are brought under attack, as they are increasingly questioned as indicators of psychological conditions, and their ideological and political implications made apparent, it becomes increasingly unclear whether such terminologies indeed have referential value. If all psychological propositions are ideology in masquerade, then what is the ontological status of mind?

In summary, as the technologies of human interchange increase in number, efficacy, and prevalence, so are we exposed to an ever expanding array of alternative intelligibilities. And as differing intelligibilities are intermingled, so do new waves of discourse and transformation in social pattern emerge. With these changes, the accepted vocabulary of the mental world is challenged, the common modes of expression are contested, the contexts of expression are ambiguated, and the ends are served by such assumptions thrown into critical relief. With this confluence of changing conditions, it becomes increasingly difficult to determine precisely what the contents of the psychological self may be, what actions constitute their expressions, where and when they occur, and what social purposes may be served by one's continued belief in such occurrences. Why, then, should one invest so heavily in knowledge, care, and training of the inner world, or identifying one's being in its terms? At some point, the very credibility of an "inner world" is colored by suspicion, the existence of a subjective center of being is rendered problematic, and the institutions justified by such assumptions are brought into critical focus.

Beyond Nihilism: Toward Relational Realities

I am not suggesting that people in large numbers are abandoning the psychological essentialism so long characteristic of the culture and central to its tradition. Rather, I am outlining what I see as a slow but profound change taking place over the current century—one that is indexed in a broad array of occurrences—for example, in the academic intrigue with the deconstruction of the self (Derrida), the disappearance of the author (Foucault), the individual as a terminal in a network of circulating images (Baudrillard), and the woman as cyborg (Harraway). In the culture more generally, we see the change manifest in the slow replacement of real persons with electronic impulses (for example, in carrying out friendships on computer networks, being entertained or intrigued by television, or achieving sexual gratification through telephone services); the ready replacement of limbs, organs, skin, and so on with technological devices; the avid enthusiasm for virtual realities, cyberpunk, and the chaotic flow of MTV images; and with the broad skepticism of psychiatry and the replacement of "talking cures" with the multimillion dollar business of psychopharmacology. I detect now a broad ambivalence regarding the reality and centrality of a uniquely inner world. It is an ambivalence that will, one may anticipate, give way to a generalized skepticism. The next obvious step would be psychological nihilism—a step that may be avoided now primarily because of the specter of a bleak and empty existence. If there is nothing there, then who am I, what is my worth, why should I live? It is better to remain absorbed with the avalanche of incoming impulses than to ask such daunting questions.

At the same time, I think we may pull short of this whimpering end. The proper comparison may not be between a full self—replete with psychological resources—and an empty one. Rather, the more promising contrast may be between self (whether full or empty) and relatedness. If we do not prove to have palpable centers within the head—autonomous and self-sufficient—then can we not turn our attention to the reality of relatedness—to forms of interdependence rather than independence? Here would be a cultural shift of Copernican magnitude— from presuming a self at the center of the social world to seeing relationships as the enduring reality of which the self is an integral part.

Is the reality of relatedness simply an idle speculation—a rabbit drawn from the hat of postmodern despair? I don't believe so. I believe there are myriad indications of a sensitivity already well in motion—within, for example, various corners of the ecology movement, the systemic movement in family therapy and organization development, the communitarian movement, and the political impulse toward regionalism. To illustrate the possibility and its potentials, it is useful to consider one significant movement currently unfolding in the scholarly domain, and then to open a conceptual space that seems resonant with widespread tendencies within the culture more generally. In the former case, there has been broad scholarly discontent with the cultural ramifications of holding the self to be the fundamental atom of social life—the central unit of description and explanation in the social sciences and within our institutions of education, law, religion, and the like. As it is variously reasoned, this abiding emphasis on the self-contained individual lends itself to an ethos of narcissism (a "me-first" orientation to social life), promotes competition of all against all, discourages attempts at understanding others (whose mental worlds are defined as remote and inaccessible), reduces relationships to a secondary status (artificial constructions of the more basic elements of single identities), and fosters a sense of ultimate isolation and despair.[4] As it is reasoned, the ideology of the self-contained individual is unserviceable in a world where the technologies of communication bring us increasingly into a state of interdependence. We can ill afford the luxury of such an ideology in a context where little that we do is without social consequence.

It is from the soil of critical appraisal that new attempts now spring to life, attempts to reconstitute the psychological terrain as a social one. Such work is inspired in part by Vygotsky's thesis of higher mental processes and in some degree by poststructural literary theory. In the former case, Vygotsky makes a strong case for mental processes as being social processes simply relocated: One carries out a mental process we might call "thinking" in the terms of the community into which one is socialized. Thought, on this account, is more radically conceived as participation in relatedness—a view that Bruner (1990), Wertsch (1985), and many others are currently exploring. At the further extreme, much poststructuralist theory places a strong emphasis on symbol systems, the collectivity of semiotic practices through which meaning is generated and sustained. These systems are genuine cultural manifestations and precede the individual. *To mean* in this view is to participate in a set of patterned relationships—again placing relatedness before individuality.

More recently, and most directly to the point, social constructionists, discourse analysts, and communication theorists have begun the task of reconstructing the various processes once believed to be "within the psyche" of the individual as constituents of relationships. For example, for investigators such as Middleton and Edwards (1990), a process such as memory—often viewed as a biologically based and universal function within the individual—is more profitably considered a form of social action—an outgrowth of social processes of negotiation, collusion, and cultural rule following. Similarly, Potter and Wetherell (1987) propose that attitudes—long held to be the basis of action—are actions themselves and, more specifically, discourse positions occupied within conversations. In the same vein, Billig (1987) shows how "thinking" can be seen as a participation in the social process of argumentation, and depending for its efficacy on rhetorical skills. And in work with Mary Gergen, we demonstrate how emotions are necessary constituents of broader scenarios of interaction (Gergen & Gergen, 1988). Without the scenario, an elaborate form of social dance, what we call an "emotional expression" would cease to make cultural sense.

Toward a Relational Sublime

These various writings begin to point the way to a palpable sense of relatedness. With effective articulation, we must believe that relational being could become at least as compelling as our traditional beliefs in a psychological self. It is in this context that I wish, in this final section, to take the liberty of exploring, through evocation, the edges of articulation. That is, I wish, by drawing on scholarly, literary, and poetic traditions, to carve out a semiotic space, enabling us further to index and elaborate our activities in terms of a fundamental relatedness. I realize this is not a mode of scholarship traditional to the social sciences, but as we move into the world of "interminable semiosis," as we begin to challenge the boundaries of disciplinary modes of expression, it is also clear that our long-standing traditions of discourse truncate our own modes of relating with each other. To paraphrase Wittgenstein, our languages form the boundaries of our relational worlds. So I hope my idiosyncratic impulse can be indulged momentarily, in hopes that new discursive and relational ground can be broken.

What I wish to do, specifically, is to resuscitate and resignify a concept that has been part of the Western tradition for at least 18 centuries, which has resurfaced at different intervals in our history—with differing meanings and differing formations. In my view, this concept of the sublime can again be revived, and play an important function in our contemporary world. Although variously understood over the centuries, the *sublime* was consistently used to refer to a power or force that was both beyond and prior to the human capacity for rational articulation. Thus, in the first-century writings of the Greek critic Dionysus Longinus, the concern was to locate the source of "great writing," that which "brings power and irresistible might to bear" (1945, sec. 1.4) in the written (or spoken) word. The source of great writing, then, was not the words themselves but an ineffable something in authors that they carried or expressed. This was the power of the sublime—a power that Longinus traced to the "inward greatness of the soul" blessed by nature.

Longinus's writings were rediscovered in the seventeenth century and gave rise to a broad number of disquisitions on aesthetics, typically a discourse of the "superhuman"—of vastness, awe, and, in the case of Edmund Burke (1844), pure terror. For Kant (1911), attempting to resist the imperious threat of a materialistic empiricism, the sublime was a particular state of mind—one in which the imagination grappled with "the unattainability of nature as a presentation of [reason's] ideas" (p. 99). For later romanticists—Wordsworth, Coleridge, Schiller— the sense of the sublime was evoked by the extremes of nature—the grandeur, power, and horror—in which conventional meanings were challenged. One sensed some transcendent order of meaning behind the moment and the taken for granted. And for American authors, such as Ralph Waldo Emerson (1940), the sublime is an ecstasy of release, in which the author allows the "ethereal tides to roll and circulate through him; then he is caught up into the life of the Universe" (p. 210).

Perhaps these phrases are sufficient to call forth a possibility—the glimmering sense of something beyond our words that grants them force, something beyond reason that causes reason to leap up. And if there is a power that gives shape to our words, to all that is intelligible, then this power is beyond all that we "know to be the case." For everything we propose to exist is itself constructed in language. It is language that furnishes the capacity to distinguish this from that, me from you, up from down, in from out. "There is . . ." is a move in linguistic space. And if all that we take to exist cannot be derived from a world independent of language, then how are we to understand the forms taken by our understanding? We confront the unnameable in this case, a "force," a "power," a "telos" that is beyond rational articulation. We confront the sublime.

Yet, although this realm of the sublime cannot be captured in language, we can appreciate its dimension. How are sounds and markings converted to what we take to be language? For how does language acquire its intelligibility? Here we must envision primordial processes of relationship—the pulsing coordination of movements and sounds—that slowly turn the amorphous into the meaningful. For what is it that gives language its meaning outside a relationship? Thus, if we are struck with the power of a given passage of writing, it is not the "inward greatness of the soul" (with Longinus) that we should credit, but the process of relatedness that enables such passages to carry us with them. Likewise, the source of "awe," "inspiration," or "terror" is not to be found in nature (with Wordsworth), or in the person (with Emerson), but within unfathomable processes of relatedness that make meaning possible. The capacity to give life to words, and thus to transform culture, is usefully traced not to internal resources but to relatedness—which serves as the source of all articulation and simultaneously remains beyond its reach. We confront, then, the possibility of a new order of sublime—suited to the technoworld of the postmodern—a *relational sublime.*

Can consciousness of the relational sublime live outside the world of letters? I believe so. There are already myriad cultural artifacts that subtend its presence. Consider the movement in the sphere of popular culture from a prevailing focus on single individuals (heroes, heroines, villains) to interdependence and complex domains of relationship. In the former case, there are the "buddy films" *(Butch Cassidy and the Sundance Kid, Trading Places, Thelma and Louise, Mambo Kings, White Men Can't Jump)*—treating the close interdependence of two individuals of the same or opposite sex. Broadening the scope of relatedness, there is the plethora of television depictions of families *(The Waltons, Beverly Hillbillies, Bill Cosby, The Simpsons, Married With Children)* and the emerging genre of film and television stories exploring extended groups *(Enchanted April, The Summer House, City Slickers, Cheers, Hill Street Blues)* and, indeed, entire communities *(Do the Right Thing, Gilligan's Island, Love Boat, Northern Exposure).* To be sure, there are many accounts to be made of these simultaneous movements in the media; at the same time, they are all consistent with a view of society as becoming increasingly sensitive to processes of relatedness. As research on women's magazines also reports (Prusank, Duran, & DeLillo, 1993), articles in the 1950s and 1960s were directed at taking care of either the relational partner or the self. In the 1970s and 1980s, a new vision is found in which "the relationship" is now created as an object for the readers.

Further, I believe the sense of the relational sublime is increasingly present in our daily experience. When rock concert goers experience the power and ecstasy of their common immersion, when city crowds gather to shout welcomes to their championship team, when the throngs gather on the Washington mall to chant their cause, and when gays join the annual parade in San Francisco, they know they are participating in an event the significance of which eclipses the single participant. I believe the relational sublime hovers close to consciousness as we click into the vast network of the computer bulletin board and add our entry to the unending conversation. It begins to make itself manifest in collaborative classroom activities, cooperative scientific projects, and community watches. Further, as multinational organizations grow in scope and size, regions of Europe and North America join in trade accords, and national governments become increasingly dependent on international opinion, we confront the potential inherent in the relational sublime. As we succeed in losing the self, the security of single rationalities, the fixation on univocal goals, and give way to the fluid and many-streamed forms of relationship by which we are constituted, we may approach a condition of the relational sublime.

Notes

1. For a more complete detailing of the process of mental reification, see Gergen (1994).
2. For further elaboration of the history of emotional discourse, see Gergen (in press).
3. For more detailed description of subcultural appropriation of symbols, see Fiske (1989).
4. For illustrations of this critical dialogue, see Sampson (1977), Bellah et al. (1985), and Lasch (1979).

References

Bellah, R. N., et al. (1985). *Habits of the heart.* Berkeley: University of California Press.

Billig, M. (1987). *Arguing and thinking.* London: Cambridge University Press.

Bruner, J. (1990). *Acts of meaning.* Cambridge, MA: Harvard University Press.

Burke, E. (1844). *Of the sublime and beautiful.* New York: Harper.

Emerson, R. W. (1940). *Complete essays by Ralph Waldo Emerson.* New York: Modern Library.

Fiske, J. (1989). *Understanding popular culture.* London: Unwin Hyman.

Gergen, K. J. (1991). *The saturated self.* New York: Basic Books.

Gergen, K. J. (1994). *Realities and relationships.* Cambridge, MA: Harvard University Press.

Gergen, K. J. (in press). Metaphor and monophony in the history of emotional discourse. In C. F. Graumann & K. J. Gergen (Eds.), *Psychological discourse in historical perspective.* New York: Cambridge University Press.

Gergen, K. J., & Gergen, M. M. (1988). Narrative and the self as relationship. In L. Berkowitz (Ed.), *Advances in experimental social psychology* (Vol. 21, pp. 17-56). New York: Academic Press.

Kant, I. (1911). *Critique of aesthetic judgment* (J. C. Meredith, Trans.). Oxford: Oxford University Press.

Lasch, C. (1979). *The culture of narcissism.* New York: Norton.

Longinus, D. (1945). *On the sublime.* Chicago: Packard.

Middleton, D., & Edwards, D. (1990). Conversational remembering: A social psychological approach. In D. Middleton & D. Edwards (Eds.), *Collective remembering* (pp. 23-45). London: Sage.

Potter, J., & Wetherell, M. (1987). *Discourse and social psychology: Beyond attitudes and behaviour.* London: Sage.

Prusank, D. T., Duran, R. L., & DeLillo, D. A. (1993). Interpersonal relationships in women's magazines: Dating and relating in the 1970s and the 1980s. *Journal of Social and Personal Relationships, 10,* 307-320.

Sampson, E. E. (1977). Psychology and the American ideal. *Journal of Personality and Social Psychology, 35,* 767-782.

Wertsch, J. V. (1985). *Vygotsky and the social formation of mind.* Cambridge, MA: Harvard University Press.

9

Therapy and Identity Construction in a Postmodern World

Sheila McNamee

The vast expansion of technological capabilities in this century has had a tremendous impact on our identity construction. With a simple flip of the television channel or radio station, or a turn of the newspaper or magazine page, we have at our disposal an enormous array of possible identity models. Specifically, we can learn by watching *Dallas* how wealthy Texans live, including a view of their backstage (Goffman, 1959) attempts to craft the desired image.[1] In contrast, we have the "personalities" of the rural, small town characters of television's *Northern Exposure*. These differing portrayals are only a small fraction of the hundreds available. Contrast these fictional identities with the varied images we can view daily of national and local leaders, news reporters, economists, talk show personalities, and so forth. Any specific person filling one of these "roles" is very likely to be seen at some time or another "out of character." That is, we might see an interview with the president in which the focus is on his family, not on his political identity.

What technology has done for us is expand our ideas of what is possible. Gergen (1991) argues that years ago, when the majority of people lived in small, isolated communities and membership in the community was based on similarity, it was difficult to imagine the "other." Now, however, the "other" is vividly portrayed via the media, and the image of the other is not unidimensional as it has been in previous decades. For example, classic television characterizations of family life (i.e., *Father Knows Best*), which featured upper-middle-class, white families, generally omitted depictions of more impoverished groups. When those "others" *were* portrayed, however, it is fair to say that those depictions were stereotypically unidimensional (e.g., maids, service employees). In contrast, today's technological capabilities provide us with multifaceted representations of a wide variety of people all of whom symbolize multiple ethnicities, races, economic classes, educational backgrounds, interests, professions, sexual orientations, and so forth. Our easy access to various lifestyles, communities, and cultures—thanks to technological development—quite literally thrusts multiplicity at our feet. Along with such diversity comes myriad styles for leadership, family life, partnering—the list is endless. In other words, the technological advances made in the current century have virtually expanded the web of possible forms of relating simply by offering seemingly infinite characterizations of diverse groups of people.

These media offerings say nothing of the increase to our sense of identity that is provided by other forms of technology such as fax machines, electronic mail, voice mail, telephone answering machines, conference calls, and so on. All these technological apparatuses provide the means for connection with a multitude of "others." And with connection (i.e., conversation), the possibility for identity construction expands ever more rapidly.

As just one illustration, electronic mail networks provide instant friendships with persons who share hobbies, interests, fears, theoretical concerns, and a multitude of other possibilities. These "chatlines" or bulletin boards provide the means by which virtual strangers can converse (sometimes quite intimately) and, thus, build relationships. This potential puts to rest long traditions of social scientific research in which the focus has been placed on documenting common, successful ways to develop and manage relationships. A brief conversation on the electronic networks quickly dispels the otherwise coherent steps presented in much of this research. And just as relationships are forged with great rapidity via electronic connection, the possibility to sustain them (without the trappings of day-to-day interference) is greatly enhanced. Also, because there is no physical contact or limited, if any, visual image of our conversational partners, many find it all the more tempting to adorn long-desired identities. As those in the conversation respond, these identities become less and less "fantasy" and instead take shape, rapidly becoming "real" possibilities.

The ways in which technology has potentiated such "population of the self" (Gergen, 1991) are central to a discussion of therapeutic practice in a postmodern world. The ability to populate ourselves with a multitude of identities, all constructed in the ever expanding relational possibilities we engage, changes our traditional notion of identity and, thus, calls for changes in our view of therapy.

The Centrality of Identity

This century has generated a self-consciousness about identity. It is difficult (and perhaps unimportant) to catalog the seeds of such self-consciousness. They are as multiple and varied as the participants who describe them. Despite the varied explanations for our current concern with identity construction, we have little difficulty agreeing that the essence of a person's identity or selfhood is a central aspect of our contemporary culture. We are surrounded by illustrations of this preoccupation: advertisements for, movies and television programs about, and call-in radio programming all devoted to self-understanding, self-improvement, and self-celebration. Add to this list the ever growing accumulation of self-help books, each geared toward improving one's relationships, self-esteem, business know-how, parenting abilities, or social competencies—in a word, all attentive to our consuming interest in who we are, in our *identity.*

As highlighted earlier in this volume, the study of identity or selfhood has emerged most fervently within this century as a modernist project. The modernist adherence to individuality, objectivity, and reason has been so widely accepted as "the way things are" that it is difficult for us to shift our way of talking about the world. As Shotter and Gergen (1994) argue:

It still seems only "natural" to conduct our inquiries into ourselves in terms of analytically structured theories, thought of as representing a hidden, underlying, ahistorical human essence, a human "reality" that could be discovered either by focusing upon self-contained individuals themselves (psychology) or upon the "systems" within which they live (sociology). (p. 11)

The consequence of such a discourse is that we are quick to assume that problems can be solved with the correct method. This problem carries over quite dramatically in our commonly adopted notions of identity. For example, there are few who would describe a "good person" as someone who appears to have a particular set of values and morals in one situation and vastly different values and morals in another. Such a description is commonly correlated with the terms *duplicitous, fake,* and *dishonest,* even *immoral* or *unethical.* And yet, our daily connection with diverse ways of being—including diverse moral and ethical codes—suggests that a situational/relational identity would be a more reasonable by-product of our day-to-day lives than a universal, objectively grounded one.

This argument, or versions of it, has been articulated elsewhere (Anderson, 1990; Gergen, 1991). My concern in the current chapter is with the implications this multiplicity has for identity as it relates to the therapeutic professions. Specifically, I am concerned with the place and meaning of the therapeutic profession, which is centered on the premise of "fixing" identities, in a postmodern world where identity can no longer be universally rational, moral, or objectively "good." What are the features of postmodern therapy when stable, essential selves become conversational resources rather than entities in themselves? Because therapy as a profession developed within the modernist project (although in many respects identified as a romanticist, Freud is credited with making psychology scientific and thus modernist), the emphasis has been placed largely on developing techniques or methods that will move a "client" toward some preferred state or goal. The importance of obtaining certain ends via correct or appropriate methods—methods that get at the underlying structure of a person's psyche (i.e., identity)—celebrates the modernist project with its "grand narrative of progress" (Gergen, 1991).

The following section provides an overview of modernist therapeutic practice. The basis upon which this profession is built, however, is called into question as technological possibilities and realities make multiplicity rather than unity commonplace. My own concern and interest with this topic is part of a broader, long-standing conversation and, as it is personal, so it is relational. This story sets the stage for my own scholarly work, and much of it revolves around interdisciplinary interests. Developing professionally within the social sciences and simultaneously with a keen interest in "nonscientific" forms of therapeutic practice has presented a continuing challenge to me. Perhaps my own resonance with postmodern characterizations is born of my immersion in a continual sea of shifting contexts. I have spent my professional career as a communication researcher examining (and practicing) therapy.

As a student, my interest in the therapeutic process was so keen that I found myself enrolled in clinical courses where, being the only nonclinician, I inevitably felt alien. Yet being a foreigner was not unique to that context. Armed with the discourse of the therapeutic context and also equipped with the *practical* resources of communicative interchange, I would return to my "home" in the communication discipline only to feel myself again "different"—different now because of my therapeutic language skills but, more so, different by virtue of my "applied" and nonscientific interests. Eventually, I felt I was not truly a clinician in therapeutic contexts and not truly a social scientist in the communication domain.

This kind of multiphrenia (Gergen, 1991) was troubling until I developed—through my relations with others—a way of talking about my interests and my work in a nonpathologizing manner. By this I mean a way of talking that did not engender feelings of inadequacy or inferiority but fostered a celebration of the different voices that could contribute to the examination of social life. The multiplicity of conversational resources afforded by being variously situated gave me license to question what was being cast in any conversation as unquestionable truths or premises—a useful skill for life in the postmodern world. It is this personal narrative that serves as context for the argument that follows.

Modernist Therapy

Although the list of competing therapeutic models is vast, the general sentiment is that this extensive list is indicative of more or less fruitful attempts to accurately assess mental (and, subsequently, social) life. Each psychotherapeutic model has been generated within a context where progress, rationality, and objectivity have been taken for granted. That is to say, to develop a coherent and viable therapeutic model, the tradition has been to assume some representation of an objective, rational account of the distinction between abnormal and normal and provide remedial measures for moving from the former to the latter. If each model developed proposes a coherent, rational, and objective way of "curing" a mental deficit, then it is sensible to conclude that these therapeutic models are in competition with one another. Each one claims to move us along as a community or culture toward some "greater good" in terms of who we are as individuals.

This general assumption is worth noting because it is in sharp contrast to the contextually situated sensibility that is common to postmodernism. It is not exactly fair to cast all therapeutic models as competing for a universal claim to truth, however. Models are parsed into categories depending on criteria such as population being served (e.g., families, children, married couples, men, women, African Americans, Hispanics) and nature of the problem (e.g., psychotic, neurological, affective, interactional). Yet, once within any of these categories, the competition is keen for the right to claim success in the restoration and/or correction of identity.

The competition among therapeutic models mirrors the competition in the natural and social sciences at large. Science, in general, is devoted to advances—advances in knowledge and advances in control of our environment. With science as a guiding metaphor for the study of human life, it should not be surprising that therapeutic models are built on the premise of advancing human functioning. If each model claims such an advance and if human nature has an assumed (or potential) universality, then the possibility for one therapeutic model to emerge as more correct in its ability to advance human capabilities is implicitly acknowledged.

To this point, I have argued that, although there are multiple possibilities for therapeutic treatment available to us today, most of these treatments are based on the assumption that one treatment is or could be the correct one (at least within a particular population). This belief is a by-product of modernist thought where the emphasis on progress issues us toward a utopian goal of "knowing" how best to understand and operate in the world.

Within this grand view of therapy, a cultural narrative about identity has emerged. This narrative includes some vision or standard of normality and some method by which abnormality (and its severity) can be assessed. And then, consistent with the rational, progressive narrative of modernism, our cultural story about identity informs us that, with the proper treatment, any abnormal identity can be brought closer to—if not completely within—the expected norm. One of the more acceptable means for achieving this form of "identity adjustment" is psychotherapy.

In sum, the cultural story we embrace tells us, as we speak it, that who we are is central to our success or failure in living our lives. And our success and our failure can be measured against some standard. Thus, we live a story that invites, at the same time that it creates, a world where homogeneity is privileged over difference and where our attempts to be unique individuals require that we fit in with everyone else. One of the most important perpetuators of this cultural story is the therapeutic profession. It is to the therapeutic context that we run when we fail to feel consistent or coherent or when the evaluative voices—either from self or others—drown the voices that celebrate who we are or want to be *in that moment.*

Within a modernist discourse, we are quick to assume that problems can be solved with the correct method. This modernist emphasis on "technique" is a natural by-product of a modernist attention to progress, outcomes, and goals. When our conversations (whether those conversations are research conversations, therapeutic conversations, or everyday conversations) begin with the assumption that there are essential features of individuals that can be known or discovered with the proper tools or methods, it is not surprising to find ourselves developing techniques that we believe are better suited in meeting particular goals. Similarly, the goals we establish are presumed to fall within the reaches of progressive action. Our modernist belief that we can objectively assess a person, a situation, or a relationship is based on the notion that there are (or could be) some clear standards of evaluation. Such constant self-monitoring—self-assessment—presupposes an active observer (i.e., therapist or expert) who is equipped with the proper assessment tools. In Bakhtin's (1981, 1984, 1986) terms, such an orientation is monologic.

From Monologue to Dialogue

Bakhtin distinguishes monologue from dialogue as an attempt to provide another way of talking about and critiquing the long-celebrated objectivist (i.e., modernist) tradition. Bakhtin introduces the term *dialogic* as a way of identifying *social processes* as central to any understanding of our worlds. Sampson (1993) summarizes Bakhtin's position: "Neither meaning nor self is a precondition for social interaction; rather, these emerge from and are sustained by conversations occurring between people" (pp. 98-99).

Bakhtin's insistence that meaning emerges in dialogue is contrasted with a monologic view of meaning construction. In short,

> monologism denies that there exists outside of it another consciousness, with the same rights, and capable of responding on an equal footing, another and equal *I* (*thou*). For a monologic outlook (in its extreme or pure form) the *other* remains entirely and only an *object* of consciousness, and cannot constitute another consciousness. No response capable of altering everything in the world of my consciousness, is expected of this other. The monologue is accomplished and deaf to the other's response; it does not await it and does not grant it any *decisive* force. Monologue makes do without the other; that is why to some extent it objectivizes all reality. Monologue pretends to be the *last word*. (Bakhtin, 1984, p. 318)

The inevitable conclusion of monologue is for the speaker to assume the position of objective observer, evaluator, and an intentional agent/actor whose actions have certain effects on their objects. Even a "silent" therapist (i.e., one who spends most of his or her time listening) could be cast as an intentional agent and thus as illustrative of Bakhtin's monologism. To many therapists, there is purpose, evaluation, and objectivity in their silence. These features characterize Bakhtin's monologism. Action emerging from an implied notion of agency, individuality, objectivity, and consequently evaluation assumes that monologic voice rather than the dialogic voice of relationship. Thus, it is important to point out that it is not necessarily the case that a therapist who adheres to a monologic epistemology or ontology will actually *do* things differently than a therapist who adheres to the dialogic principle. Yet the interplay of the therapist's and client's actions will be qualitatively different in both cases, with the dialogic therapeutic context serving as an illustration of attentiveness to relational processes (i.e., processes of *social* construction).

Another way of discerning monologism from dialogism is to recognize that a monologue locates our investigation within the person. To that end, any attempt to discover, assess, or adjust identity is directed toward an investigation of a self-contained individual (Sampson, 1977, 1993). Dialogism, on the other hand, locates our investigations in relational patterns. We enter into our conversations, our investigations, our therapeutic contexts privileging processes rather than individuals. Such an emphasis means that

> people's lives are characterized by the ongoing conversations and dialogues they carry out in the course of their everyday activities, and therefore that *the most important thing about people is not what is contained within them, but what transpires between them.* (Sampson, 1993, p. 20, italics in the original)

Consequently, the *conversational practices* that engage therapists and clients become the focus of dialogic therapy, whereas studying what are assumed to be *features of the client* becomes the focus of monologic therapy. In the latter, there is little or no consideration given to the *relational* creation of identity that emerges in (a) the therapeutic relationship and in (b) the client's *telling* of his or her story. The telling of a story is always constrained and potentiated, as are its meanings, by the relationship (real and imagined) in which the telling occurs. Consequently, a story told to one's therapist might construct a different identity than the same situation storied in another relational context.

Psychotherapy, because it is considered the "talking cure," could all too quickly be identified as dialogic. Conversation is already a central component of psychotherapy. It is easy to deduce from this realization that, by its very nature, therapy is dialogic. A return to the distinction between dialogue and monologue, however, illustrates that despite its largely conversational nature, most forms of psychotherapy are, as illustrated above, monologic.

Monologue implies or suggests that a therapist can evaluate another through his or her ability to objectively determine and intervene in the other's life, and this *can* be and often *is* a therapist's stance even when/if she or he proclaims a "process" orientation. For example, a therapist who attends to interpersonal processes in families but claims that the family has diffuse boundaries and is therefore enmeshed does not speak as one engaged in relational construction but as one who is the objective observer of complex family patterns. On the other hand, a therapist who "plays" with the idea of boundaries, who invites clients to "try on" this discourse as a way of talking about the current problem situation, is engaging in dialogic interplay. In other words, the dialogic therapist does not levy a diagnosis or evaluation on his or her clients. Rather, the therapist suggests a way of talking about the client's situation that draws on that therapist's array of conversational resources (i.e., ways of talking). The limits and constraints of these resources, to the postmodern therapist, are always featured.

Let us take, for example, what has become the cornerstone of psychotherapeutic treatment: the American Psychiatric Association's (1987) *Diagnostic and Statistical Manual of Mental Disorders* (third edition, revised; *DSM-III-R*). This manual lists 200 categories of mental disorder and discusses several other related problems. The very generation of such a manual—created for use as a definitive guideline in assessing mental health—presumes that the clients in therapy are not part of a dialogue but are, instead, objects to be studied, classified, and subsequently treated. Within this realm, the "stories" told by clients in psychotherapy are not thought of as told for purposes of co-constructing with therapists new life narratives or new interpretations. Instead, they are heard as evidences of relatively enduring features of personal character in need of cure, adjustment, realignment, or fine-tuning. The "talk" of the "talking cure" is no different in this respect than the data analyzed by scientists in a traditional scientific investigation. Thus, the prominent cultural narrative of science permeates our therapeutic talk about identity.

This is clearly a problem constructed within the diagnostic/evaluative context. In other words, diagnosis, itself, becomes a focal point within modernist discourse where emphasis is placed on progress. To progress, we must take stock of "what is," evaluate it, identify (i.e., diagnose) the degree to which it impedes movement (i.e., progress) toward the culturally preferred state, and ultimately develop a treatment plan. This plan (or "cure") might, in fact, resonate with dialogism particularly in the therapeutic domain where conversation is central to "cure." Yet diagnosis—particularly as exemplified by the *DSM-III-R*—distances and objectifies the focus of study and thus takes on a monologic character.

This distinction between diagnosis (as monologic) and cure/treatment (as perhaps tending toward more of a dialogism) might present a useful way to think about therapy. The more important issue here, from a postmodern sensibility, however, is the recognition that *both* diagnosis and cure are language games (Wittgenstein, 1963). For example, diagnosis is not an objective science. It is a discursive possibility. To invite others into a conversation about a problem could take, as we well know, many forms that could serve diagnostic purposes but would not necessarily be considered "real" diagnoses. For example, I could discuss my problem with a friend and in the course of that conversation generate an explanation that characterizes my quickness of temper as a sign of commitment and passion. In the therapy room, however, a discussion about the same situation might yield a diagnosis of premenstrual syndrome. Thanks to modernism, it is the language game in the therapeutic context that gains a greater audience. It is the language game of diagnosis. Yet is that game any more real than the language game enjoyed with my friend? And, we must ask, what are the ensuing conversational and relational possibilities engendered by each language game? Is it necessarily the case that the language game of diagnosis will generate better interactions?

What has contributed to the elevation of modernist ways of talking? It is a cultural narrative that is in great part possible because of the technological advances made in this century. As illustrated above, media have expanded the potential for conveying to large segments of the population three important features that contribute to the modernist notion of a secure, stable identity. First, media contribute to the idea that there is a proper way for a person to be by providing numerous and consistent illustrations of "normal" individuals. Second, media have in recent years contributed to the popularization of psychotherapy as a form of identity adjustment by featuring various therapeutic modes as legitimate cultural discourse: by viewing "favorite characters" in therapy, by offering programming like *The Oprah Winfrey Show*, and by making on-line therapy available via electronic networks. Finally, both by legitimizing the notion of "typical" ways of being (i.e., normal identity) and by legitimizing therapy as a means to achieve and/or maintain normality, media—and technologies in general—have contributed to the necessity of psychotherapy.

The irony of this situation is that although technological advances provide the grounds upon which modernism has been able to flourish, these same advances have generated the potential for a major deconstruction of our current notion of identity. Simultaneous to the features just listed, the multiplicity of images and connections made possible through technological advancement expands our notions of who we are, of what it means to be an ethical or moral person, a wife, a husband, a lover, a friend, a daughter, a son, a professional, a neighbor. The uniform image presumed to be an unquestionable rationality is now easily juxtaposed with two or three or four alternative possibilities. For example, the legal institution—an institution previously believed to be built on a solid and unshifting foundation of reason and justice—is displayed as a complex criss-crossing of narratives all vying for a voice. On television, lawyers are all crafting a story that fits coherently within one community but is deemed illegal or unethical within another. If such a significant cultural institution as the law can be portrayed as multivocal, what are the implications for similar portrayals of a good parent, or a good spouse, or a good friend?

Beyond media-represented images, we now have a multitude of ways to speak with each other. With these increasing formats is the possibility for increasing intimacy. As Gergen (1991) argues, relationships formerly kept superficial because of geographic distance now have the potential to blossom and expand in an infinite number of ways. What does the onslaught of such multiple relationships imply about our selfhood? If we believe, as modernists do, that there are essential characteristics that constitute the self, then an expansion of our relational network would do little to alter our identities. If we talk about selfhood as a relational construction, however, then this swelling web of relatedness has a significant bearing on who we are and how we talk about ourselves.

The Discourse of Relationship

It is not only the advances in technology that warrant a move away from a modernist conception of identity. We must examine what it is that such techno-logical capabilities have introduced to our way of talking about the world. We have already explored how technology brings us in contact with various ways of shaping an argument, constructing a description, and accomplishing a goal. In each of these arenas, it is a way of talking that is introduced. Simply put, the multiplicity offered through technology is not a multiplicity of essences or objects (i.e., things that exist) but a multiplicity of discourses (i.e., ways of talking). We have access to a wide variety of conversations. Some are congenial with the ones in which we already participate; others are foreign and disparate. Our current ability to participate in (even as observers) multiple conversations, many with diverse rationalities, presents us, however, with a forum for realizing, or at the very least recognizing, competing discursive forms.

Our ability to listen to these competing discursive traditions and become curious about their *local* coherence invites us into the conversational domain of postmodernism. Here, the modernist attempt to objectify the social world gives way to the postmodernist attempt to attend to the various ways of talking that construct our social worlds. Identity, from a postmodern perspective, is not an object to be examined but is a reality constructed in the interactive moment. It is an emergent by-product of persons in relation, each drawing upon his or her conversational resources (i.e., his or her networks of relationship) as the moment unfolds.

The shift this represents is a shift from the study of objects to the study of conversation. A central feature of this shift is relationship. Simply put, conver-sation is a relational accomplishment. Meaning is created as the actions of one person are supplemented by the actions of another (Gergen, 1990). This relational orientation to meaning construction is what Bakhtin captures in his notion of dialogism. Regardless of an actor's intentions, meaning emerges only at the moment another responds to that person's actions, for it is in the connection to another's response that a *performance* takes shape.

The emphasis on performance is in keeping with Wittgenstein's (1963) notion of language games. To Wittgenstein, words do not represent a world "out there," nor do they represent the nature of the speaker's mind. Rather, words gain their significance through their *use* in social interplay. Consequently, the construction of a world, a reality, an identity is contingent upon how language is used in particular contexts. *How* language is used is dependent, in turn, upon how others respond to (supplement) each action. The forms of action and supplementation in any given context or relationship are themselves contingent upon the discursive traditions (i.e., histories) and discursive communities (i.e., cultures/relationships) with which the participants are engaged.

To return to the topic of identity, we can reiterate that, to a modernist, identity is seen as an object to be examined, evaluated, and adjusted (if need be). Although the question of what counts as identity varies dramatically among modernist theorists (e.g., it can be thought of as cognitive, behavioral, psychic, neurological, biological, cultural, and so on), all share in their attempts to objectively analyze identity by studying its various representations in isolation. This, to Bakhtin, is monologism.

The discourse of relationship provides the means by which identity becomes the accomplishment of situated activity. Thus, it is a by-product of relationships rather than a precursor to the construction of any relationships. Bakhtin refers to this as *dialogism.* The implication for therapy then is that, armed with a dialogic understanding of identity, a therapist must consider and question his or her own part in pathologizing or not pathologizing clients. That is, a therapist must see his or her descriptions of clients as relationally achieved constructions and thereby assume some relational responsibility (McNamee & Gergen, 1994) for any pathologizing as well as for any "cure." Relationally speaking, identity is created in conversation and conversation is always culturally and historically situated. Talking this way about identity, we quickly slip away from the idea that anyone could have an essential, stable identity. To talk of an essential self is to engage in a particular form of discourse. That is to say that modernist discourse itself is not wrong from a postmodern perspective. It is simply one of many competing discursive alternatives.[2] The question we must ask concerns how well people can coordinate their activities within any discursive style at any given time in any given relationship.

This question suggests that, unlike the modernist or monologic adherence to one ultimate form of rationality, postmodernism or dialogism provides the forum for entertaining multiple rationalities. Rhetoric then becomes a central feature of the postmodern (see Shotter & Gergen, 1994) because the evaluation or acceptance of one's rationality will depend in large part on one's ability to warrant one's position (Gergen, 1989) in light of the competing voices. Whereas modernism provides us with the tools necessary for deciding whose voice will be heard, postmodernism directs our attention to the *processes* through which one voice eventually emerges as sustainable over others. Thus, processes of negotiation, coordination, and performance are centralized in postmodernism.

Therapeutic Practice With/in a Postmodern Sensibility

Now, confronted with the postmodern dilemma of multiple and often competing realities, we must question what purposes therapeutic practices serve. If
advances in communication technology have given us access to diverse ways of
knowing the world and, thus, of constructing our sense of identity, what then
becomes the task of postmodern therapy? Rather than uncovering and adjusting
an essential self (which is the modernist project), postmodern therapy entertains
and privileges the construction of multiple selves as emergent by-products of
situated action—for both clients *and* therapists. This constitutes a radical adjustment in our thinking about therapeutic practice. If the therapeutic profession
itself developed as a modernist project, why or how can we hold on to this
profession in a postmodern world? Some may even wish to ask if we *should* want
to hold on to the therapeutic profession.

One of the first points to be made concerns the term *identity* itself. Identity is
conceptualized as an *entity* in modernist discourse. Although from a postmodern
approach we would want to deessentialize such a term, we would not attempt to cast
it aside. Our concern is not with the object status of any suggested concept. Instead,
and consistent with Wittgenstein, we are concerned with the way in which terms are
used and the ways in which they gain significance in particular discursive contexts.
To that end, identity as a topic of investigation maintains its centrality in a postmodern, highly technological context if only by virtue of its historical and cultural
salience. Here, identity is described as a conversational resource—a way of talking
that we quite often find useful in our attempts to coordinate with others. Identity as
a conversational resource differs dramatically from descriptions of identity as a
possession of self-contained individuals. If identity is a person's possession, then
that person is (and should be) held responsible for the character of his or her identity.
Consequently, if there is a problem located within a person, that person is held
accountable and, thus, becomes the nexus of control and potential change. Such a
view has spawned our commonly accepted economic, moral, and ethical cannons in
which individualism is featured and held in high esteem.

To describe identity as a conversational resource used by participants in their
situated activities, however, implies that it is the discourse itself that becomes
open to investigation as well as the relational context in which it emerges.
Questions focus on *how* (not *why*) a particular way of talking/acting gains
viability and sustainability in *this* particular interactive moment. How do the
actions of all participants join to constrain certain ways of talking/acting and
potentiate others? How does this specific interactive moment make particular
lines of action possible while excluding others? What might have happened if
the participants in the given interaction had been different, or if the situation was
different, or if the way of talking had been different? These are the types of
questions raised when we place our emphasis on the process of relating (i.e.,
discourse). Thus, postmodern therapy is not equated with *no* therapy. In both
traditional and postmodern therapy, a therapist can be seen as an active participant in the conversation. What distinguishes the two is that in traditional,
modernist therapy, the "conversational role" of the therapist emanates from his

or her predetermined understanding of particular problems and the remedial actions that are believed to be the best ensuing from this understanding of the problem. On the other hand, the postmodern therapist engages not in a conversational role but *in* the conversation itself, seeing it as a contingent, indeterminant dance within which meanings, actions, and identities emerge.

Postmodern therapy provides a different way of talking about what counts as therapy and what the cultural purpose of therapy is. Therapy is no longer viewed as a professional service sought by individuals, couples, or families who need to understand their core identity, their true feelings, or their denied problems. Therapy in a postmodern mode seeks to explore the multiple possibilities for identity construction and how they fit with the significant relational networks with which a client or clients engage. Most pragmatically, clients might leave this therapeutic context armed with a variety of ways to comfortably talk about themselves and their relationships. Most important, they might leave such a therapeutic experience with a sense of curiosity for the local coherence of not only their own but others' stories and with a concomitant tolerance and respect for these stories (although not necessarily an agreement with them). Such curiosity and respect demand a relational sensibility. They demand, in other words, at least a gesture of recognition to the relational contexts within which certain ways of talking and acting emerge and become viable and sustainable.

To this end, the relational focus on process can be described as a form of "interested inquiry" (Gergen & Kaye, 1992), a kind of "not knowing approach" (Anderson & Goolishian, 1992), or curiosity. In this spirit, there is emphasis on questions rather than answers, on multiple interpretations rather than any singular meaning, on the historical, cultural, and situational nature of any description of identity. The relational attention to process suggests that a client's descriptions voiced in therapy are just as relationally, historically, and culturally specific to that particular therapy context as the "events" or interactive moments they are attempting to characterize. They are not heard as factual descriptions, nor are they heard as symptoms of pathology. Rather, they are viewed as conversational resources made possible by the therapeutic conversation itself. In these terms, the metaphor of therapist as conversational partner takes precedence over the metaphor of therapist as objective knower.

Postmodern therapy attempts to achieve a conversational domain where participants begin to supplement their own and each other's behaviors in ways that allow failures, difficulties, and problems, as well as successes, to be recognized as *relational accomplishments*.

Therapeutic Possibilities

The multiplicity of meaning, a plurality of voices/discourses, attentiveness to process, and the historical, cultural, and situational nature of identity can be, and often is, explored in all forms of therapy. In modernist therapy, however, there is a foundationalist premise urging both therapist and client to uncover or unlock the root of the client's problem. The problem, here, becomes an object to be dealt with or treated in some way. Although postmodern therapy may find this conversational mode useful as the therapeutic narrative unfolds, it is not a necessary selection.[3] What is necessary is the original commitment to exploring many voices because selection of one method, one form of conversation, one set of beliefs, adorns a relational sensibility when it is selected for its "good fit" from among many, and in a particular, interactive moment. As exemplars of this postmodern commitment, Penn and Frankfurt (1993) use letter writing as a way to engage clients in a different kind of dialogue with themselves, as therapists, as well as with the client's web of significant relationships. Letters (or journal entries) become processes of construction for alternative conversations by virtue of the client's ability to imagine different supplements from those typically emergent in daily interactions. As clients read their written materials in the therapy sessions, the therapist can provide yet another array of supplements. Thus, both the writing and the reading become significant interactive moments. The possibilities generated in the use of this different conversational style provide the potential for both client and therapist to attend to the processes through which certain identities have been constructed as well as how these processes might encourage new constructions.

The reflecting position or process described by Andersen (1991, 1992) offers another illustration of postmodern therapy. He asks clients in therapy to listen to the therapist or therapy team "reflect" on the clients' stories. After listening, clients comment on the therapist's or therapy team's discussion. Andersen (1992) notes that "the listener is not only a receiver of a story but also, by being present, an encouragement to the act of making the story. And that act is the act of constituting one's self" (p. 66). By constantly shifting one's position from that of speaker to that of listener, clients and therapists engage in an interactive process where multiple meanings are given voice. Shifting positions eliminates the notion of therapists as scientific, objective professionals who discuss only what they observe of their clients with colleagues behind closed doors. This shift in the way therapy is enacted aids both therapist and client in attending to the processes of construction themselves.

Conclusions

In the brief descriptions of alternative therapeutic conversations, it is the construction of a multiplicity of accounts that is featured rather than the selection of any one account. Commitment to one account is a practical matter, but there is a vast difference between a situational/relational commitment and a universal commitment. That is to say that therapist and client will select a certain interpretation so that they "know" how to go on in their situated activities. Yet, to adopt a particular discursive form as opposed to another, regardless of the relationship in which one is engaged, would imply an adherence to monologism.

Dialogue, where we curiously enter into conversation, allows us to *do* different things in our interactions. We focus on how certain interpretations and lines of action become sanctioned as viable and sustainable while others are negated. We move our assessment, therefore, from one of the individual to one of the conversational arena. In such a move, we must adopt a tolerance for uncertainty. We will not be able to provide definitive answers to questions of one's identity. Yet, we can provide situated answers. Even these, however, can be provided only in dialogue with clients and others. The therapist, in the course of conversation, invites participants to question their own assumptions about mental health, identity, relationships, and so on by questioning his or her own as well as the broader cultural assumptions that have become our traditions.

When we place our emphasis on what people do together, we abandon the individual as our unit of investigation and replace it with relational practices. Such a move underscores the often competing interpretive communities that participants bring to any particular relationship. These interpretive communities are expanded daily by virtue of the vast array of mediated interactions. And, thus, each interactive moment is full of uncertainty, multiplicity, and potential conflict. The chore of coordinating our lives within this complex web of relatedness is daunting if we are constantly pathologized by the voice of objectivity, universality, rationality, and progress. Alternatively, attentiveness to the process by which we create different (and often competing) rationalities and truths provides us with a way of talking about identity, therapy, and social life as culturally, historically, and relationally situated. Such a way of talking provides the means by which we can comfortably entertain the plurality of identities and moralities with which we engage. These are necessary survival skills for constructing identities in a mediated world, and the therapeutic profession can play an important role in mediating identity construction.

Notes

1. The reference here to Goffman's notion of backstage is not meant to imply an allegiance to his work. One problem with the frontstage/backstage dichotomy is that it harbors a modernist ideology and in so doing positions one identity or performance against the other in an attempt to locate the "true" self.

2. Shotter and Gergen (1994) discuss the project of social constructionism as an alternative, not as a view of knowledge that is superior to the dominant tradition.

3. It is not my attempt here to cast modernist therapy as evil or wrong. My project focuses simply on casting a variety of readings onto the stage for consideration.

References

American Psychiatric Association. (1987). *Diagnostic and statistical manual of mental disorders* (3rd ed., rev.). Washington, DC: Author.

Andersen, T. (Ed.). (1991). *The reflecting team: Dialogues and dialogues about the dialogues.* New York: Norton.

Andersen, T. (1992). Reflections on reflecting with families. In S. McNamee & K. J. Gergen (Eds.), *Therapy as social construction* (pp. 54-68). London: Sage.

Anderson, W. T. (1990). *Reality isn't what it used to be.* San Francisco: HarperSanFrancisco.

Anderson, H., & Goolishian, H. (1992). The client is the expert: A not-knowing approach to therapy. In S. McNamee & K. J. Gergen (Eds.), *Therapy as social construction* (pp. 25-39). London: Sage.

Bakhtin, M. M. (1981). *The dialogical imagination* (M. Holquist, Ed.; C. Emerson & M. Holquist, Trans.). Austin: University of Texas Press.

Bakhtin, M. M. (1984). *Problems of Dostoyevsky's poetics* (C. Emerson, Ed. and Trans.). Minneapolis: University of Minnesota Press.

Bakhtin, M. M. (1986). *Speech genres and other late essays* (C. Emerson & M. Holquist, Eds.; V. W. McGee, Trans.). Austin: University of Texas Press.

Gergen, K. J. (1989). Warranting voice and the elaboration of the self. In J. Shotter & K. J. Gergen (Eds.), *Texts of identity* (pp. 70-81). London: Sage.

Gergen, K. J. (1990, March). *From heteroglossia to communication.* Keynote Address, Temple University, 11th Annual Conference on Discourse Analysis, Philadelphia.

Gergen, K. J. (1991). *The saturated self.* New York: Basic Books.

Gergen, K. J., & Kaye, J. (1992). Beyond narrative in the negotiation of therapeutic meaning. In S. McNamee & K. J. Gergen (Eds.), *Therapy as social construction* (pp. 166-185). London: Sage.

Goffman, E. (1959). *Presentation of self in everyday life.* New York: Doubleday/Anchor.

McNamee, S., & Gergen, K. J. (1994). *Relational responsibility.* Manuscript in preparation.

Penn, P., & Frankfurt, M. (1993). Creating a participant text: Writing, multiple voices, and narrative multiplicity. *Family Process, 33*(3), 217-233.

Sampson, E. E. (1977). Psychology and the American ideal. *Journal of Personality and Social Psychology, 35,* 767-782.

Sampson, E. E. (1993). *Celebrating the other.* San Francisco: Westview.

Shotter, J., & Gergen, K. J. (1994). Social construction: Knowledge, self, others, and continuing the conversation. In S. Deetz (Ed.), *Communication yearbook 17* (pp. 3-33). Thousand Oaks, CA: Sage.

Turner, B. S. (Ed.). (1990). *Theories of modernity and postmodernity.* London: Sage.

Wittgenstein, L. (1963). *Philosophical investigations* (G. Anscombe, Trans.). New York: Macmillan.

10

Parallel Lives:
Working on Identity in Virtual Space

Sherry Turkle

In a recent *New Yorker* cartoon, one dog, paw on keyboard, explains to another: "On the Internet, nobody knows you're a dog." Obviously, the point of the cartoon is humor; here I take seriously some of the cultural practices to which it refers. I describe virtual communities on the Internet in which people are acting as authors not only of text but of themselves. I take as my case study a class of computer environments known as MUDs (short for *multiuser dungeons* or *multiuser domains*).[1] In the early 1970s, a role-playing game called Dungeons and Dragons swept the game culture. In this game, a "dungeon master" created a world in which people created characters and played out complex adventures. A Dungeons and Dragons style of game was interpreted for computational space in a program called Adventure. There, players proceeded through a maze that was presented to them through text description on a computer screen. The term *dungeon* has persisted in the high-tech world to refer to a virtual social space that exists on a machine. MUDs are social virtual realities. On them, players logged on from all over the world, each at his or her individual machine, join communities that exist only "in" the computer.[2] Players find themselves in the same "space." They communicate with each other either in large groups or privately.[3]

There are many hundreds of multiuser games based on at least 13 different kinds of software on the international computer network known as the Internet. Here, for simplicity, I use the term *MUD* to refer to all of them. Although MUDs differ in their theme and structure, in general, when you "start life" on a MUD, you create a character and specify its gender and other physical and psychological attributes.[4] Other players can see "you" only through this description. It becomes your character's self-presentation. The created characters need not be human and there may be more than two genders. Indeed, in many MUDs, characters may be multiple ("a swarm of bees"; "Laurel and Hardy") or mechanical (you can write and deploy a program in the game who will present itself as a person or, if you wish, as a robot).

Beyond character creation and role-playing, in many MUDs, players are invited to help build the virtual world itself. Using simple programming languages, they can make "rooms" in the game space where they are able to set the stage and define the rules. That is, they make objects in the computer world and specify how they work. So, for example, in one MUD, an 11-year-old player builds a room she calls "the condo." It is beautifully furnished; she has created magical jewelry and makeup for her dressing table. When she visits the condo, she invites her friends; she chats, orders pizza, and flirts. Other players have more varied social lives on MUDs: They create characters who have casual and romantic sexual encounters, hold jobs, attend rituals and celebrations, fall in love and get married. To say the least, such goings-on are gripping: "This is more real than my real life," says a character who turns out to be a man playing a woman who is pretending to be a man. In MUDding, the rules of self-construction and social interaction are built, not received.

MUDs are a new "blurred genre"[5] of collaborative writing, with things in common with performance art, street theater, improvisational theater, commedia dell'arte, and script writing. My focus here is on the way MUDs serve as places for the construction and reconstruction of identity. I report on people who consider MUDding a significant part of their lives.[6] I believe that although such people are relatively rare today, their experiences of constructing selves in cyberspace will become increasingly important in our psychological culture. When it comes to thinking about identity in a culture of simulation, the citizens of MUDs are our pioneers.

MUDs, like other experiences in cyberspace, blur the boundaries between self and game, self and role, self and simulation. One player says, "You are the character and you are not the character, both at the same time," and "You are who you pretend to be. . . . You are who you play." But people don't just become who they play, they often play who they want to be. Diane, 26 years old, says:

> I'm not one thing, I'm many things. Each part gets to be more fully expressed in MUDs than in the real world. So even though I play more than one self on MUDs, I feel more like "myself" when I'm MUDding.

Players sometimes talk about their real selves as a composite of their characters and sometimes talk about their MUD characters as means for working on their "real life."

Of course, some players use MUDs to "act out" rather than "work through" their problems. In psychoanalytic thinking, "acting out" involves staging old conflicts in new settings. We reenact the past in fruitless repetitions. In contrast, "working through" usually calls for a moratorium on action to facilitate thinking about things in a new way. It is precisely by not stirring up the real that we are best able to effect inner change. In this chapter, I present case materials that show how MUDs offer possibilities for both acting out and working through.

Beyond their importance as "identity workshops,"[7] MUDs are also playing a part in undermining our traditional notions of identity, for so long tied to notions of authenticity, which simulation actively subverts. *Identity,* after all, refers to the sameness between two qualities—in this case, between a person and his or her persona. But in MUDs, one can be many. "Playing in the MUD," playing multiple characters within one MUD or across several MUDs, contributes to a larger cultural negotiation with ideas about identity that include the idea of identity as a society of selves. MUDs imply multiplicity, heterogeneity, and fragmentation. A one that must be multiple, heterogeneous, and fragmented is a contradiction in terms. But this contradiction increasingly defines the conditions of our lives, and not just on MUDs.

In the MUDs, all projections of self are engaged in a resolutely postmodern context. There are parallel narratives in the different rooms of the MUD; one can move forward or backward in time. The cultures of Tolkien, Gibson, and Madonna coexist and interact. Authorship not only is displaced from a single, solitary voice, it is exploded. The MUDs are authored by their players, thousands of people in all, often hundreds of people at a time, all logged on from different places. The self is not only decentered but multiplied without limit. We can use MUDs as objects to think with for thinking about postmodern identity.

My method of investigation of MUDding has been ethnographic and clinical: visit the games, "hang out" with game players in virtual as well as real space, interview game players in person both individually and in groups. Some of my richest data came from a series of weekly "pizza parties" for MUDders within the Boston area. There the topic was open and conversation turned to what was on the players' minds: most often love, romance, and what can be counted on as real in virtual space.

Distributed Identities

MUDs make possible the construction of an identity that is so fluid and multiple that it strains the very limits of the notion. People become masters of self-presentation and self-creation. There is an unparalleled opportunity to play with one's identity and to "try out" new ones. The very notion of an inner, "true self" is called into question. This idea is well captured by the player who said:

> You can be whoever you want to be. You can completely redefine yourself if you want. You can be the opposite sex. You can be more talkative. You can be less talkative. Whatever. You can just be whoever you want really, whoever you have the capacity to be. You don't have to worry about the slots other people put you in as much. It's easier to change the way people perceive you, because all they've got is what you show them. They don't look at your body and make assumptions. They don't hear your accent and make assumptions. All they see is your words. And MUDs are always there. Twenty-four hours a day you can walk down to the street corner and there's gonna be a few people there who are interesting to talk to, if you've found the right MUD for you.

On MUDs, the obese can be slender, the beautiful can be plain. The "nerdy" can be elegant. The anonymity of MUDs (you are known only by the name you gave your characters) provides ample room for individuals to express unexplored "aspects of the self." In role-playing games, one steps in and out of a character. MUDs offer something more: a parallel life. The boundaries of the game are fuzzy, and the routine of playing them becomes part of their players' real lives.

In writing about personal computers, I have analogized them to the psychologist's Rorschach inkblot test because they allow for the projection of personality. I have also said that they are more than a Rorschach—because, unlike the Rorschach, they enter into an individual's everyday life. To pursue the metaphor, role-playing games are emphatically more than a Rorschach, because not only do they allow projection and enter everyday life, but they can become everyday life.

One college sophomore explains how he cycles in and out of MUDs and "real life," or what MUD players call "RL." "When I am upset I just . . . jump onto my ship [the spaceship he commands in a MUD] and look somebody up." He does this by logging on to the game in character and "paging" a friend in the game space. Then, he explains, he goes to class, and by the time he comes back, the friend or friends he had paged would now be on the game and ready to talk. This player has become expert at using MUDs as a psychological adjunct to RL: "I was always happy when I got into a fight in the MUD," he says. "I remember doing that before tests. I would go to the MUD, pick a fight, yell at people, blow a couple of things up, take the test, and then go out for a drink." If a particular game closes down, players can take their characters to other games; players tend to "migrate" together.

One group of players joked that they were like "the electrodes in the computer," trying to express the degree to which they feel part of its space. "Part of me, a very important me, only exists inside of PernMUD," says one player. Players are often people who work with computers all day at their "regular" jobs. As they play on MUDs, they will periodically put their characters to "sleep," remaining logged on to the game but pursuing other activities. From time to time, they return to the game space. In this way, they break up their workdays and experience their lives as a "cycling through" between the real world and a series of simulated ones. A software designer who describes himself as "never not playing a MUD" describes his day this way:

> I like to put myself in the role of a hero, usually one with magical powers on one MUD, start a few conversations going, put out a question or two about MUD matters, and ask people to drop off replies to me in a special "inbox" I have built in my MUD "office." Then I'll put my character to sleep and go off and do some work. Particularly if I'm in some conflict with someone at work it helps to be MUDding because I know that when I get back to the MUD, I'll probably have some appreciative mail waiting for me. Or sometimes I use a few rounds of MUD triumphs to psych myself up to deal with my boss.

This kind of interaction with MUDs is made possible by the existence of what have come to be called "windows" in modern computing environments. Windows are a way of working with a computer that makes it possible for the machine to place you in several contexts at the same time. As a user, you are attentive to only one of the windows on your screen at any given moment, but in a certain sense, you are a presence in all of them at all times. You might be writing a paper in bacteriology and using your computer in several ways to help you: You are "present" to a word processing program on which you are taking notes and collecting thoughts; you are "present" to communication software that is in touch with a distant computer for collecting reference materials; and you are "present" to a simulation program that is charting the growth of bacterial colonies when a new organism enters their ecology. Each of these activities takes place in a "window" and your identity on the computer is the sum of your distributed presence. This certainly is the case for Doug, a Dartmouth College junior, for whom a MUD represents one window and RL represents another. Doug says: "RL is just one more window, and it's not usually my best one."

Doug plays four characters distributed across three different MUDs. One is a seductive woman. One is a macho, cowboy type whose self-description stresses that he is a "Marlboros-rolled-in-the-T-shirt-sleeve kind of guy." Then there is a rabbit of unspecified gender who wanders its MUD introducing people to each other, a character he calls "Carrot." Doug says, "Carrot is so low key that people let it be around while they are having private conversations. So I think of Carrot as my passive, voyeuristic character." Doug tells me that this "Carrot" has sometimes been mistaken for a "bot," a computer program on the MUD because its passive, facilitating presence strikes many as the kind of persona of which a robot would be capable.

Doug's third and final character is one that he plays only on a FurryMUD (these are MUDs in which all the characters are furry animals). "I'd rather not even talk about that character because its anonymity there is very important to me," Doug says. "Let's just say that on FurryMUDs I feel like a sexual tourist." Doug talks about playing his characters in "windows" and says that using windows has enhanced his ability to "turn pieces of my mind on and off."

> I split my mind. I'm getting better at it. I can see myself as being two or three or more. And I just turn on one part of my mind and then another when I go from window to window. I'm in some kind of argument in one window and trying to come on to a girl in a MUD in another, and another window might be running a spreadsheet program or some other technical thing for school. . . . And then I'll get a real-time message [that flashes on the screen as soon as it is sent from another system user], and I guess that's RL. It's just one more window.

The development of the windows metaphor for computer interfaces was a technical innovation motivated by the desire to get people working more efficiently by "cycling through" different applications much as time-sharing computers cycle through the computing needs of different people. But in practice, windows have become a potent metaphor for thinking about the self as a multiple, distributed, "time-sharing" system. The self is no longer simply playing different roles in different settings, something that people experience when, for example, one wakes up as a lover, makes breakfast as a mother, and drives to work as a lawyer. The life practice of windows is of a distributed self that exists in many worlds and plays many roles at the same time. MUDs extend the metaphor; now RL itself, as Doug said, can be just "one more window."

To address what is psychologically most powerful about MUDding, it helps to take one step back to more general considerations of how traditional role-playing games enable people to work through issues of identity. By "traditional" role-playing games, I mean games that take place in physical space, where participants take parts or "roles" in an unfolding drama. There are many different kinds of role-playing games. They differ in theme, the degree to which they are prescripted, the degree to which players "act out" the parts. In some games, players sit in a circle and make statements that describe their characters' actions. In others, they wear costumes, engage in staged swordplay, and speak special languages that exist only within the game. MUDs enhance the evocative potential of traditional games by further blurring the line between the game and "real life."

Traditional Role-Playing Games

As identity workshops, MUDs have much in common with these more traditional role-playing games, for example, those played by Julee, a 19-year-old who has dropped out of college after her freshman year and moved to New York, where her best friends are among a group of people who run weekend role-playing games. Part of the reason for Julee's leaving college is that she found herself in an increasingly turbulent and personally disruptive relationship with her mother, a devout Catholic, who broke all ties with Julee when the mother discovered that Julee had had an abortion the summer before beginning college. From Julee's point of view, her mother has chosen to deny her existence. "My mother is trying to make me disappear."

Julee's favorite style of role-playing game begins with each character being handed a book that contains that character's description and the starting structure and assumptions of the game action. Although the characters and starting point are provided, the drama that unfolds is in the control of the players. Among Julee's friends, the plots usually involve intrigue and espionage. When asked about her most important experience playing role-playing games, Julee described a game in which she had been assigned to play a mother facing a conflict with her daughter. Indeed, in that particular game, the script said that the daughter, a double agent on the mother's team, is going to betray, even kill, the mother.

In that game, played over a weekend on a college campus, Julee and her "daughter" talked for hours: Why might the daughter have joined her mother's opponents—how could they stay true to their relationship and the game as it had been written? Huddled in a corner of an empty classroom, Julee was having the conversation that her own mother had not been willing to have with her. There were anger, tears, and embraces. In the end, Julee's character chose to ignore her loyalty to her team to preserve her daughter's life. "I'm sorry," she said to her team, "I'm going to forfeit the game for our team."

Clearly, Julee projected feelings about her "real" mother's choice onto her experience of the game, but more was going on than a simple reenactment. Julee was able to reexperience a familiar situation in a setting where she could examine it, do something new with it, and revise her relationship toward it. In many ways, what happened to Julee in that game was resonant with the psychoanalytic notion of "working through."

Julee's experience of using a game to work with the materials of her life stands in contrast to images of role-playing games that are prevalent in the popular culture. A first popular image portrays role-playing games as depressing, even dangerous environments. It is captured in the now legendary story of an emotionally troubled student who disappeared and committed suicide during a game of Dungeons and Dragons. Another popular image turns the games into places of escape. Players are seen as leaving their "real" lives and problems behind to lose themselves in the game. Julee's story belies both stereotypes. For her, the game is psychologically constructive. She uses it not for escape but as a vehicle for engaging in a significant dialogue with important events and relationships in her life.

Role-playing games are able to serve in this evocative capacity precisely because they are not simple escapes from the real to the unreal, but because they stand betwixt and between, both in and not in real life. But in the final analysis, what puts Julee's game most firmly in the category of game is that it had an end point. The weekend was over and so was the game. MUDs present a far more complicated case. In a certain sense, they don't have to end. Because their boundaries are more fuzzy, the routine of playing them becomes part of their players' real lives. As I have said, the roles played in the game become not so much an alternative as a parallel life. Such blurring of boundaries between role and self present new opportunities to use the role to work on the self. MUDs take the possibilities that Julee found in role-playing games and raise them to a higher power.

You Are Who You Pretend to Be

The notion "you are who you pretend to be" has a mythic resonance. The Pygmalion story endures because it speaks to a powerful fantasy: that we are not limited by our histories, that we can be re-created or can re-create ourselves. In the real world, we are thrilled by stories of dramatic self-transformation. Madonna is our modern Eliza Doolittle; Michael Jackson the object of morbid fascination. But, of course, for most people, such re-creations of self are difficult. In MUDs, however, you can write your character's self-description any way you wish. Virtual worlds provide environments for experiences that are hard to come by in the real world.[8]

Stewart is a 23-year-old physics graduate student. His life revolves around his work in the laboratory and his plans for a future in science. He says that his only friend is his roommate, another student whom Stewart describes as even more reclusive than himself. This almost monastic life does not represent a radical departure for Stewart. He has had heart trouble since he was a child; his health is delicate. One small rebellion, a ski trip during his freshman year at college, put him in the hospital for three weeks. His response has been to circumscribe his world. He lives within a small compass.

In an interview with Stewart, he immediately makes it clear why he plays on MUDs: "I do it so I can talk to people." He MUDs exclusively on a variant of the adventure-style "hack and slay" games. Stewart found these attractive because they demanded no technical expertise, so it was easy both to get started and to achieve "Wizard" status, the highest level of player. Unlike some players for whom becoming a wizard is an opportunity to get involved in the technical aspects of MUDding, Stewart likes being a player with status because wizard privileges allow him "to go anywhere and talk to anyone" on the game. He says: "I'm going to hack and slash the appropriate number of monsters so that I can talk to people."

Stewart is logged on to one MUD or another for at least 40 hours a week. It seems misleading to call what he does there "playing." He spends his time constructing a life that is more expansive than the one he lives in real life. Stewart, who has traveled very little and has never been to Europe, explains with delight that his favorite MUD is physically located on a computer in Germany and has many European players.

> And I started talking to them [the inhabitants of the MUD] and they're like, "This costs so many and so many Deutschmarks," and I'm like, "What are Deutschmarks? Where is this place located?" And they say: "Don't you know, this is Germany." It hadn't occurred to me that I could even connect to Germany. . . . All I had were local Internet numbers, so I had no idea of where it was located. And I started talking to people and I was amazed at the quality of English they spoke. . . . European, European and Australian MUDs are interesting. . . . Different people. Completely different lifestyles. And at the moment completely different economic situations.

It is from MUDs that Stewart has learned what he knows of politics and economics. He was thrilled when he first spoke to a Scandinavian player who could see the northern lights. On the German MUD, Stewart shaped a character named Achilles, but he asks his MUD friends to call him Stewart as much as possible. He wants to feel that his real self exists somewhere between Stewart and Achilles; he wants to feel that his MUD life is part of his real life. Stewart insists that he does not "role-play" but that MUDs simply allow him to be a better version of himself.

On the MUD, Stewart creates a living environment suitable for his ideal self. Life in a dormitory has put him in modest circumstances. The room he has built for Achilles on the MUD is elegant, romantic, heavily influenced by Ralph Lauren advertising. He has named it "the home beneath the silver moon." There are books, a roaring fire, cognac, a cherry mantel "covered with pictures of Achilles' friends from around the world." "You look up . . . and through the immense skylight you see a breathtaking view of the night sky. The moon is always full over Achilles' home, and its light fills the room with a warm glow."

Beyond expanding his social world, MUDs have brought Stewart the only romance and intimacy he has ever known. At a social event held in virtual space, a "wedding" of two regular players on the German-based MUD I call Gargoyle, Achilles met Winterlight, a character played by one of the three female players. Stewart, who has known little success with women, was able to charm this desirable player.

On a first virtual date, Achilles took Winterlight to an Italian restaurant close to Stewart's dorm where he had often fantasized being with a woman. Stewart describes how he used a combination of MUD commands to simulate a romantic evening at the bistro. He picked Winterlight up at the airport in a limousine, drove her to a hotel room so that she could shower, and then proceeded to the restaurant.

> So, you just kinda get creative. . . . I described the menu to her. I found out she didn't like veal, so I asked her if she would mind if I ordered veal . . . because they have really good veal scallopini . . . and she said that "yes, she would mind," so I didn't order veal.
>
> We talked about what her research is. She's working on disease . . . the biochemistry of coronary artery disease. . . . And so we talked about her research on coronary artery disease and at the time I was doing nuclear physics and I talked to her about that. We talked for a couple of hours. We talked. And then, she had to go to work, so we ended dinner and she left.

The intimacy Stewart experiences with Winterlight on the MUD is unknown to him in other contexts. "Winterlight . . . she's a very, she's a good friend. I found out a lot of things—from things about biochemistry to the color of nail polish she wears." The dinner date led to a brief courtship in which Achilles was tender and romantic, chivalrous and poetic. One is reminded of Cyrano, who could find his voice only through another's persona, even though that persona was his "true self." It is Achilles, Stewart's character on the MUD, who could create the magic and win the girl. Finally, Achilles asked for Winterlight's hand. When she accepted, they had a formal engagement ceremony on the MUD. In that ceremony, Achilles testified not only to the importance of his relationship with Winterlight but to the extent to which Gargoyle MUD had become his real home.

> I have traveled the lands of MUDs for almost four months. I have traveled far and wide across these lands. . . . I have met a great deal of people as I wandered. I feel that the friendliest people of all are here at Gargoyle. I consider this place my home. I am proud to be a part of this place. I have had some bad times in the past . . . and the people of Gargoyle were there. I thank the people of Gargoyle for their support. I have recently decided to settle down and be married. I searched far and near for a maiden of beauty with hair of sunshine gold and lips red as the rose. With intelligence to match her beauty. . . . Winterlight, you are that woman I seek. You are the beautiful maiden. Winterlight, will you marry me?

Faced with the notion that "you are what you pretend to be," Stewart can only hope that it is true for he is playing his ideal self.

Stewart plays what in the psychoanalytic tradition would be called an "ego ideal." Other players create a character or multiple characters that are closer to embodying aspects of themselves that they hate or fear or perhaps have not ever consciously confronted before. One male player describes his role-playing as

> daring to be passive. I don't mean in having sex on the MUD. I mean in letting other people take the initiative in friendships, in not feeling when I am in character that I need to control everything. My mother controlled my whole family, well, certainly me. So I grew up thinking "never again." My "real life" is exhausting that way. On MUDs I do something else. I didn't even realize this connection to my mother until something happened in the game and somebody tried to boss my pretty laid-back character around and I went crazy. And then I saw what I was doing.

My past research into the experiences of individuals working with computers has led me to underscore the power of this technology as a medium not only for getting things done but for thinking through and working through personal concerns (Turkle, 1984). Engagement with computational technology facilitates a series of "second chances" for adults to work and rework unresolved personal issues and, more generally, to think through questions about the nature of self, including questions about definitions of life, intentionality, and intelligence.

What is true of individuals working alone with a computer is raised to a higher power when people use computers to communicate with other people as they do on the MUDs. In the first case, the person alone with the computer, I have found that individuals use computers to work through identity issues that center on control and mastery; in the second, in a case such as Stewart's in which the computer functions as a communication medium, there is more opportunity for the technology to be used to increase the capacity for personal relationships.

Both Julee and Stewart appropriate their games to work on their relationships as a way of remaking the self. Stewart logs onto his MUD in physical isolation (he sits alone as he reads and writes text on a computer in his dorm room) while Julee's playing has the powerful quality of real-time psychodrama. She has face-to-face encounters with "real" people with whom she can laugh and cry, all of which evoke the issues and people in her life outside the game. On the other hand, Stewart's game is ongoing and provides him with anonymity and potential multiplicity. It is ongoing in the sense that he can play it as much as he wants, all day if he wants, every day if he chooses to, as he sometimes does. He has a long time, months, even years, to develop the character he is playing. The game is anonymous in the sense that once he creates his character, that is Stewart's only identity in the game. His character need not have his gender or share any recognizable feature with him. Stewart can be who he wants and play with no concern that "he," Stewart, will be held accountable in "real life" for his character's actions.[9] And Stewart can create many characters, simultaneously playing out and playing with different aspects of his self.

The possibilities the medium offers for projecting both conscious and unconscious aspects of the self suggest an analogy between MUDs and psychotherapeutic milieus. The goal of psychotherapy is not, of course, to simply provide a place for "acting out" behavior that expresses one's conflicts but to furnish a contained and confidential environment for "working through" unresolved issues. The distinction between acting out and working through is crucial to thinking about MUDs as settings for personal growth. To explore this distinction, I return to Stewart's case and contrast it with that of Robert, another MUD player.

Acting Out

Stewart, quite self-consciously, has tried to put MUDding in the service of developing a greater capacity for trust and intimacy, but he is not satisfied with the outcome of his efforts. MUDding offered him a safe place to experiment with new ways, but he sums up his experience on MUDs by saying that it has been "an addicting waste of time." Stewart's case, where MUDs led to a net drop in self-esteem, illustrates how complex the psychological effects of life lived in cyberspace can be. And it illustrates that a safe place is not necessarily all that is needed for self-transformation.

Stewart came to MUDding with serious problems. Since childhood he has been isolated both by his illness and by a fear of death he felt that he could not discuss with other people. Although Stewart loves his mother, she has always been terribly distressed by his illness. He always felt that he had to protect her and was never able to talk freely with her. Stewart says that his mother has serious migraine attacks for which he feels largely responsible. Stewart's father protected himself by emotionally withdrawing and losing himself in fix-it projects on lawn mowers and cars, the reassuring things that could be made to work the way a sick little boy could not. Stewart resented his father's periods of with-drawal; he says that they too often left him "the head of the household." Nevertheless, whenever possible, he now emulates his father's style. Stewart says that his main defense against depression is "not to feel things." "I'd rather put my problems on the back burner and go on with my life." Before he became involved in MUDs, for Stewart "going on with his life" usually translated into throwing himself into his schoolwork or into fixing cars. He fondly remembers a three-week period during which a physics laboratory experiment took almost all of his waking hours. He finds respite and reliability in science and technology; he does not know how to take comfort from the more volatile and unpredictable world of people.

> I have a problem with emotional things. I handle them very badly. I do the things you're not supposed to do. I don't worry about them for a while and then they come back to haunt me two or three years later. . . . I am not able to talk about my problems while they are happening. I have to wait until they have become just a story.
>
> If I have an emotional problem I cannot talk to people about it. I will sit there in a room with them and I will talk to them about anything else in the entire world except what's bothering me.

Stewart was introduced to MUDs by Carrie, an unhappy classmate whose chief source of solace was talking to people on MUDs. Although Stewart tends to ignore his own troubles, he likes to connect with other people by helping them with theirs. Carrie had troubles aplenty: She drank too much and had an abusive boyfriend. Yet Carrie rejected Stewart's friendship. Stewart described how Carrie turned her back to him when he visited her in her dorm room and she talked to "the people in the machine."

> I mean when you have that type of emotional problem and that kind of pain, it's not an intelligent move to log onto a game and talk to people because they are safe and they won't hurt you. Because that's just not a way out of it. I mean there is a limit to how many years you can spend in front of a computer screen.

Shortly after this incident in Carrie's room, Stewart precipitated the end of their relationship. He took it upon himself to inform Carrie's parents that she had a drinking problem, something that she wanted to sort out by herself. When Carrie confronted him about his "meddling," Stewart could not see her point of view and defended his actions by arguing that "morality was on his side." For Carrie, Stewart's intrusions had gone too far; she would no longer speak to him. By the fall of his junior year in college, Stewart's emotional resources were strained to the limit. His friendship with Carrie was over, his mother was seriously ill, and he himself had developed pneumonia.

The pneumonia in his junior year caused Stewart to be hospitalized for several weeks and then bedridden at home for an additional 10 days. His illness brought back the fears of death he had tried to sweep under the carpet. When Stewart finally returned to his dormitory, he felt utterly alone. He couldn't even manage to throw himself into work because he felt too far behind to even try to catch up. In desperation, he tried Carrie's solution. He turned to MUDs. Within a week, he was spending 10 to 12 hours a day on the games. He became a wizard on several of them, but their real appeal was that they were a place where he could "talk" about his real life troubles. In particular, he "talked" to the other players about Carrie, telling his side of the story and complaining that her decision to break off their friendship was "unjust."

> I was on the game talking to people about my problems endlessly.... I find it a lot easier to talk to people on the game about them because they're not there. I mean they are there but they're not there. I mean you could sit there and you could tell them about your problems and you don't have to worry about running into them on the street the next day.

On the one hand, MUDs helped Stewart find a way to talk about his troubles while they were still emotionally relevant. But on the other hand, Stewart says that MUDding has made him feel worse about himself. Despite his MUD "socializing," despite the poetry of his MUD romance and the pageantry of his MUD marriage, despite the fact that on MUDs he actually talked about his troubles before they became "just a story," MUDding did nothing to alter Stewart's sense of himself as withdrawn, unappealing, and flawed; just as in the Rostand play, Cyrano's "romantic success" through writing love letters for another never made him feel worthy of love himself. Stewart says of MUDding:

> The more I do it, the more I feel I need to do it. Every couple of days I'd notice it's like, "Gee in the last two days, I've been on this MUD for the total of probably over 28 hours." ... I mean I'd be on the MUD until I fell asleep at the terminal practically and then go to sleep and then I'd wake up and I'd do it again.

Stewart has tried hard to make his MUD self, the "better" Achilles self, part of his "real life" but he says that he has failed. He says, "I'm not social. I don't like parties. I can't talk to people about my problems." We recall together that these things are easy for him on MUDs and he shrugs and says, "I know." The integration of the social Achilles who can talk about his troubles and the asocial Stewart who can cope only by putting them out of mind has not occurred. From Stewart's point of view, MUDs have stripped away some of his defenses but have given him nothing in return. In fact, MUDs make Stewart feel vulnerable in a new way. Before he was depressed; now he sees himself as addicted—and to MUDs. Although he hoped that MUDs would cure him, it is his time on MUDs that makes him feel sick. "When you feel you're stagnating and you feel there's nothing going on in your life and you're stuck in a rut, it's very easy to be on there for a very large amount of time."

Popular conceptions of what goes on during psychotherapy tend to see it as a "safe place" to talk, air problems, admit to fears, depression, and insecurity. But although MUDs provide a place for people to talk freely, they illustrate that therapy has to be more than a safe place. There is considerable disagreement among psychotherapists about what that "more" has to be, but within the psychoanalytic tradition, there is fair consensus that it involves a special relationship with a therapist in which old issues can come up and be addressed in new ways. When elements from the past are projected onto a relationship with a therapist, they can be examined. Distortions become data for better self-under-standing. A psychotherapy is not just a safe place, it is a work space or, more exactly, a "reworking" space.

For Stewart, MUD life gradually became a place not for reworking but for "reenacting" the kinds of difficulties that plagued him in the real. On the MUD, he declared his moral superiority over other players and lectured them about their faults, the exact pattern he had fallen into with Carrie in real life. He began to violate MUD etiquette by revealing certain players' real life identities and real life "bad behavior" to others. For example, he has "taken on" one prominent player, Ursula, a woman whom he thinks has taken advantage of her husband (in real life) and is trying to expose her as a "bad person" to other MUDders. Again, Stewart justifies his intrusive actions toward Ursula, as he justified his intrusions on Carrie's privacy, by saying that morality is on his side. "Ursula deserves to be exposed because of her outrageous behavior." A psychotherapist might try to help Stewart reflect on why he needs to be in the position of policeman, judge, and jury. Does he try to protect others because he feels that he has so often been left unprotected? How can he find ways to protect himself? In the context of a relationship with a therapist, Stewart might be able to address such painful matters. On the MUDs, Stewart avoids them by blaming other people. When other players point out that it is now Stewart who is crossing the threshold of inappropriate behavior, he becomes angry and self-righteous.

When most players talk about sharing confidences on MUDs more freely than in real life, they usually make reference to using anonymity to modulate their "exposure." In contrast, Stewart virtually renounced anonymity on MUDs and talked nonstop to anyone who would listen. Not surprisingly, this wholesale discarding of his most characteristic defenses (of withdrawal and reticence) made Stewart feel out of control. He compensated by trying even harder to "put things out of his mind" and denying that MUDding had been of any value. Again, the comparison with psychotherapy is illuminating. A skillful therapist would have treated Stewart's defenses with greater respect. They are tools for Stewart to use, and are potentially helpful if used with appropriate force.[10] A little withdrawal can, after all, be a good thing. But a naive psychotherapist might have encouraged using therapy to toss away defenses and "tell all." And that therapist would likely have had a similar unhappy result as Stewart achieved from his MUD confessions. Stewart's defenses would end up more entrenched than before, but it would be the psychotherapy rather than the MUDding that would be denigrated as a waste of time.

Stewart cannot learn from his character Achilles' experiences and social success because they are too different from the things of which he believes "himself" capable. Despite his efforts to turn Achilles into Stewart, Stewart has "split off" his strengths and sees them as possible only for Achilles in the MUD. In making this split between himself and the character he animates, Stewart denies or minimizes certain realities, for example, that he has made some steps toward turning his MUD-based virtual friendships into real life ones. He has visited other American MUD players and has had a group of the German players visit him in Boston, where he took them around the Freedom Trail.[11] Like an unsuccessful psychotherapy, MUDs have not helped him to learn how to bring good things "inside." MUDs can be a transitional tool, but not for everyone and in every circumstance.

In psychoanalytic language, Stewart has used MUDs to "act out" rather than "work through" his difficulties. The presence of a therapist can help to contain the impulse to simply repeat old patterns as well as encourage an examination of the meaning of the impulse itself. The relationship with the therapist, the transference, provides a context in which they can be most clearly examined. MUDs provide rich spaces for both acting out and working through. There are genuine possibilities for change and there is room for unproductive repetitions. The path chosen depends on the persons doing the MUDding, the kinds of emotional challenges they face, and the kind of emotional resources they bring to the game.

Stewart tried and failed to use MUDs for "therapeutic" purposes. Robert, whom I met after his freshman year in college, presents a contrasting case. Although Robert went through a period during which he looked equally if not more "addicted" to MUDs than Stewart, in the end, his time on MUDs provided him with a context for significant personal growth. It was therapeutic.

Working Through

During his final year of high school, Robert had to cope with severe disruptions to his family life. His father, a fireman, lost his job because of heavy drinking. The fire department helped him to find a desk job in another state. "My dad was an abusive alcoholic," says Robert. "He lost his good job. They sent him somewhere else. He moved, but my mom stayed in Pennsylvania with me. She was my security." College in New Jersey took Robert away from his high school friends and his mother. It was his first extended separation from her. He was lonely during the early days of his freshman year. Calls to his mother felt unsatisfying; they were too short and too expensive. And then Robert discovered MUDs.

For a period of several months, Robert MUDded over 80 hours a week. "The whole second semester, 80 hours a week," he says. During a time of particular stress, when a burst water pipe and a flooded dorm room destroyed all his possessions, Robert was playing for over 120 hours a week. He ate at his computer; he generally slept 4 hours a night. Much of the fun, he says, was being able to put his troubles aside. He liked "just sitting there, not thinking about anything else. Because if you're so involved, you can't think about the problem, your problems."

Much of Robert's play on MUDs was serious work because he took on responsibilities in cyberspace equivalent to those of someone with a full-time job. Robert became a highly placed administrator of a new MUD. It needed to be built and maintained. Players needed to be recruited and trained. Robert told me that he had never before "been in charge of anything." Now his MUD responsibilities were enormous.

Building and maintaining a MUD is a large and complicated task. There is technical programming work. New objects made by individual players need to be carefully reviewed to make sure that they do not interfere with the basic technical infrastructure of the MUD. There is management work. People need to be assigned jobs, taught the rules of the MUD, and put into a chain of command. And there is political work. The MUD is a community of people whose quarrels need to be adjudicated and whose feelings need to be respected. On his MUD, Robert did all of this, and by all accounts, he did it with elegance, diplomacy, and aplomb.

> I had to keep track of each division of the MUD that was being built, and its local government, and when the money system came in, I had to pay the local workers. All the officers and enlisted men and women on each ship got paid a certain amount, depending on their rank; I had to make sure they got paid on the same day and the right amount. I had to make sure people had the right building quota, not wasting objects, not building too much.

Robert's use of MUDs has something in common with Julee's constructive role-playing. Both nurtured themselves "in displacement." By helping others, they were able to get something for themselves.

Prior to taking this administrative job in a MUD, Robert had been known as something of a "cutup" on MUDs, someone accustomed to thumbing his nose at authority. He had gotten the administrative job because he was good at handling people and because of the amount of time he was willing to commit to MUDding. Robert says that his MUD responsibilities gave him new respect for authority ("Everyone should get to be a higher-up for a day," he says) and taught him something about himself. Robert discovered that he excels at negotiation and practical administration. He MUDded like a "man obsessed."

> When I MUDded with the computer I never got tired. A lot of it was like "Oh, Whoa, it's this time already." . . . Actually it is very obsessive. I remember thinking up at college, I was once thinking: "Boy, I was just on this too much. I should cut down." But I was not able to. It's like a kind of addiction. . . . It was my life. . . . I was like living on the MUD. . . . Most of the time I felt comfortable that this was my life. I'd say I was addicted to it.
> I'd keep trying to stop. I'd say, "OK, I'm not going on. I'm going to classes." But something would come up and I wouldn't go to my class; I wouldn't do what I wanted to do.

But at the end of the school year, Robert's MUDding was essentially over. Now he was working as a salesman, had gotten his first apartment, and had formed a rock band with a few friends. One week, he was MUDding "12 hours a day, for seven days." And then, the next week, he was not MUDding at all.

> Ever since I stopped MUDding I notice that this [real life] is more fun than virtual reality. I'm getting more active in my music. I notice a big difference between computer time and music time. I'm actually getting outside, seeing the sunlight. It's a lot different now, seeing the sun. . . . You can be more involved with friends, when you play frisbee, football, softball, whatever, you get involved in sports. . . . On the computer, you don't have sounds at all. . . . I do a lot with sound in the band. That's kind of become my focal point.

How had Robert's MUDding ended? For one thing, a practical consideration had intervened. At the end of the school year, his college took back the computer they had leased him for his dorm room. But Robert says there is another side to the story. He recognizes that by the time his computer was taken away, MUDding had already served several important emotional purposes for him.

First of all, Robert believes that during the period he was MUDding most intensively, the alternative for him would have been "partying and drinking," that is, getting into his father's kind of trouble. He says: "I remember a lot of Friday and Saturday nights turning down parties because I was on the computer. . . . Instead of drinking I had something more fun and safe to do." Robert drank to excess during high school and was afraid that he might become an alcoholic like his father. Mudding helped to keep his fears at bay.

Second, MUDding gave Robert a way to think about his father with some sympathy but reassured him about ways he was not like his father. Robert's behavior on MUDs reminded him of his father's addictions in a way that both frightened him and increased his compassion.

> It made me feel differently about someone who was addicted: I was a different person on the MUD. I didn't want to be bothered when I was on the MUD about other things like work, school, or classes. . . . I suppose in some way I feel closer to my Dad. I don't think he can stop himself from drinking . . . maybe with a lot of help he could. But I don't think he can. It's just like I had a hard time stopping MUDs.

Like Stewart, Robert acted out certain of his troubles on the MUDs—the fascination with pushing an addiction to a limit, for example. But unlike Stewart, after he was confident that he could function responsibly and competently on MUDs, he wanted to try the same behaviors outside of MUDs. And unlike Stewart, he was able to use MUDding as an environment for constructive self-revelation. In the "real," Robert found it painful to talk about himself because he often found himself lying about such simple things as what his father did for a living. Because it was easier to "walk away" from conversations on the MUD, Robert found that it was easier to have them in the first place.

> I talk about anything on the MUD . . . the computer is sort of practice to get into closer relationships with people in real life . . . the only thing you don't get from [communications on] the computer is emotions, but sometimes, that's good. If something is bothering me, you don't have to let the person know, or you can let the person know.

In sum, MUDs provided Robert with what Erik Erikson (1963) would have called a *psychosocial moratorium,* a central element in how Erikson thought about identity development in adolescence. Although the term *moratorium* implies a "time-out," what Erikson had in mind was not withdrawal. On the contrary, the adolescent moratorium is a time of intense interaction with people and ideas. The moratorium is not on significant experiences but on their consequences. Of course, there are never human actions that are without consequence, so therefore there is no such thing as a pure moratorium. Reckless driving leads to teenage deaths; careless sex, to teenage pregnancy. Nevertheless, during the adolescent years, people are generally given permission to try new things. There is a tacit understanding that they will experiment. Although the outcomes of this experimentation can have enormous consequences, the experiences themselves feel removed from the structured surroundings of one's normal life. The moratorium facilitates the development of a core self, a personal sense of what gives life meaning. This is what Erikson called identity.

Erikson developed these ideas about the importance of a moratorium during the 1950s and early 1960s. At that time, the notion corresponded to a common understanding of what "the college years" were about, a sense that was heightened with the mass availability of contraceptives and more open attitudes about sexual experimentation in the 1960s. Today, 30 years later, the idea of the college years as a consequence-free "time-out" seems remote. College is preprofessional and AIDS has made sexual experimentation a potentially deadly game. The years associated with adolescence are no longer a "time-out." But if our culture no longer offers an adolescent moratorium, virtual communities do. It is part of what makes them so attractive.

Erikson's ideas about stages did not suggest rigid sequences. His stages describe what people need to achieve before they can easily move ahead to another developmental task. For example, Erikson pointed out that successful intimacy in young adulthood is difficult if one does not come to it with a sense of who one is. This is the challenge of adolescent identity building. In real life, however, people frequently move on with incompletely resolved "stages," simply doing the best they can. They use whatever materials they have at hand to get as much as they can of what they have missed. MUDs are dramatic examples of how technology can play a role in these dramas of self-healing or self-repair. Stewart's case makes it clear that they are not a panacea. But they do present new opportunities as well as new risks.

Once we put aside the idea that Erikson's stages describe rigid sequences, we can look at the stages as a description of modes of experience that people work on throughout their lives. Thus, the "time-out" of an adolescent moratorium is not something that people pass through but a mode of experience that is necessary throughout functional and creative adulthoods. We take vacations to escape not only from our work but from our habitual social lives. They are a time during which adults are allowed to "play." Vacations give a finite structure to periodic adult "moratoria." Time in cyberspace reshapes the notion of vacation and moratoria because they may now exist as an always-available "window." Erikson (1963) wrote that "the playing adult steps sideward into another reality; the playing child advances forward into new stages of mastery" (p. 222). In MUDs, adults do both: They enter another reality and develop new dimensions of self-mastery.

Unlike Stewart, Robert came to his emotional difficulties and his MUDding with a solid relationship with a consistent and competent mother. This good parenting enabled him to identify with other players he met on the MUD who had qualities he wished to emulate. Even more important, Robert, unlike Stewart, was able to identity with the better self he played in the game. This constructive strategy is available only to people who are able to "take in" positive models, to bring other people and images of their better selves inside of them. When people like Stewart get stuck or become increasingly self-critical and depressed on

MUDs, it is often because deficits in early relationships have made it too hard for them to have relationships that they can turn to such purposes. From the earliest days of his life, Stewart's illness and his parents' response to it (his mother's breakdowns and his father's withdrawals) made him feel unacceptable. In his own words, "I have always felt like damaged goods." Life in cyberspace, as elsewhere, is not fair. Are MUDs "good or bad" for psychological growth? The answer is unreassuringly complicated. If you come to the games with a self that is healthy enough to be able to grow from relationships, they can be very good. If not, you can be in for trouble.

Deconstruction and Reconstruction

Within the psychoanalytic tradition, theorists write and talk about decentered selves and self as a cacophony of internalized objects; in cultural studies, theorists routinely use notions of decentering and fragmentation as a way to think about the self. This kind of metaphor has also found its way into computational images of the minds of machines and people; for example, in the computer world, people meet ideas about decentered selves through theories of "emergent" AI in which a community or society of agents or entities creates a sense of self through their interaction. There is a convergence of such decentered notions of self in the intellectual culture, but in the main, these ideas have remained confined to seminar rooms. That is, they have remained within the academy. Today, this state of affairs is changing. Experiences in cyberspace carry the notion of decentered and multiple ideas about the self.[12]

Ideas about mind come to be a living presence in the culture at large in many ways. In my view, one of the most powerful is when they are carried by evocative objects, "objects to think with" (Lévi-Strauss, 1960). They need not be material. For example, dreams and slips of the tongue were the "objects to think with" that brought psychoanalytic ideas into everyday life. People could "play" with their dreams (and others') and their slips (and those of their friends). MUDs are these kinds of objects. People are helped to construct ideas about identity-as-multiplicity by a new practice of identity-as-multiplicity in everyday life. With this comment, I am certainly not arguing that MUDs are causally implicated in the dramatic increase of people who are presenting with symptoms of what has come to be called "multiple personality disorder" (MPD)—or that people on MUDs have MPD, or that MUDding is "like" having MPD. What I am saying is that these two manifestations of multiplicity in the culture contribute to a general reconsideration of our traditional, unitary notions of identity.

A recent work on postmodernism and multiple personality by James Glass (1993) uses experiences of MPD to criticize postmodern notions of a fragmented self. Glass argues that, although postmodern theory reads like a great celebration of fragmentation, patients who suffer from MPD live that fragmentation, and it is nothing to celebrate. I read the relationship between postmodernism and multiple personality differently. Severe and repeated trauma leads a dissociative self to "split" and have its various aspects take on defensive roles, each walling itself off from the others, exclusively carrying certain memories and thereby protecting the rest of the "self-system" from their burden. If the *disorder* in MPD is the need for the rigid walls between the selves and the secrets they protect, then renewed interest in the multiple's society of selves may have a great deal to teach us about how to think about healthy selves. It may help us conceptualize healthy selves that are not unitary but that have flexible access to their many aspects. Similarly, MUDding and other ways of playing with "aspects of the self" in cyberspace are helping to construct a notion of identity as multiplicity.

Thus, MUDs are a context for constructions and reconstructions of identity and they are also a context for the deconstruction of the meaning of identity as "one." Through theories that stress the decentered subject and through the fragmented selves presented by patients, contemporary psychology confronts what is problematic and probably illusory in traditional notions of a unitary self. What is the self when it functions as a society?[13] What is the self when it divides its labors among its constituent "alters"?[14] Those burdened by post-traumatic dissociative disorders suffer the question; inhabitants of MUDs play with it. Experiences such as those that people are having in MUDs are giving more and more people an experience of talking about oneself in the third person and of seeing identity in terms of multiplicity. To put it too simply: In the MUD, one is not oneself.

Notes

1. This chapter draws on materials that have appeared in Sherry Turkle (1995), *Life on the Screen: Identity in the Age of the Internet.* For a general introduction to LambdaMOO and MUDding, see Pavel Curtis (1992), "Mudding: Social Phenomena in Text-Based Virtual Realities," and Amy Bruckman (1992), "Identity Workshops: Emergent Social and Psychological Phenomena in Text-Based Virtual Reality." On virtual community in general, see Allucquere Rosanne Stone (1992), "Will the Real Body Please Stand Up?" Amy Bruckman, a graduate student at MIT's Media Laboratory, was my research assistant and dialogue partner during a first summer of intensive work on MUDs in 1992; my understanding of this activity and its importance owes much to our collaboration.

2. You join a MUD using a "telnet" command from your home computer, which creates a connection to another computer where the MUD software "resides."

3. At this point, MUD participants on the Internet communicate through typing; systems in development will enable them to speak to and see each other through audio and video connections. This may well enhance the uses of MUDs for work collaboration. But MUDding may need to retain invisibility and anonymity to keep its appeal as an "identity workshop." Some graphical MUDs allow users to "buy" heads and bodies; proposals for future development include allowing players to use computer graphics techniques to create their physical representations in cyberspace.

4. MUDs can be built around a medieval fantasy landscape in which there are dragons to slay and gold coins and magical amulets to collect, or it can be a relatively open space in which you can play at whatever captures your imagination, both by playing a role and by participating in building a world.

5. This term is from Clifford Geertz (1983), cited in Gergen (1991, p. 113).

6. I have interviewed more than 200 persons who consider MUDding part of their daily lives. I typically meet with them for two interview sessions of 1 to 1½ hours.

7. This felicitous phrase was coined by Amy Bruckman (see Bruckman, 1992).

8. The Well, a virtual community, has a "topic" (discussion group) on "On Line Personae." In a March 24, 1992, posting to this group, F. Randall Farmer noted that in a group of about 50 Habitat users (Habitat is a MUD with a graphical interface), about a quarter experienced their on-line persona as a separate creature that acted in the same ways these people act in real life, and a quarter experienced their on-line persona as a separate creature that acted in ways these people do not in real life. A quarter experienced their online persona not as a separate creature but as one that acted like them; and another

quarter experienced their online persona not as a separate creature but as one that acted in ways unlike them. In other words, there were four distinct and nonoverlapping groups.

9. A rare exception here is the case of cyberspace "rape." When such extreme violations occur, the virtual community sometimes moves to forbid the offender to rejoin the game.

10. Defenses are usually born of situations where they were badly needed. But they can take on a life of their own. Our situations may change but the defense remains. For example, while Stewart was growing up, it may have been functional for him not to dwell on his difficulties, but the wholesale denial of his feelings is not serving him well. Therapy aims to give patients greater flexibility in dealing with the world as it is and a sense of distance, even a sense of humor, about their particular ways of distorting things. If one can look at one's behavior and say, "There I go again!" adjustments and compensations become possible. It becomes easier to see one's limitations yet maintain one's self-esteem.

11. Stewart attended a series of "pizza parties" that I held for MUDders in the Boston area. These were group sessions during which MUD participants had a chance to meet face-to-face and talk about their experiences. There, Stewart met a group of MUDders who used the games for role-play set in several cultures and time periods: They played medieval ladies, Japanese warriors, Elizabethan bards. Stewart said that he felt little in common with these players; in some ways, they threatened his sense that MUDding was a simple extension of life. Stewart repeatedly insisted that, despite the fact that his character was "technically" named Achilles, he was playing himself, and reminded the group several times that when he MUDded he actually asked other players to call him Stewart. But during one group session, after insisting for several hours that he plays no role on MUDs, a member of the "role-playing" MUDding group asked Stewart if he was married. Stewart immediately said yes, and then blushed deeply because he was caught in the contradiction between his insistence that he plays no roles in Gargoyle and his deep investment in his MUD marriage.

12. Other experiences with technology do this as well. See, for example, Gergen (1991) and Poster (1990).

13. See, for example, Minsky (1991).

14. See, for example, Ross (1989).

References

Bruckman, A. (1992, March). *Identity workshops: Emergent social and psychological phenomena in text-based virtual reality.* Unpublished manuscript. (Available via anonymous ftp from medialab.mit.edu., pub/asb/papers/Identity Workshop.)

Curtis, P. (1992). Mudding: Social phenomena in text-based virtual realities. *Proceedings of DIAC '92.* (Available via anonymous ftp from parcftp.xerox.com, pub/MOO/papers/DIAC92. {ps,txt}.)

Erikson, E. (1963). *Childhood and society* (2nd rev. ed). New York: Norton.

Geertz, C. (1983). *Local knowledge: Further essays in interpretive anthropology.* New York: Basic Books.

Gergen, K. (1991). *The saturated self: Dilemmas of identity in contemporary life.* New York: Basic Books.

Glass, J. M. (1993). *Shattered selves: Multiple personality in a postmodern world.* Ithaca, NY: Cornell University Press.

Lévi-Strauss, C. (1960). *The savage mind.* Chicago: University of Chicago Press.

Minsky, M. (1991). *The society of mind.* New York: Simon & Schuster.

Poster, M. (1990). *The mode of information: Poststructuralism and social context.* Chicago: University of Chicago Press.

Ross, C. (1989). *Multiple personality disorder: Diagnosis, clinical features, and treatment.* New York: John Wiley.

Stone, A. (1992). Will the real body please stand up? Boundary stories about virtual cultures. In M. Benedikt (Ed.), *Cyberspace: First steps* (pp. 81-118). Cambridge: MIT Press.

Turkle, S. (1984). *The second self: Computers and the human spirit.* New York: Simon & Schuster.

Turkle, S. (1995). *Life on the screen: Identity in the age of the Internet.* New York: Simon & Schuster.

Part V

The Mediated Self and Inquiry

11

Seeking a Path of Greatest Resistance: The Self Becoming Method

Thomas R. Lindlof
Autumn Grubb-Swetnam

If Anthropology is to embrace [the] relationship between Subject and Object (or between "Self" and "Other") it must, as it pursues the Other, also become able to pursue the Self. . . . Yet anthropologists, perhaps sensing that to expose the Self is necessarily to place it in jeopardy, have for the most part been unwilling to take such a gamble. Avoiding this risk with unusual virtuosity, they have refused to admit that the very possibility of dealing squarely with the Other is tied to the capacity to put the Self at stake. (Dwyer, 1979, p. 205)

The problem that Dwyer criticizes in anthropological practice is one that also haunts the still-emerging study of mediated communication: how researchers account for their situated encounters with those they study, and how this accounting must necessarily put their own self at risk. By denying the relationships that underpin the methodology of fieldwork, Dwyer asserts that researchers frame cultural scenes in the image of their own deeply held beliefs of scientific objectivity and progressive knowledge. The encounter simply becomes a means to this end. It is the theoretical project that prefigures the space a researcher carves out to meet the Other.[1]

The great irony is that it is only through this specific and always uncertain encounter between them that an objectified explanation can be produced at all. But how could it be otherwise? Or, as Dwyer (1979) asks, "What might the anthropological project look like when it begins consciously to embrace its special vulnerability?" (p. 206).

In this chapter, we ask: What might the project of studying mediated communication look like when it begins consciously to embrace its special vulnerability? Our question carries much the same urgency that Dwyer saw for his discipline.[2] During the past decade and a half, communication researchers have adopted the strategies of fieldwork to learn how mass media are received and woven into everyday life. Since the groundbreaking work of David Morley's *The 'Nationwide' Audience* (1980), Janice Radway's *Reading the Romance* (1984), and James Lull's (1990) naturalistic research of family television, qualitative studies have thrived partly because they have done what communication science was formerly reluctant to do: make some sustained contact with users of media on their own turf, record their actions and utterances in some realm of mediated experience, and construct readings of what these events mean. To an extent, the choice of taking trips to the worlds of people-being-audiences has produced its own sensuous rewards that the more remotely deployed techniques of quantitative science cannot match. Fieldwork is not just labor-intensive, it is socially intensive, and this can be a gratifying purpose in its own right.

The turn to qualitative research also refurbished the theoretical project of media studies. Questions about the cultural and ideological roles of the media now began to be answered in local contexts, with the concepts of polysemy and situational sense-making operating together as engines of a thoroughly semiotic process. Focus shifted to the lived process of being an audience. Instead of having a status as a category or variable, *audience* could be conceptualized as the cultural work of people enmeshed in their ongoing associations of family, subculture, gender and racial differences, and so on. For some scholars, even the name of the *audience* was replaced with such ideas as that of "discursive formations" of media language (Ang, 1991) or "interpretive communities" of people whose common tie is a repertoire of strategies for interpreting certain kinds of media texts (Jensen, 1991; Schroder, 1994). People could be characterized as sly "poachers" of the television commodity (Jenkins, 1988) or as cultural members who "accommodate" the texts and technologies of media in the routines of their life worlds (Anderson & Meyer, 1988). The empirical linchpin for advancing these and other designer constructs was the emergence of qualitative studies in their various forms.

Notably absent from most of the new audience literature, however, is very much consideration of the consequences of an embodied research presence on the actual production of knowledge. Researchers have turned out to have remarkably little to say about their own social selves in relation to what they experience and report. When they do appear, such discussions usually account for the negotiations of entry into a scene or the impact of field relations on access to informants or settings. Problems in the field are often depicted as a series of technical decisions that can be foreseen because our methods texts tell us to expect them and provide rules for managing them. Surprising problems can be coped with in an untroubled way by shifting their locus "out there," to the realm of an obtuse question or a difficult interviewee. In the rest of the research text, the writer recedes from the open view of readers, leaving the participants to act their parts in a theoretical play orchestrated from behind the curtain, à la *The Wizard of Oz*.

Arguably, the researcher's own perspective is a privileged species of the metakind that takes the naively performed perspectives of the Other as its object, and seeks to live vicariously inside, or beside, them long enough to understand their situated rationality. In this classic image, the researcher is a chameleon who can change demeanor and physical or social distance as the situation demands. By adjusting the "color" of his or her participation to match the distinctive qualities of each of the scenes being studied, the researcher hopes not only to fit easily into the action and observe with minimal disturbance, but that the process of changing the researcher's self-presentations to others also becomes invisible to the analysis.

At this point, we revisit the problem of what it means to describe the Other if a researcher's investment is only vicarious, part-time, or bracketed as a perspective belonging to someone else. What kind of knowledge is generated when researchers can adjust their investigative equipment freely and assuredly, while the Other continues to be constrained by the traditions and politics of their life worlds? What if the researcher realized that it is the unpredictable construction of his or her own Self that must be staked, or put at risk, so as to encounter the Other?

The recent interest in mediated cultures calls for another look at the assumptions underlying the researcher's own capacities and relationships in the field. If our subjects are ones of cultural identity and the codes and crossings characterizing the performance of identity, then we may need to rethink the research intervention as a strategy of subjecting the self to the risks of misunderstanding. The self becomes a method, in which the researcher's confrontation with insecurity not only is not avoided but is pursued.

Toward Dialogical Audience Research

In this section, we start to build a framework for a *dialogical* practice of inquiry. What we have in mind specifically is a version of "radical empiricism" (Jackson, 1989) in which the researcher's relations with what is observed are included in the tasks of description and interpretation, and in fact drive the greater part of those tasks. First, we look critically at the more familiar modes of researcher-participant relationship and thereby highlight some of the key differences (and points of contention) among methodologies.

The Monological

Traditional quantitative and cultural scholars of the critical issue and hegemony branches have typically conceived the audience as the site of exposure to media content. Content is viewed as either a causal or a catalytic agent that starts a cycle of behavioral, cognitive, or ideological effects. In these formulations, the concept of the audience is built up out of the terms of *location, presence, frequency, duration, fixed meaning, common engagement,* and *overdetermination of interpretation.*[3]

The concept of location accomplishes two tasks: (a) It establishes the place of the enabling agent of content—*on* television, *at* the movies, *with* the radio; and (b) by setting place as the site of content, it requires the process of *attendance,* which then becomes the explanation for the actions of viewing television, going to the movies, or listening to the radio. The presumptive character of the audience's action, then, goes like this: Attendance is required for "exposure" to occur as media content is always in a location.

Because exposure—the required condition of any media effect, according to the traditional view—requires attendance, the terms of presence, frequency, and duration come into the research purview. Individuals are considered audience members by their presence at the site of the content, and differences among audience elements are noted by virtue of their duration (e.g., how long an event of television exposure occurred) and frequency (how many such exposure events have occurred over time).

Any audience approach that includes an analysis of content also requires some belief in fixed meanings that inhere in the characteristics of content, so that the researcher's "reading" can be the basis of audience response. This belief can be asserted in several ways: by an empiricist study of a range of atomized content elements (content analysis); by a formalist inquiry of message signification (semiotic analysis); or by an essentialist argument founded on commonsense appeals (e.g., saying that a message is pornographic because of a presumed popular consensus that it is pornographic). Behind all of these techniques lies a belief in media content as a limit-setting field for whatever we can know of the audience. Even the liberating or audience-empowering claims of polysemy or openness enable an audience's interpretive moves by virtue of content characteristics: It is the *text* that is open or polysemic.

Audience surveys and the global claims of critics also assume that the methods of engaging media content practiced by an individual will have no, or at least trivial, impact on the relationship between the media content and the interpretation of it. The simplest way to accomplish this assumption is to presume that the content/medium presentation requires a common (or canonical) practice of engagement for an exposure to be authentic. In terms of methodology, this assumption makes an audience response easily transportable to the lab or the questionnaire or the focus group, because the meaning of exposure can be enacted anywhere and for anyone in generic form.

Finally, interpretation stands as a prime difficulty for all audience analyses. Many traditional hypothetico-deductive approaches deny interpretation by ignoring the possibility. Critical studies generally recognize that individuals do interpret content, but then do not account for how it occurs locally. Silverman (1983) sets the dilemma for us by describing "readerly" and "writerly" interpretations. Readerly interpretations are overdetermined by the text. Meaning is invoked as a cognitive reflex in response to characteristics of the content. Writerly interpretations view the text as a resource to be assembled and reassembled in accordance with the interpretive achievements of the audience member. Most traditional frameworks in media research, however, grant writerly interpretations to the analysts and assume readerly responses from the audience.

What we see in this brief overview is that for traditional and many critical analysts, with their emphasis on content, the audience itself is often a neglected site of analysis. Questions of how audience members actually engage with content on their own time, or what they do in relation to media discourse but *without* exposure to content, usually go unasked, let alone unanswered. In much of the research derived from this paradigm, "human subjects" function as tokens of some set of audience elements that is consistent with the exposure model cited above. To be brought off successfully, these studies must honor a "contract" of role incumbencies governing the researcher's performances as *the agent of inquiry* and the subjects' performances as *objects of study:* the researcher, by directing the subjects' attention to certain features in their perceptual field, most of which are organized around a reference to media content; the human subject, by selectively performing many of the norms of good faith, civility, attentiveness, and obedience to authority that are followed in similar situations of obligation.

How well the research subject performs depends on how closely he or she co-orients with the presentation of the audience construct, understands his or her part to play in the protocol, and conforms behaviorally to expectations. In other words, the subject should follow instructions in the strict sense (which, of course, assumes the moral obligation to cooperate in the first instance). Beyond these basic role requirements, which are essentially passive, the subject is not held responsible for the outcomes of the project or even for the value of his or her own participation in it. The researcher bears the burden of proof for demonstrating high-quality data by determining the correct type and level of measurement, ensuring adequate testing conditions, and controlling against unwarranted variance in the key measures.

In faithfully playing a part in this protocol, the subject can contribute only what the researcher is prepared to expect. An individual may state an opinion in a way meant to be taken ironically. But if irony is not an element of the coding scheme, then irony will not constitute any part of what is coded. With the customary use of closed-ended response options or coding schemes applied to "free" responses, the subject's creative act will either go unrecorded or be edited to fit an existing category.

Moreover, specifics of the subject's identity are either deemed irrelevant or placed in the anonymous confidence of the investigator. The history of the individual has importance only to the extent that it can be refined and aggregated as an attribute (e.g., marital status or race) for later analysis. The net effect of this use of the human subject is to reduce the varied contextual and biographical features of the audience phenomena under study. The researcher thus colonizes the human subject by constraining the individual's means of expression and by enforcing specific definitions of the research project at all points in its execution.

This colonization is successful if data can be obtained without any serious "contamination" resulting from wayward readings of the research situation (Krieger, 1991). In their use of such precautions as rewards for compliance, concealed or misdirected cues to the study's hypotheses, and the use of redundancy and very simple structure in the language of questionnaire items, such projects betray a degree of cynicism in their view of unrestrained human behavior. These precautions are basically hedges against the inclinations of ordinary folk to be lazy or stubborn, to be mischievous, or to fail to get the "same message" that everyone else gets. Shortcomings of validity are the price researchers must be willing to pay if people are induced into contexts not of their choosing, *without* using the standard precautionary tools.

Most of these observations apply to objectivist inquiry, but a similar contract is evident in many critical audience studies. The original interests in such studies are often the ideological properties of a media text. *Duration* and *frequency of exposure* may not be familiar terms for these inquiries, but a background of attendance and common engagement at a text's location is generally assumed. Discourses already operating in the text, usually at a more latent level than its denotative signs, provide a stable reference for eliciting audience discourse. Themes of interpretation are then explained in terms of selected social-structural positions such as class or gender that cut broadly and unevenly across the media-using population. The main reason for studying the audience, then, is to gauge the text's "effectivity" in fostering subjectivity. Some of the actual sayings of these audience members may be reported, but the researcher often frames them in terms of the critical theory imported into the study. Readers may be given some of the subjects' personal background or their ideas about the project, but this material does not usually enter very far into the analysis itself. It is enough to know the individual by his or her representation of a social category, which itself is a proxy for an ideological subject position. Evidence of the researcher's own role in the joint constructions of meaning in the research project is rarely provided.

To the extent that one actor speaks univocally for the representations of the other, the protocol just described is a *monological* contract. The monological contract privileges the researcher as an agent of inquiry who is duty-bound to repress his or her ability to make the project an ongoing object of critical study by all who participate in it. Conversely, the subject is positioned as an alert, but passive object of study who is barred from engaging creatively and collaboratively with others as an agent of inquiry into his or her own media practices or the project itself. In fact, discussion of the project as an event of arbitrary convention is usually discouraged. Both parties uphold the fiction that the artificial, even perverse, nature of their relationship is actually quite necessary. In the jargon of today's popular therapy, the two are "codependents" in an inquiry that refuses to recognize its own conspiracy.

The Dialogical

The monological contrasts with those theorists and researchers who consider the *social action* of receiving and using media (e.g., Anderson & Meyer, 1988; Ang, 1991; Jensen, 1991; Lindlof, 1988; Lull, 1988; Radway, 1988). To start with, these theorists organize their analysis not around exposure to media content but around the situated relationship: individuals who are situated in historical time, place, and social reference. Generally, they assume a socially constructed reality that is the emergent product of local discursive action. Their analyses have as their explanatory objects the accomplishments of meaning that empower that reality. None of the audience terms useful in describing the traditional and most critical approaches would be denied importance by this view. Social action analysts, however, hold these terms as problematics for which there could be local and recognizable empirical traces.

For example, the study of media effects does not depend on a location in which the totality of effects *must* occur, although location can be important. That is, media texts are not only, or even primarily, objects found in some locations; they are also subjects dispersed throughout social discourse. One did not have to attend the *Forrest Gump* film circa 1994 to know the character of Forrest Gump or to be able to appropriate signs of the character for a social purpose. Fragments of Gump turn up in casual conversation, speeches, stores, clothing, and television and print venues, all of which attest to the ramifying power of a modern cultural commodity. Our "exposure" to a text is not specifically located; we can always turn to it as a situated resource well beyond the limits of the artist's invention or the initial product release.

By questioning exposure and location, the givens of attendance, frequency, and duration also come into question. It may be that "heavy" users of media are different from "light" users. But until we know how heavy use and light use are actually practiced, and how those practices inform the differences of frequency or duration we observe, the distinctions are of little explanatory value.

Meaning, methods of engagement, and interpretation are, of course, the center of study of social action. As already noted, media texts are engaged in widely dispersed social contexts that are only partially under our control. But media texts are not only material objects of attention and use in social life, they are also appropriated as subjects in imaginative constructions of the self. An audience, then, is constituted in the social action that accommodates media content both as objects and as subjects.

This move away from a site-based exposure model may be due to some extent to actual shifts in the reception infrastructure. Arguably, our postmodern epoch is marked by an intensifying penetration of social scenes by media technologies (Gergen, 1991; Harvey, 1989). We experience little surprise at encountering television at the sports stadium, doctor's waiting room, or fast-food restaurant; or the CD kiosk in the bookstore; or the jogger following her route with audiocassette player in hand. As media become more mobile, interactive, and niche-marketed, users' ordinary literacies—or (to use a less print-biased term) *competencies* of media knowledge that people cultivate and apply informally— may become more situational, fluid, and self-reflexive. These changes do not mean the dissolution of relationships as an object of study. Families, peer groups, and so forth continue to function as more or less bounded contexts for contacting media. It does mean, however, that these relational bonds are now subject to continual morphological change and vigorous public debate, particularly at the intersections between them, and partly as they have to adapt to new media systems.

This social action approach—of analyzing the practices by which an audience comes into being—brings forward a critique of the normative protocol we termed the *monological*. In particular, it suggests the futility of investigating the expo- sure-effect (or exposure-interpretation) circuit so as to explain *how* meanings are achieved. Radway (1988) writes:

> In so constructing the circuit of exchange as the crucial site for research, we inevitably begin by assuming that individuals in the audience are already stitched into a particular kind of relation with the speaker or writer. . . . Because they appear in our discourse only as the receivers of messages which are themselves both temporally and theoretically privileged, those individuals are rarely if ever presented as active subjects, let alone as producers of culture. (pp. 361-362)

Strategies of ethnographic inquiry, in particular, claim to start from the *practices* of media engagement, not the text, and give priority of study to the panoply of social-contextual and historical determinants of individual interpre- tation. As mentioned in the introduction, however, naturalistic media research has typically sought to make its methods transparent. By disturbing the scene minimally, so the argument goes, one is better able to move around freely and thus achieve a greater descriptive realism. With its promise of the rewards that come from detachment, there is of course more than a passing resemblance to the monological contract.

But any act of research is always a socially accomplished intervention. Therefore, any knowledge we have of communication technologies, texts, and their uses in local cultures reflexively embeds a certain stance or perspective in its own description. We cannot get rid of the embodied perspective by becoming more diligent scribes who can be trained to write more accurately or neutrally about the events we witness. We do often learn to write more competently *within* the codes of the perspective, but it is not possible to write our way *out* of a perspective. Nor is it simply a matter of making relativistic claims about the equivalence of *our* understandings and *their* understandings. Certainly cultural scenes are literally peopled with perspectives, so the more perspectives we (as researchers) are enabled to learn about, the less derivative our accounts will be. But a perspective is a highly practical device that articulates where we stand in relation to others, and, therefore, it always enacts a power claim; we can only postulate the type of original mode of language practice in which a given perspective can be presentable or negotiable without constraint (see Habermas, 1984). By denying an embodied research stance, or by claiming special protection for it under the mantle of a disinterested, colonizing inquiry, researchers decide implicitly to ignore or edit the power-laden terms of engagement that would permit them to hear the Other's voice in at least some of its contextual determinations.

Alternatively, the inquirer might actually embrace the coeval ontology of the ethnographic situation: that is, the temporally contingent action of creating and managing a "project" within the circumstances of the Other's life world. By inhabiting a shared dialogical frame, researcher and participant can mutually experience the breakdowns of communicative coherence (events of not-under-standing and understanding-repair) that often lead to a surer analytic grasp of social rules or cultural meanings (Agar, 1982; Fabian, 1979; Lindlof, 1995). If the participant had to learn at one time to be culturally competent, what will the researcher miss by not going through at least some of the same faltering encultura-tion? If the participant does not always act "correctly," why should the researcher resist being incorrect? Why should the researcher avoid the throat-catching tension of not knowing the right utensil to pick up, the right word to use?

It follows from this reasoning that the researcher's *positioning* must be a key part of this learning methodology. Positioning, here, is what Davis and Harré (1991) call "the discursive process whereby selves are located in conversations as observably and subjectively coherent participants in jointly produced story lines" (p. 48). As a process of fashioning a self in the critical and supportive presence of others, positioning is accomplished in the stories we tell for making sense of our own and others' lives. Like all other selves, the researcher-self strives to formulate actions that are consistent and morally accountable within contexts and, to a lesser degree, across contexts. Efforts at positioning receive essential support from others because the communicative work of any discourse situation requires granting a "self" to each of the interlocutors. Unless the others who are with us also understand and practice the local rhetorics of self, our own efforts will prove absurd. The self also undergoes critical supervision: who one purports to be finally comes down to the test of how convincing (and situationally warranted) others judge "the story of me" to be.

What is special about the social action researcher's positioning is the willingness to strategically forgo some of the usual aversions to risk to ontological security that undergird the production of a social self (Giddens, 1991). In effect, the researcher *wagers* his or her scarce resources of insecurity to confront and, we hope, understand the Other (Dwyer, 1979). These are moments when the method is literally working very hard. The researcher's own need to sustain some personal stability, and a periodic longing to tell the familiar self-stories of one's own community, however, prevent a total commitment to dialogic confrontation, which is why the research intervention must be strategic, and why the resources for doing it are scarce.

Problematics from the researcher's autobiography often start the chain of thinking that leads to an idea for inquiry. Consciously or not, the researcher may seek some partial solution to a predicament of self in the work of the project. Sometimes drawing upon familiar resources or informants from his or her local world (imbricating personal attachments with the demands of the inquiry), the researcher tries to craft a persona so as to *normalize* a job that might otherwise be perceived by the participants as alien (Van Maanen, 1981). By being genuine, or socially useful to them in some way, the researcher aims to put their anxieties or skepticism to rest, to present the self in the best light as the kind who can and should be trusted. The researcher's power to impose this, however, is always chimerical: The normalization of a project is more a struggle over rights, appearances, tastes, definitions, labels, ethics—in short, over identity.

Dialogue is the model for this inquiry, but it is different than the warm sentimentality often evoked by "dialogue" (Crapanzano, 1992). Dialogical theory conceives the self as the multiple themes of agency that animate the utterances, genre, and body performances of social communication (Conquergood, 1991; Holquist, 1990; Taylor, 1991). Each party participates in the rhetorical positioning of the other through coordinated, embodied action, and it is only by explicating dialogical process that a project achieves its purpose of understanding (Conquergood, 1991; Taylor, 1991). This process of facing, doubting, explicating, accepting, and reporting *difference* in joint action is described by Jackson (1989) as radical empiricism:

> We make ourselves experimental subjects and treat our experience as primary data. Experience, in this sense, becomes a mode of experimentation, of testing and exploring the ways in which our experiences conjoin or connect us with others, rather than the ways they set us apart. In this process we put ourselves on the line; we run the risk of having our sense of ourselves as different and distanced from the people we study dissolve, and with it all our pretensions to a supraempirical position, a knowledge that gets us above and beyond the temporality of human existence. (p. 4)

Feminist inquiry, in particular, strives to locate and understand concrete experience by the use of collaborative research strategies. Through its critical interrogations of such deeply ingrained social science oppositions as subject/object, body/consciousness, and value/knowledge, feminism has opened awareness of the discursive bases of gendered identity and power (Smith, 1990a; Westcott, 1979). In doing so, it challenges the social practices by which subordinated selves are rendered invisible or inadequate in the routine languages of the dominant.

Such research practice "decolonizes" its human subjects by recognizing the agency of the participants and by including them as partners in the process of inquiry. Confrontation and risk are its distinguishing marks. For the participants, it is mostly a risk of their interest being misunderstood, neglected, or abused. They may come to know who *we* are (as friends or apprentices or hangers-on or whatever), but they may be unsure, even apprehensive, about what we "do" as analysts. The researcher's own immediate risks run the gamut from the psychological to the physical but finally end up in the terrain of epistemological uncertainty: the crossing of cultural borders and the prospect of facing an indeterminate process of sorting second-order, analytic interpretations from the first-order coeval experience (Rose, 1990; Van Maanen, 1979). We may come to know who *they* are (as friends or mentors or whatever), but we frequently wonder how the relationships we've developed cloud or clarify our access to the "authentic." The relationship is both a method and an object of analysis, and in that duality lie the inevitable ambiguities of ethnographic knowledge.

In the rest of this chapter, we engage in dialogues about the dialogical mode. The context of these dialogues is the second author's dissertation (Grubb-Swetnam, 1994), which centered on the ways in which women negotiate their identities of body, sexuality, and race through their experiences with magazines marketed to women. As supervisor of her dissertation, the first author was one of many voices in Autumn's "shadow dialogues" (Crapanzano, 1992), paralleling, intersecting with, and ultimately informing her flows of experience in the primal scenes of research.[4] We met at regular intervals over a period spanning April 1993 through February 1994.[5] In these transcribed conversations, field dilemmas are told, expanded, and worked upon, but rarely resolved. Other texts bring out telling incidents or comment on issues of research practice. Most of what follows, unless noted otherwise, is narrated by Autumn. It is not our desire to show an ideal practice but to illustrate—by way of stories, conversations, and commentaries—how the varied biographical, political, and interpersonal positionings of a researcher's self constitute much of the work of inquiry.

Shadow Dialogues

Origins and Decisions

This dissertation project began to take shape in conjunction with my growing awareness of the many ways women have been and are silenced in mainstream philosophy, history, education, medicine, familial relations, media, and professions. The awareness of their silencing came from personally experiencing the act of being silenced as well as reading a variety of texts that discussed, made visible, and theorized about this silencing within various institutions.

The initial connection between the silencing of women's experiences in our culture and the dissertation was made in a personal journal entry dated 6/3/92. I wrote:

> I am awakened into being as a woman, reading and consuming material that is unlike anything I've experienced before in an educational setting. The classes I am taking expose me to new ways of understanding myself and my relationships with others. And yet this excitement comes tainted with sadness, for I become more aware, with each new article or book, of the level to which the silencing of women's lives has been sustained. As I learn more, I mourn more for the loss of women's history, the untold stories of the millions of women before me. Maybe an important reason to do the dissertation . . . as a way to make visible and document women's stories.

Clearly from this journal entry, I was beginning to realize I wanted to make a contribution by breaking that silence, in some fashion, through documenting and analyzing women's stories. As this idea began to develop, I was exposed to the work of feminist scholars Dorothy Smith, Ann Ferguson, and Patricia Hill-Collins. These women moved me intellectually with powerful theoretical and methodological concepts that later served as foundations for my "female-centered" dissertation.

Smith's (1987, 1990a) methodology compelled me to begin from the standpoint of women. In addition, it required me to have knowledge of myself as a researcher, and to extend that knowledge to include my own subjectivity, my experiences, and location in the everyday world. Smith points out that beginning from the standpoint of women opens the investigation to include the perspectives and experiences of those who are interviewed. This in turn propels the researcher to locate these testimonies in the social organization that gives meaning to the experiences from which they arise. Smith's (1990b) explication of femininity as discourse helped me to understand and "crack open" the gendered communications the women and I participated in during the interviews.

Ann Ferguson (1991) offered the phrase *sexual/affective production,* which identifies the material labor women are expected to provide in our culture when engaged in relationships of a familial, marital, or sexual nature. This phrase was used in the dissertation to identify information informants read in the magazines that indicated aspects of that material labor. During the interviews, sexual/affective production was a topic the women often described with anger, disappointment, or despair.

Patricia Hill-Collins (1990) provided the concept "outsider-within": individuals who are personally identified with one culture but must survive in another culture that is dominant (African Americans, lesbians, women). This concept was useful when attempting to describe the interpretive communities of lesbians and African American women who use women's magazines that inscribe the ideal woman as white and heterosexual.

Two other important influences on the dissertation project were the cultural studies theorists Stuart Hall and Janice Radway. Both of these writers argue that we interpret the media in ways that are influenced by our local and particular positions in society. Their contributions to understanding media audiences helped me to interpret the influence of race, class, gender, and sexuality on the informants' media use, and to understand how the women made sense of that media use.

The impact of these five writers is evident in a journal entry dated 1/26/93:

> I've got it! I'm going to look at what women do with magazines marketed to them. And I want to explore how a variety of women make use of these magazines. For example, how do lesbians and African Americans describe and make sense of their use of women's magazines in comparison to white and heterosexual women? What are the similarities and differences? What are the similarities and differences in women's interpretations of the magazines' textually mediated discourse of femininity? My own use and interpretation of these magazines can help me understand the women's experiences.

Little did I know then how these women's experiences and interpretations would affect my understanding of my own magazine use and interpretation! The impact those stories had on me, I think, is hinted in the purpose of the dissertation: to make visible women's diverse stories about media use so we are more mindful in our own media choices, to learn that we can be more of an active agent in choosing and creating media that promote who we *really* want to be as women.

While I was interviewing, I was very naive about the risks I would be taking in the interview process. I perceived the project and process as exciting and fun. I looked forward to talking with each woman about using women's magazines. I did not anticipate, at that point, the intensity of the interviews or the critical reflection that the process of interviewing and doing the dissertation would prompt in me.

Tom Lindlof became my dissertation committee chair in spring 1992. I had originally requested that he and another faculty member cochair my committee. Both of them nixed the cochair idea. Because policy required the chair to be a tenured faculty member, I chose Tom. This decision made me somewhat uncomfortable because he was a male and I feared negative reactions to my female-centered dissertation ideas. I also was worried about our ability to develop a relationship that would foster an acceptable level of understanding whereby I would get my needs met by him as a mentor and he would receive a contribution from me that met his standards. He scared me. I viewed him as a great academic guru and questioned my ability to produce work he thought to be worthy. But I didn't let this fear overwhelm me. I was bound and determined to "give it a go." At that time, creating work that was of quality *in his eyes* was the only risk I perceived.

Origins and Decisions—Tom

My hesitance to sign on as chair of Autumn's committee stemmed from some long-overdue thinking about my own practices. Over the years, my position had been that students should consider dissertation subjects that have salience for them personally in addition to being significant theoretically. Knowing that this endorsement of identity articulation could pose dangers to the successful (read: disciplined) prosecution of a project, if left unchecked, I adopted a kind of tough-love persona who offers ideas and critical comment but withholds solutions and ultimately lets them go to do what they said they would do. If the dissertation *as a process* is to mean something, the student should be able to make mistakes. Let them go through the preparations, drills, and simulations, then pull a few of the safety nets for the main performance. Such was my creed.

Yet I saw in Autumn and a few others I was advising that this style could incur costs. I was wary that they might expect more empathy, attentiveness, and "ego reinforcement" of me than I could give, or would even want to give. My deskside manner, I was finding out, was not my strong suit. Maybe my persona was more tough than love. And as a man advising a woman on a project involving women's communication issues, there might be dimensions to the relationship that escape me until it is too late. Autumn wrote to me,

> So, how do I feel about a man directing my dissertation? It scares the hell out of me. . . . I must believe that you will try to understand, that you will see this as important to do and to trust your expertise in guiding me through this process to help me in reaching my goal. Trusting you is a part of my growth.

I began to realize how profoundly this trust exposes a student to the failings of the adviser.

I also felt that students might start to live so far *inside* their work, if conceived as a personal project, that they might not be ready for those outside voices who must be addressed, such as other committee members, the human subjects board, and the informants themselves, to name just a few. The danger, as Krieger (1991) remarks, is that

> we [social scientists] use standard terms and depersonalized voices that camouflage the self and make it conventional in order to make it acceptable and in order to communicate our thoughts. Yet curiously, these very attempts at protection exacerbate vulnerability problems. For if a work that was supposed to protect the self is criticized by an outsider, the greatest threat is not that the work will be found faulty, but that the self behind the work will be exposed. (p. 32)

For Autumn, in July 1993, it was the human subjects board that questioned the self behind the work:

Autumn: The human subjects board—a story of power-over, masculinity, and homophobia. No introductions. "Welcome to the Inquisition," was the greeting I received. Opened for questions, the all-white participants stared at the table except for the male at the opposite end who engaged me in eye contact and began, "I understand you will develop a first set of informants who will then identify a second group, who you will then introduce yourself to and ask them if they would be willing to participate?" I answered yes. "No," he replied forcefully. The chair began to explain how it would be inappropriate for me to identify as "one of them"—meaning, I assumed, African Americans and lesbians. Making the assumption that I, like them, viewed these groups as "others," they seemed to be trying to counsel me as one of their own as to how I might be perceived by my informants as "othering" them. Feeling uncomfortable, I simply closed down and responded with, "No problem. I will ask that all informants contact me first if they are interested in participating. I understand the importance ethically of letting them 'self-identify' their race and sexual minority status to me as a researcher." Unfortunately, the board members made visible their lack of participation with these communities and obviously could not imagine for a moment that as a white female I might regularly engage with these communities on a social and personal level.

I found myself uneasily agreeing both with her and with them. I knew the board's purview in this matter: A dissertation is an institutional undertaking, and Autumn must act as the institution's agent. The board was just not ready to approve a stance that foregrounds her self in solidarity with her subjects. But I also believed in the rightness of her approach to recruiting informants. I knew Autumn would not abuse her informants, no matter what they ended up disclosing to her. And I felt sure the style of interviewing she used was not intended to marginalize or objectify them but to encourage a common goal of understanding their life contexts (for a sampling of this view, see Kauffman, 1992; Kleinman, Stenross, & McMahon, 1994; Lindlof & Grodin, 1990). In the end, I decided, here was a situation in which she would perform without a net. She would make her own judgment of what it means to align or not align with *their* interests.

Not long afterward, I got this e-mail message from her:

> I have great news! I escaped to the big pond today to study. Before I left the house a friend of mine called and said she would like to introduce me to a new friend of hers. She brought her out to the pond this afternoon and she's a black lesbian. Not only is she willing to be interviewed but offered to give me names of other black lesbians in the area!!! Hurrah! I was most worried about identifying this population and I have finally made a contact. I knew you could relate to the exciting feeling of successfully gaining entrance into a community you desire to study.

She was right; I could relate.

Beauty Must Suffer

Autumn in dialogue with Tom: My mother gave me contradictory signals about what it meant to be an adult woman. Sometimes she would tell me I didn't need a man in my life. She assured me I could do and be whatever I wanted. At other times she would contradict those messages and tell me I was required to wear restricting undergarments such as bras, girdles, and pantyhose, or high heels, makeup, and a particular hairdo. When I would attempt to bring together those two types of messages, they didn't make sense. They didn't fit. So, in my own personal way, I tried to ignore the messages, "You should wear certain clothes and look a certain way." I paid more attention to the "you can do whatever you want" and "you don't need a man to succeed" messages.

When I ask the informants to tell me stories about things their family of origin told them about what it means to be feminine, I shared a story about my mother. When I was little she would curl my hair in brush rollers and put me to bed. I would cry and whine because those rollers hurt my head and made it very difficult to sleep. When I complained my mother would tell me to "dry up . . . beauty must suffer." I remember thinking when I grow up, *this* beauty wasn't going to suffer!

This story got a reaction from the informants every time, ranging from, "Well that's nothing! I tried to sleep with my hair rolled on orange juice cans!" to "My mother never did anything like that to me, but she always told me to act like a lady, and be nice, smile."

The cultural messages we hear about "appropriate" women from family members, the media, mentors, and partners sometimes generate anger. The ongoing struggle between the "beauty must suffer/be nice, smile" dogma and honoring our personal voice in the journey to discover who we are and who we really want to be is painful. As the women in the dissertation described their struggles between these external and internal messages, I supported their stories by sharing a journal entry:

> I have come to realize in myself that I could not and did not begin to generate (let alone hear) my original thought and voice until I accepted my natural, wild beauty. Until I quit cinching my waist and chest into confining, uncomfortable clothing; until I quit hating myself as an imperfect commodity; until I explored that pain and gently laid it down I could not hear and know and believe in my original thought and voice. I could not breathe in whole breaths and could not move in freedom and grace as long as I accepted the commodity model for my Self. Now that I know this, I must constantly re-create this knowing of self-acceptance that struggles against some unseen ideological circle that is maintained in cultural systems.

I think, in my own struggle, I began to feel angry when I could not sustain or choose environments that allowed me to honor my internal voice of who I am. The dissertation helped me to further develop strategies of creating environments where I thrive and grow. The process of doing the dissertation was, in fact, one of those environments:

Tom: What does Mark [Autumn's partner] think of you while you are doing this research?

Autumn: Well, once I sat him down and said, "Here's what I've come up with, Mark. What do you think? Do you think I'm being true to who I am?" His response was, "Yes, Autumn, the way I see you is all this time in your life you have been like a fish out of water, and then feminist theory came along and now you are fish out of water with a purpose."

I showed Mark this statement in the transcripts and asked him to explain what he meant. He told me he had observed me, before my graduate work, in ways that suggested I was out of my environment (fish out of water), angry and frustrated, flopping around without any real direction. He told me he felt my coursework and the process of doing the dissertation helped me to begin finding ways of creating environments that were healthier for me, turning my anger in directions that would encourage positive change (fish out of water with a purpose).

One of the informants, named Rose, met with me after I had finished writing the dissertation and listened to me explain the analysis chapters. Upon finishing my explanation, she smiled and said,

> You've shown how they [the culture] have given us things to wear [socially acceptable characteristics of the "appropriate" woman], but that those things have nothing to do

with who we really are. You have made our voices visible so others can understand this relationship.

Although Mark's and Rose's comments are true, they do not reveal the anger and frustration I felt during the interview process. These feelings are revealed in the conversations I had with Tom:

Autumn: I've been thinking about when you talked about using critical theory. You said we should be cautious that we don't force the story, that we don't see something or believe something that is not there [in the data]. I've thought about that a lot and what I wanted to be there are "wild women" who are autonomous and that don't buy into the male-described view of femininity, and that's where my anger and frustration come in. Asking those questions like, "What do you like about your body?" I ask them to describe characteristics they perceive to be feminine beauty. Then I turn right around and ask them which of those characteristics they think they exhibit. Sitting there again and again and not one of them saying, "All of those characteristics," or "I love my whole body." Not a single one of them. And when I reflect on that, I wish just one of them would say, "I love my whole body and being in my body." But it is just not there in the interview transcripts. I don't want to see women who hate themselves.

Tom: But so far you haven't come across women who care to be autonomous?

Autumn: On certain levels, I wouldn't say absolutely not. On certain levels there are women who are reflecting that autonomy, but regarding their bodies they certainly aren't. When I ask those questions and I get that nonverbal facial reaction that's become so familiar to me, it's like I slapped them and they literally pull back. Then they sit there for a long time and maybe pull out one or two of all the ones they have mentioned and say, "Well, maybe I'm compassionate, " or "Maybe I reflect a self-assurance about myself some of the time." But there is not a lot of energy in their tone of voice. At least that is how I am interpreting those kinds of answers. When I ask them to reflect . . .

Tom: How do you ask them?

Autumn: The way I get into it is, I say, "What images in the media would you say reflect feminine beauty? Who do you see in the media that reflects those traits?" Some immediately give names and traits. Others would say, "What I perceive as feminine beauty is not in the media." They are very clear about that and I ask them to explain what they mean. And then I say, "For you, what characteristics exemplify feminine beauty? Of those characteristics, what ones do you exhibit?" The other questions about their bodies come after the magazine questions. I just ask, "What do you like about your body?"

Tom: And that's where they break down a bit and don't come up with an answer right off?

Autumn: Well, there is this dead pause. A major dead space there. And I'm sitting there in the chair, and now it's getting to the point where when I get to those questions, I'm starting to think, "Oh, let's skip this one."

Even though I obviously had moments in the interviews when I yearned for the women to be something they weren't feeling at the time, other moments affirmed a positive experiencing of ourselves in our bodies. Those moments are exemplified in one of my talks with Tom as we discussed how informants reacted to the interview process.

Autumn: They want to be reassured that what they did [in the interview] was appropriate and they are not going to be put in the "weird" category. I had a lot of them at the end of the interview ask me, "I hope that what I said was what you wanted." I had some ask, "Was I normal?" or, "Did I say really odd things compared to what others have said about that question?"

Tom: So, when people ask you if they are normal, what do you say?

Autumn: The first time a woman asked me that, well, she was 19 years old, anorexic, and bisexual . . . an interesting identity all packed into 19 years old. When she asked me if her answers were normal, I looked back at her with her youthful skin, her whole appearance a lovely feminine youth, and I smiled and said, "Every individual that I have interviewed, they have absolutely blown me away in their beauty while struggling with these issues. You did an excellent job and I really appreciate you being willing to share this stuff." She got this big smile on her face and everything was great. I tried to use that afterward when people would ask that. It seemed to work so well and that really was my honest feeling. The women really did strike me as intensely beautiful when they struggled with trying to make sense of their life as a woman and what magazines have meant to them throughout their lives.

Passing

Another thread weaving in and out of my personal relationships and the act of doing the dissertation involved creating the self moment by moment. I interviewed women who talked about choosing new ways of presenting their selves and experiencing resistance from their loved ones and friends. I watched my own friends in this struggle and experienced the struggle myself. I discussed this in dialogue with Tom:

Autumn: I believe that part of the way we relate to people is grounded in whether they are married or single, heterosexual or homosexual, white or black, male or female. This has all come home very closely to me. Last month, one of my friends left her husband. Two weeks ago, another one of my friends told her husband to move out. What I've noticed in myself and my other friends is that it becomes different for us to deal with these women. Because now we have to deal with them in a different way. One of the women leaving her marriage is in a period of transition, becoming an out lesbian, and I recently observed one of our friends asking her, "So, is this lesbian thing in your head or is it really in your heart?" And I just clapped my hand over my mouth. You know, here are these friends of mine trying to come to terms with what all this means, but what they are not realizing is that no one has ever asked them that question about heterosexuality. Why in the hell are they asking her that question about lesbianism?

The tensions between my friends had a particular familiarity when listening to the informants talk about times in their lives when they chose new ways of being as well as in my own life experiences as a graduate student. When I started back to school in 1991, I took a three-year leave of absence from my job and decided I was going to live in Lexington during the week. I ventured home only on weekends. My partner, Mark, had just started a new job and was driving 120 miles round trip each day. I knew we would have serious problems (and arguments) over who could and should address the mundane chores around the house. To divert these uncomfortable discussions, we agreed to move a recently divorced and unemployed male friend and his 5-year-old son into our home. This individual was responsible for running the household, making sure we had clean clothes, food, and a warm house to come home to.

This arrangement was closely scrutinized by my female friends. They wanted to know whether this arrangement meant Mark and I had split up. They wanted to know what Mark thought about this arrangement, and was he annoyed and angry? These same friends were regularly annoyed at my unwillingness to get together with them socially. This was a period in my life when I *was* forsaking many important people and relationships in order to develop new relationships that I felt were critical to my growth.

The struggle of making meaning of the self moment by moment, as well as experiencing resistance and acceptance in the larger culture, involves a phenomenon called "passing," which became especially salient for me after reading an article in an issue of *Utne Reader* (Powers, 1993).

Autumn: Oh, did I give you a copy of the article in *Utne Reader* called, "Queer in the Streets/Straight in the Sheets"?

Tom: No.

Autumn: The author refers to them as queer straights. But she's describing perfectly what I call a hetero-dyke. She claims that heterosexuals are out there "passing" as homosexuals. Passing is another word I've been reflecting on during this project, and how women pass.

Tom: But not how you pass? How *they* pass?

Autumn: At first I reflected on how I passed in this particular project; being very out front, not wearing my heterosexuality. And then I began to realize how the informants passed in particular situations that are directly connected to the magazines.

Passing as a concept became important to me in two ways: my own passing (personally, and as a researcher) and the informants' stories of passing. Tom and I discussed my critical reflections about passing and the politics involved in passing.

Autumn: My friend, who I mentioned is struggling to come out as a lesbian, had this party. She told everyone it was a birthday party for her new lover. No men attended. We are talking fifty dykes in the house. The next morning several women, myself included, commended her on a great "coming out" party. She immediately flushed a bright red and started rejecting the idea verbally. You can well understand there is a lot of tension there when a woman comes out. But it seems to me that once a "heterosexual" decides to come out, then the lesbians will back off and be very supportive. They quit the bantering.

Tom: What's the purpose of the bantering?

Autumn: Power, I think.

Tom: To see how tough they are about the decision they are making?

Autumn: I didn't perceive it like that. I perceived it as an act of power as soon as she started to squirm.

Tom: It's kind of interesting when you find yourself in a place you're not supposed to be, and things get said around you, or don't get said for that matter.

Autumn: Lesbians don't like it when I call myself a hetero-dyke. And they don't like it when I call myself a theorizing lesbian. Both those labels are like putting salt into a wound. Some women have gotten in my face about it and said, "Either you are [a lesbian] or you aren't."

Tom: When do you use those terms?

Autumn: If they ask me, "How do you define yourself?" Or, "Why do you seem to be spending a lot of time here?" The women who ask this aren't normally my informants. These women who challenge me on this are lesbians who have seen me around a lot and then have found out I'm not one of them. I use the labels so they will quit questioning me. I explain that hetero-dyke is a woman who prefers sex with a man but prefers emotional connections with women.

Tom: Not necessarily lesbian women, but women.

Autumn: No, for me I mean lesbian women. Heterosexual women do not tend to provide that for me. They are consumed with the sexual/affective production in their home, and I don't get the kind of nurturance that I get from these lesbian women who don't have that kind of stuff, things, requirements in their lives. The heterosexual women tend to abandon me because of those requirements whereas lesbian women don't. I call myself a theorizing lesbian because I agree and connect with a lot of the radical lesbian feminist philosophers' writing. They just put it out on the table. They don't dress it up. They don't get out the china to say that women are oppressed. They don't feel they have to put it in a way that wouldn't piss men off. They don't care about them. These theorists make a lot of sense to me and help me understand my life experience. That's why I call myself a theorizing lesbian. It sort of disappoints me that some lesbians get angry about me calling myself that because I'm not trying to present myself in the way they perceive, that is, that I'm co-opting only the good things for myself and I'm not having to experience the bad things. I understand their perspective, but that certainly is not my goal. I just don't go out and have a good time and then go back to the farm.

Tom: Right. This is not just a field trip.

Autumn: Right, exactly!

During the interviewing process, the informants described the act of passing in myriad ways. Many of them discussed their frustration in attempting to pass as acceptable women. For example, one informant said, "I tried to look like the women in the magazines, but never could." Others described studying the magazines so they could successfully pass as a homemaker, mother, and heterosexual lover. Still others spoke of rejecting women's magazines and their images of being feminine, and sought out new ways of being through alternative media.

Robinson (1994) argues that passing "poses the question of identity as a matter of competing discourses of recognition" (p. 728). For a pass to be successful, she claims, members of the passer's original culture cannot be present, and if they are, they must cooperate with the pass. I tried throughout the course of my project to pass as a lesbian, a heterosexual, a single woman, a married woman, a working-class woman, a middle-class woman, a student, a professional, and a scholar. Some of these attempts worked, others did not, but I quickly learned that the action of passing could not succeed if a member of my former culture was present and refused to cooperate with my pass.

I remember one particular evening I was attending a poetry reading. Several of my lesbian friends were in attendance as well as several heterosexual women friends who had known me for years. The problems started exploding around me when we all went outside for a smoke. My heterosexual friends were behaving in ways with me that suggested, from a lesbian point of view, they were former lovers of mine. My heterosexual friends (the very ones who had quizzed me about the status of Mark and me) perceived my new lesbian friends as prospective lovers of mine. This experience was quite traumatic for me. I felt incapable of passing as either a lesbian or a heterosexual, which in turn silenced me.

My Power Words

Autumn: I'm a theorizing lesbian, not a practicing dyke . . .

Autumn: I'm a gynergetic shero and a wild virgin . . .

Autumn: I'm a hetero-dyke . . .

Autumn: She is an outsider-within . . .

Autumn: The women read magazines to discover how to perform sexual/affective production . . .

These quotes reveal many of the "power words" I used in the research process and to define myself socially. These words served three purposes: to connect me with the participants, to connect the women's life experiences to the academic world, and to provide for myself feminine ways of knowing that incorporated strength, wisdom, and agency.

The word *gynergy* is explained in a footnote of the dissertation:

Gynergy refers to positive female agency, energy, and resistance generated in the feminine core of self and grounded in the personal experience of living in a patriarchal society. The word is conceived and used in direct opposition to such words as "hysterical" and "emotional," which connote femaleness that is out of control and dangerous, irrational and in need of silencing. (p. 213)

Tom and I discussed these power words further:

Autumn: I would argue that a lot of the words we internalize that describe us or explain us as women aren't very nice. So, [gynergy] is a word I've claimed that is still a good word for me. It goes against what seems to be our socialization, like being clumsy, sort of living up to people's expectations of how I should be, and if I really think about it and focus on it, I'm not clumsy. In fact, I'm graceful and feel good in my body. That word provides a meaning that helps me to refocus because you can lose it real easy being in the culture.

Tom: So that word is a personal word?

Autumn: Very personal.

Tom: So you did feel comfortable lending a personal word, a power word, to your dissertation?

Autumn: Yes. It sort of put my stamp on it.

Tom: Where did that word come from?

Autumn: Mary Daly and her book *Gyn/Ecology*. As far as I know, that is the first place I've come upon it. Then Marilyn Frye, a feminist philosopher, wrote a book called *Willful Virgin*. She talks about the definition of virgin having nothing to do with a woman being penetrated by a male's penis, but a woman, a willful virgin, being a woman who is not possessed or controlled or connected in a financial or social and therefore sexual way to men. It doesn't necessarily mean lesbians. Heterosexuals can be willful virgins, although it's difficult. So I put those together—gynergetic virgin. Another word is *shero*. I learned that word in a workshop. This guy, the presenter, said this word four or five times. I sat there and thought, "What are you saying?" And then finally it got through and I realized this guy's talking about a female hero. So, those three words are the ones that when I remember them, they get me back to a place that is positive rather than feeling negative while I try to survive in a male-defined world.

As described in the "Passing" section, some of my power words were not accepted as such by my lesbian informants, and, in fact, some of them were offended by my use of *theorizing lesbian* and *hetero-dyke*. In one instance, an African American lesbian explained one of her power words, and why it fit her sense of self, by saying, "I'm not a lesbian, I'm a queer. Lesbians are white, middle-class women with lots of time on their hands." Other informants found my words to be strange and mysterious, and many of them embraced *lady* or *good girl* as power words. I think our choice of power words can signal our underlying assumptions of what it means to be a woman in this culture.

Writing

I see the writing of the dissertation as a type of labor, similar to that of childbirth, but which takes eight months to complete, rather than 36 hours. In addition I saw the writing as not only giving birth to a document but also giving birth to myself.

To do this work, I created a "womb" room. This involved co-opting our newly built basement room, laying carpet, hanging lace curtains, placing a wicker rocking chair next to the window looking out onto the woods, setting up a long wooden table, setting up the computer and printer, getting a comfortable office chair on casters and a futon. This is where I spent 10- to 16-hour days.

In my dialogue with Tom, I realize now, I revealed a premonition regarding this work. We were discussing what I wanted the informants to do as a result of reading the study.

Autumn: I have sat and thought about that for a long time. What do I want them to do? I hadn't thought about that before. Thinking about the interviews, what seemed to happen over and over again was at some point in the interview the women would say in reaction to a question or story, "Well, I never thought of that before." Or, "In saying that you made me remember . . ." So, reflection I guess. Reflecting on, "Do we do things because we have thought them out and is this something we really want to do?" Or, "Do we do things because we think that it is the appropriate thing to do?"

Tom: So you're looking for some kind of connection or opening into their consciousness to some themes that you are discussing . . .

Autumn: That's just too scary of a thing to think about. I could see myself going, "Oh my gosh, are they going to think that I described them in a positive light?" And just freezing. It is very important to me to present them in the way that they are to the best of my ability, because some of the groups are very different from who I am. And it makes me very uncomfortable to think that I am able to do that.

This freezing up in fear over my concern to present the women as they are, did occur once I started writing the analysis chapters. I would regularly leap out of the office chair in front of the computer and throw myself onto the futon, curling into a fetal ball under the covers. When it happened, I would tell myself to just "roll with it." This reaction occurred when I would enter a long passage with informants' quotes and then try to synthesize or interpret what they meant. This process always sent me to the futon because I was so afraid I was not representing them in the way they would have wanted to be presented to the reader. This part of the work was probably the most difficult and painful.

The Defense—Tom

One of my last jobs was to get Autumn ready for the defense. I walked her through the sequence of events she should expect. We went over the roster of committee members, anticipating where each might be "coming from" with their questions. " 'Defending' means you discuss what you did and why you did it," I told her. "You are facing a critical, responsive audience, but we're not here to intimidate." She said that she would prepare a prefatory statement, as is the custom, but that she wanted to discuss the experiential aspects of the dissertation as well as its substantive content. No problem. Finally, I said, "Give it another reading, but don't overstudy."

A week later, the defense: Huddling briefly before inviting Autumn in, the other members of her committee and I agreed that we saw no significant problems with her work. It promised to be a lively intellectual conversation, not the sort of high-wire act that these meetings sometimes become. Nevertheless, my pulse quickened as it always does when a candidate I've supervised enters the room. Autumn looked rested and calm. For a moment, I thought of the 19-year-old informant Autumn had spoken of months before, "with her youthful skin," the one she complimented for being beautiful.

The accomplishment was clear for all to see. It was not even conceivable just four years ago. Yet it would not have turned out in this particular form without the precarious moments, resistances, and affirmations of her partner, friends, informants, committees, and numerous others, including the authors whose writings helped her to articulate a problem in journal entries. Even her memories of growing up, the ones that disturbed her sense of female agency, had an influence. These events positioned her differently than she had first imagined, just as the specificity of her own embodied presence altered, and made visible in certain interpretable ways, the self-positionings of those whom she studied. Her project emerged in the space where these identities were recognized. Whatever other form the dissertation *could have* turned out to be in is now an immaterial issue for the reader, and a private, evolving footnote in Autumn's life story.

Conclusion

Much like the investigative journalist, the ethnographer is a quintessential knowledge worker of our time who goes on forays to a "margin" and reports on the peculiar or problematic customs of some other people for a cosmopolitan audience. Unlike the reporter, the ethnographer's choices respond to a market that produces and consumes the same specialized discourse. What is brought back to the center is a work whose claims are crafted to meet standards valuated and policed vigorously by its agents in journals and other outlets. In communication, it is the cottage industry known as cultural (or interpretive) media studies that sets the exchange value for the commodity.

That the work of understanding depends on establishing and maintaining personal relationships cannot be disputed. Method becomes visible as such in events of discourse, and results in discursive artifacts. But in most cases, the work-as-commodity bears few traces of a relational passage. If it did, we might well be treated more often to contingent claims, tales of bad faith as well as good, and even a little incoherence (in what is described, if not how it is written). Instead, the relationship is typically a means of stabilizing the researcher's persona in the imagined eyes of the participants so that their actions can be disclosed in a manner that is also stable and recordable. With the aid of compliant, anonymous subjects and a fair-weather study site, the researcher is altogether grateful to merge into a zero-degree self with only "theoretical" assumptions to declare. And further helping to elide the analyst's presence is the common belief that any media text is capable of yielding many readings, each of which is somehow a signature of a different social formation. It becomes improbable to think the analyst intervened at all in these acts of interpretation.

What might the project of studying mediated communication look like when it begins consciously to embrace its special vulnerability? Simply stated, it proposes the self as a site of experimentation because it is the investigator's own preconceptions that must be faced and wagered. A dialogical project begins by recognizing the existential interdependencies of the Self and Other as these are confronted in the Other's world. Dwyer (1979) cites three criteria for the conduct of such studies:

> First, the confrontation is "recursive": that is, its meaning at any moment both depends upon, and may call into question, the meaning of what has preceded. Second, the confrontation is "contingent": its continuity must not be taken for granted and its meaning, at any moment, must entail the fact that rupture, until that moment surmounted, may always ensue. Third, the confrontation is "embarked"; that is, it is necessarily tied to specific forces which transcend personal activity and, at the very least, to those forces which perceive human groups as different and which encourage direct contact between certain of their members. (p. 215)

Recursivity grounds Self-Other encounters in a history that is jointly produced. The stories we tell cycle and proliferate through this continually updated fund of meanings. Recursivity in fieldwork experience refers us back to all of the events that are constitutive of *this* encounter, making them available to being interrogated with respect to an interest or conflict. In the "Beauty Must Suffer" dialogue, Autumn narrated her "fish out of water with a purpose" story as key to the meaning of dissertation work. A variety of moments are retrieved and bracketed recursively, acquiring new meanings as a result: Autumn's data analyses constructed through feminist theoretical ideas; a talk with Mark about those constructions; the making of their talk into a transcript; Mark's subsequent interpretation of that transcript; and, finally, our use of it in this chapter. Recursivity in inquiry means to resist fixing meanings to content once and for all as well as to "resist irretrievably distorting the text by cutting it into bits and pieces or by playing freely with its actual sequence in time" (p. 218). Our temporal coexistence with the Other is the ineluctable basis of field experience.

The second characteristic, *contingency,* acts as a dialectical corrective for the first: Any encounter is capable of a breach, or rupture. To be sensitive to the possibility of rupture means, as Dwyer puts it, "to counter a non-dialectical project whose purported continuity requires goals and strategies elaborated prior to the confrontation" (p. 215). Particularly in media studies, where the text is often well known to both the researcher and the informant, "taste" can act as a differentiating test of culture position and knowledge, and perhaps of grounds for compatibility in the interview (Seiter, 1990). The researcher should be ready for situations in which the Other opposes, disappoints, alters, or terminates a line of action. The researcher herself can invoke questions, thus introducing rupture, which might then be deflected or otherwise managed by the informant. Autumn's meeting with the human subjects board, her sadness at not finding women who love their entire bodies, her failure to pass when both heterosexual and lesbian friends were present—as different as they were, all of these ruptures temporarily shook the coherence of her endeavor. Each contingent moment calls attention to a difference in stance, to the fact that Self and Other are each situated differently and speak asymmetrically in the unfolding dialogue. Where closure is the outcome of visualist, detached inquiry, "vulnerability and self-disclosure are enabled through conversation" (Conquergood, 1991, p. 183).

In *embarkation,* the researcher tries to examine the ties between the field encounter and the social forces that transcend it, including those of the academic discipline. Part of this effort involves using the encounter to comment on historically embedded processes. But it also involves understanding "how this fieldwork experience and the effort to transform it into a public text provide support for particular forces in today's world" (Dwyer, 1979, p. 219). Autumn's use of power words not only had a local interpersonal effect, it brought the more broadly political ambiguities of gender and sexuality directly into the confrontation. She wagered that the words would create a tension in the very phenomenon she was studying, eliciting more decisive articulations of her informants' identity work.

A dialogical inquiry joins the resources of the self to the risks of new ways of working and speaking. To commit to this vulnerability means giving up the monological power to refine, or to denature, the contextual presences of the Other. With that loss, however, comes the gain of a more honest academy that engages the worlds of social action and moral choice upon which it depends.

Notes

1. The term *Other* (or *Otherness*) is not without its problems because it may be perceived as projecting a mark of foreignness, or negative identity, on a group from a privileged perspective of normality. The term could also promote a comfortable sense of familiarity on the part of its users where none may be felt, or wanted, by the group it describes.

2. In the years since Dwyer's essay, cultural anthropologists have energetically debated issues of cultural appropriation and experimented with ways of including the presence of people they study, mostly through textual inscription (e.g., Clifford & Marcus, 1986; Jackson, 1989; Manganaro, 1990; Marcus & Fischer, 1986; Rosaldo, 1989).

3. Parts of this section are adapted from Lindlof and Anderson (1988).

4. Crapanzano's term *shadow dialogue* refers to all of those dialogues the investigator has with others, real or imagined, in the field or after the fact, in which the ethnography itself becomes an object. He states:

> The ethnographer's—or anyone's—participation in these shadow dialogues, with a colleague, an important theoretical position, or a symbolically significant person provides him with a position external to the immediate exchange, though it is never fixed or timeless, that enables him to reproduce the exchange and offer an interpretation of it. . . . [T]he other participants to the dialogue are also engaged in shadow dialogues that afford them external vantage points and enable them to reproduce and interpret the dialogue when they choose. (Crapanzano, 1992, p. 213)

5. These dialogues were transcribed with great care by Joanne Popa Lindlof.

References

Agar, M. (1982). Toward an ethnographic language. *American Anthropologist, 84,* 779-795.

Anderson, J. A., & Meyer, T. P. (1988). *Mediated communication: A social action perspective.* Newbury Park, CA: Sage.

Ang, I. (1991). *Desperately seeking the audience.* London: Routledge.

Clifford, J., & Marcus, G. E. (Eds.). (1986). *Writing culture: The poetics and politics of ethnography.* Berkeley: University of California Press.

Conquergood, D. (1991). Rethinking ethnography: Towards a critical cultural politics. *Communication Monographs, 58,* 179-194.

Crapanzano, V. (1992). *Hermes' dilemma and Hamlet's desire: On the epistemology of interpretation.* Cambridge, MA: Harvard University Press.

Daly, M. (1978). *Gyn/Ecology: The metaethics of radical feminism.* Boston: Beacon.

Davis, B., & Harré, R. (1991). Positioning: The discursive production of selves. *Journal for the Theory of Social Behavior, 20,* 43-63.

Dwyer, K. (1979). The dialogic of ethnology. *Dialectical Anthropology, 4,* 205-224.

Fabian, J. (1979). Rule and process: Thoughts on ethnography as communication. *Philosophy of the Social Sciences, 9,* 1-26.

Ferguson, A. (1991). *Sexual democracy: Women, oppression, and revolution.* Boulder, CO: Westview.

Frye, M. (1992). *Willful virgin: Essays in feminism, 1976-1992.* Freedom, CA: Crossing Press.

Gergen, K. J. (1991). *The saturated self: Dilemmas of identity in contemporary life.* New York: Basic Books.

Giddens, A. (1991). *Modernity and self-identity.* Stanford, CA: Stanford University Press.

Grubb-Swetnam, A. (1994). *Women's use, negotiation, and interpretation of women's service, fashion, and beauty magazines: Generating gynergetic tales through standpoint epistemology.* Unpublished doctoral dissertation, University of Kentucky.

Habermas, J. (1984). *The theory of communicative action* (Vol. 1.). Boston: Beacon.

Harvey, D. (1989). *The condition of postmodernity.* Cambridge, MA: Blackwell.

Hill-Collins, P. (1990). *Black feminist thought: Knowledge, consciousness, and the politics of empowerment.* New York: Routledge.

Holquist, M. (1990). *Dialogism: Bakhtin and his world.* London: Routledge.

Jackson, M. (1989). *Paths toward a clearing: Radical empiricism and ethnographic inquiry.* Bloomington: Indiana University Press.

Jenkins, H., Jr. (1988). Star Trek rerun, reread, rewritten: Fan writing as textual poaching. *Critical Studies in Mass Communication, 5,* 85-107.

Jensen, K. (1991). When is meaning? Communication theory, pragmatism, and mass media reception. In J. A. Anderson (Ed.), *Communication yearbook 14* (pp. 3-32). Newbury Park, CA: Sage.

Kauffman, B. J. (1992). Feminist facts: Interview strategies and political subjects in ethnography. *Communication Theory, 2,* 187-206.

Kleinman, S., Stenross, B., & McMahon, M. (1994). Privileging fieldwork over interviews: Consequences for identity and practice. *Symbolic Interaction, 17,* 37-50.

Krieger, S. (1991). *Social science and the self: Personal essays as an art form.* New Brunswick, NJ: Rutgers University Press.

Lindlof, T. R. (1988). Media audiences as interpretive communities. In J. A. Anderson (Ed.), *Communication yearbook 11* (pp. 81-107). Newbury Park, CA: Sage.

Lindlof, T. R. (1995). *Qualitative communication research methods.* Thousand Oaks, CA: Sage.

Lindlof, T. R., & Anderson, J. A. (1988, July). *Problems in decolonizing the subject in qualitative audience research.* Paper presented at the biennial meeting of the International Association of Mass Communication Research, Barcelona.

Lindlof, T. R., & Grodin, D. (1990). When media use can't be observed: Some problems and tactics of collaborative audience research. *Journal of Communication, 40*(4), 8-28.

Lull, J. (1988). Constructing rituals of extension through family television viewing. In J. Lull (Ed.), *World families watch television* (pp. 237-260). Newbury Park, CA: Sage.

Lull, J. (1990). *Inside family viewing.* New York: Routledge.

Manganaro, M. (Ed.). (1990). *Modernist anthropology: From fieldwork to text.* Princeton, NJ: Princeton University Press.

Marcus, G. E., & Fischer, M. M. J. (1986). *Anthropology as cultural critique.* Chicago: University of Chicago Press.

Morley, D. (1980). *The 'Nationwide' audience: Structure and decoding*. London: BFI.

Powers, A. (1993, November/December). Queer in the streets/straight in the sheets. *Utne Reader,* pp. 74-80.

Radway, J. A. (1984). *Reading the romance: Women, patriarchy, and popular literature*. Chapel Hill: University of North Carolina Press.

Radway, J. (1988). Reception study: Ethnography and the problems of dispersed audiences and nomadic subjects. *Cultural Studies, 2,* 359-376.

Robinson, A. (1994). It takes one to know one: Passing and communities of common interest. *Critical Inquiry, 20,* 715-736.

Rosaldo, R. (1989). *Culture and truth: The remaking of social analysis*. Boston: Beacon.

Rose, D. (1990). *Living the ethnographic life*. Newbury Park, CA: Sage.

Schroder, K. C. (1994). Audience semiotics, interpretive communities and the "ethnographic turn" in media research. *Media, Culture, & Society, 16,* 337-347.

Seiter, E. (1990). Making distinctions in TV audience research: Case study of a troubling interview. *Cultural Studies, 4,* 61-84.

Silverman, K. (1983). *The subject of semiotics*. New York: Oxford University Press.

Smith, D. E. (1987). *The everyday world as problematic: A feminist sociology*. Boston: Northeastern University Press.

Smith, D. E. (1990a). *The conceptual practices of power: A feminist sociology of knowledge*. Boston: Northwestern University Press.

Smith, D. E. (1990b). *Texts, facts, and femininity: Exploring the relations of ruling*. London: Routledge.

Taylor, C. (1991). The dialogical self. In D. R. Hiley, J. F. Bohman, & R. Shusterman (Eds.), *The interpretive turn: Philosophy, science, culture* (pp. 304-314). Ithaca, NY: Cornell University Press.

Van Maanen, J. (1979). The fact of fiction in organizational ethnography. In J. Van Maanen (Ed.), Qualitative methodology [Special issue]. *Administrative Science Quarterly, 24,* 535-550.

Van Maanen, J. (1981). The informant game: Selected aspects of ethnographic research in police organizations. *Urban Life, 9,* 469-494.

Westcott, M. (1979). Feminist criticism of the social sciences. *Harvard Educational Review, 49,* 422-430.

12

The Nature of the Individual in Communication Research

James A. Anderson
Gerard T. Schoening

In the various domains of communication research, individuals are our subjects, respondents, informants, associates, and colleagues. They are the repository of traits, the expression of social forces, the materialization of roles, and the acting agent. They are our statistical aggregates, the surrogates of us all, the objects of study, and the targets of explanation. For much of the discipline's science, the individual is an inviolate boundary of epistemological methodology in which explanations of the collective, of society, of the organization, and of the group must reside.[1] Beyond traditional science, individual intentions justify our critical claims, and we give voice to otherwise mute individuals in our ethnographies and reception studies. The individual is everywhere but most often nowhere as we work our naturalized practices of science and scholarship. Let us offer three recent examples.

Hansen and Krygowski (1994) describe the individuals in their study on sexy music videos as "163 male and female undergraduates" (p. 33). This terse categorical description, typical of traditional social science, deliberately denies any individuality to the people involved. This is a necessary move for the 163 respondents to stand as surrogates for us all.

Whitt and Slack (1994) offer us a different type of categorization in their critical analysis of the central role "community" plays in cultural studies. They state that the "ideal of community valorizes the tightly knit, exclusive, highly structured, hierarchical, small town or rural community, based on locale and face-to-face communication" (p. 12). In cultural studies, where an interpretive community is often the unit of analysis (e.g., Lindlof, 1988), individuals are seen as codependents, mutually complicit, molded into an organic unity of similarity. The individuals we meet in our research are simply the available representatives.

In Trujillo's (1993) ethnographic study, we meet neither surrogates nor representatives but people engaged as characters in another episode of the Kennedy-at-Dallas drama. We learn their names, some of their history; we wonder at the choices they have made that brought them together on that grassy knoll in November.

AUTHORS' NOTE: Much of this chapter was prepared as Chapter 4 of J. A. Anderson, *Communication Theory: Epistemological Foundations* (Guilford). The publisher's permission is gratefully acknowledged.

Research studies such as these examples require the researcher to hold radically different visions of the individuals who appear within them. This chapter decodes those visions that are materialized in our journals and texts to illuminate the underlying concepts by which the individual is made to appear. It presumes (a) that the concept of the individual is not self-evident; (b) that, instead, a conceptualization is required; and (c) that the conceptualization-in-place does particular epistemic work.[2]

As is typical of foundations, claims most often incorporate the accomplishments of items a through c without comment or question. We propose to use two devices and a set of four models to break this silence. We work the devices first.

Devices

The paragraphs that follow develop two sets of analytical tools that we feel are useful for constructing the models that follow. They also serve as a preface to the issues that we believe are central to the differences in the character of claim that distinguish the research we read.

The First Device: Identity, Subjectivity, and Agency

The first of the devices develops a litmus test out of the concepts of identity, subjectivity, and agency.[3]

Identity

Identity is both an inward- and an outward-looking concept. Inward looking, it provides a consideration of the existence of a unity, a coherence that extends across time and situation. This unity can be the "essence of the individual" that remains at the core of all particular manifestations, the integrated personality that is predictable (and a therapeutic goal), the acting agent of continental existentialism or American pragmatism, the impulsive "I" of Blummer's Meadian symbolic interactionism, the quarrelsome Freudian troika of the human partitioned, the self in its many conceptualizations from essentialist to dramaturgic, as well as the serial identity of psychographic attributes and traits.

Outward looking, identity is that constellation of characteristics and performances that manifest the self in meaningful action. This identity is the something(s) that actually can be observed to which the concept of a self might be attached. Different theorists will treat this identity differently. Some will postulate this identity as a sign of, say, cognitive activity or of social/cultural/genetic determinants. Others will hold this identity as the expressive site of a larger sociology. And still others will read this identity through lines of action that have recognizable eidetic qualities.

Together, the inward and outward components of identity answer the question: "Who is the I" in self/other configurations and definitions of the person?

Subjectivity

Subjectivity[4] presumes the existence of cultural paradigms of the self. They are the concepts of gender and class of cultural studies, the roles of symbolic interactionist sociology, and the figures and characters of narrative. Where the subject has epistemic standing, identity will always appear (if permitted at all) within some nexus of subjectivity.

Subjectivity is presented as being both evoked and invoked. As evoked, it is called into place by the actions of others, the power of society, or the force of culture. The degree of anonymity in the evocation and the view of subjectivity as oppression separate the lines of thought that use it. Symbolic interaction's use of the "me," for example, holds subjectivity as necessary for any expression, oppressed or not (Meltzer, Petras, & Reynolds, 1975).

Subjectivity can also be read as invoked in an opportunistic attempt to position oneself. (Our writing in these paragraphs attempts an authorized voice.) One's invocation is often coupled with a concomitant evocation of the other (say, compliant reader).

Agency

Identity pursues the transcendental character of the individual, that element (or elements), its material presence and acting force, which allows us to talk about human nature as generalization. Subjectivity begins a move to historicizing the individual as a production of a particular time and place (albeit potentially grand in its scope). Agency will allow us to complete this historicity by pointing to the local agent in action.

Agency describes the character of acting (doing) and particularly the question of immanence in human action. Part of the upheaval of postmodern thought has been the return of agency from its exile along with the reintroduction of immanence in explanation. Most of the history of modernist psychology (1850-1950) has been a drive toward determinism in which the appearance of agency was removed from explanations that instead depended upon transcendental social and material forces.

In an agency perspective, however, the action of choice is in some part a self-initiating event and can be understood only as an individual choosing. Choice, itself, raises the question of who or what does the choosing (Ellis, 1986; Ricoeur, 1992). In this question, we are turned full circle back to begin again with identity. What identity (unity) in what subjectivity do we position as the agent of choosing?

Identity, subjectivity, and agency can effectively illuminate differences among theories. Behavioral or cognitive theories as they search for the transcendental claim often emphasize identity (usually a single focal trait) to the exclusion of subjectivity and agency. Most Marxist or structuralist cultural theories focus on subjectivity, deny identity, and discount the effectiveness of agency, whereas most critical theories focus on identity and agency as the emancipation from subjectivity. And, finally, social action and structuration theories work all three as dynamic elements of a tripart relationship.

The Second Device: Material, Biological, and Semiotic Domains

The notion of the individual can also be trisected by the material, biological, and semiotic domains of explanation. In epistemologies based on multiple domains of explanation, the individual represents a material object responsive to the explanatory laws of physics and chemistry. It is also a life form invested in the explanations of change, individual difference, and the tensions between genetic potentials and materialization in action. And, third, the individual appears as a performative and discursive subject within the semiotic domain. As this subject, the individual is variously constituted within discourse and action.

It would appear vitally important in the project of theory to distinguish the domain or domains in which the individual is being theoretically approached. For example, Burgoon and Le Poire (1992) write (from deep inside their argument):

> According to EV [expectancy violation] theory, communication expectancies are a function of target characteristics, relationship characteristics and context features. Of interest here are target characteristics, which include both general traitlike attributes (such as personality or gender) and statelike attributes (such as giving positive or negative feedback or being in a humorous, entertaining mood). (p. 69)

Interesting questions arise when one attempts to determine the domains in which, say, personality and gender reside, the characteristics that entitle them as traits, and the manner of their operation within EV theory. Is the gender of issue here a biological or semiotic trait? Similar questions occur when one wonders how an action (as in giving positive feedback) is the same thing as a state (as in a humorous, entertaining mood).

For theorists who accept multiple domains of explanation, all theories are formulated in and most offer explanation for events in the semiotic domain. Many theorists (both critical and scientific), however, act as if their explanation reached into the biological and the material. And for theorists who accept reductionism as a starting place, all theories must ultimately ground themselves in materialist explanation.[5]

There is a second contrast that is at least partially embedded in the issue of multiple domains. That is the mind-body contrast (Segal, 1991). This contrast reaches back beyond Cartesian dualism, and Popper's (Popper & Eccles, 1977) transcendental mind is just one of its recent manifestations. Many applications of this contrast formulate the mind to return us to the scholastic essentialist self—one's fully formed, persisting identity—in rejection of materialist explanations (see, particularly, Lewis, 1982).

With the exception of feminist writings, the body is notably missing in communication theory (but for the kind of thing that does appear, see Meyers & Biocca, 1992; for a more complex analysis, see Bourdieu, 1978). Pain, ecstacy, discipline, carnival, expressions of the body, the body as sign, and the actual "writing on the body" of cultural differences in work, nutrition, decoration, and the like are all topics that have been met in feminist thought (Bartky, 1995) but few places elsewhere in the communication literature.

As the body is missing in deference to the mind so is action as a defining moment subjugated to mentalist determinants. Most of our theory sets essence before existence so that such constructs as attitudes, values, schemata, motivations, uses, and gratifications establish the basis for behavior. Theories based on symbolic interactionism, American pragmatism, and continental existentialism, however, reverse the order to hold that existence defines our essence. It is, therefore, action that defines our motives, not the other way around.

The relative absence of the body and action, given our materialist inclinations, appears to be strange or at least notable. But, then, many of the confusions that occur in the study of theory cannot be solved by a more careful analysis of the theory itself. The analyst must jump to the community, the paradigm, or the episteme to understand the meanings in place. The meaning of the absence of the body may well be a masculine mark of inquiry. And the absence of action may be traced to the current dominance of cognitivism in communication theory.

Models

We now turn to the underlying models of the individual (person, self) that support various forms of inquiry. We can distinguish four separate positions within communication theory: the attribute individual, the conjunctive individual, the situated individual, and the activative individual.

Attribute Model

In the attribute model, the individual is seen as the weighted sum of a finite set of attributes (intelligence, personality, and cognitive structures such as values, attitudes, and schemata). Following Hume's injunction, there is, in particular, a deliberate rejection of an "inner self," some coherent entity that is the source or seat of these attributes.[6] Each attribute is, however, its own unity, which transcends its location and expression in the particular person. In hierarchical societies, for example, all members are considered as imprinted with (something like) socioeconomic class, although its value and power will vary across individuals. The program of science is the discovery of these attributes and their functions (Anderson, 1987).

The attribute model is not limited to science. It appears in values-based textual analysis (see Trujillo & Ekdom, 1985) and in many of the audience-based critical approaches (e.g., Allen, 1987). The psychoanalytic frame of the individual also works in much the same way as the attribute model. In the psychoanalytic approach, the individual presents itself as a partitioned subject, the partitions of which—to use popular terminology—are the primal motives of the id, the socially constructed strictures of the superego, and the pragmatic, reality-tested practices of the ego. Although psychoanalysis is traditionally a clinical approach, it has been used in a variety of critical approaches (e.g., Silverman, 1983) as well as in the revelation of the politics of desire (e.g., Lacan, 1988).

The attribute model is ahistorical in that it does not locate its explanation in the particular but seeks the more general claim. In our media campaign example, the advice is meant to cover all highly educated women in low-compliance states.

We can expect the attribute model to be in place when words such as *traits, aptitudes, states, stages, attitudes, values, schemata, scripts, psychographics, inculturation, development,* or *socialization* appear, signaling the use of internalized mentalist entities as antecedents to behavior. Because of its use of mentalist antecedents, the attribute model is a psychological form. It presents the self's forms of action as the symptoms of inner processes that have taken place in more or less successful ways. Behavior has no meaning except as the end point of processes that ultimately transcend the self that behaves. It is a vision of the mind. It can be contrasted with the conjunctive model, which follows where the antecedents are exterior.

Conjunctive Model

In the conjunctive model, the individual is seen as the site of the intersection of material, cultural, and social influences. It is Durkheim's social penetration. The individual is a collective enterprise and relatively powerless alone, although one can participate (or be swept along) in movements of change. The conjunctive model has both a sociological and a cultural form.

Sociological Form

As a sociological form, it was once the expression and is now the legacy of dialectical materialism, continental structuralism, and American functionalism. It represents an emphasis on social, cultural, and ideological institutions and apparatuses that merge subjectivity and identity and provide the agency of action.

Dialectical materialism. Dialectical materialism develops out of the writings of Hegel, Engels, and Marx. The material determinism of Marxism is different than the material determinism of the natural order. Marxism arises not out of the "Big Bang" but out of our own ideational representations of reality (Marx, 1867/1959). Capitalism (or any political-economic system) is an ideology—a reality representing a system of ideas—supported by knowledge-producing practices and the means of distribution of the structured discourse that results.[7]

As a dialectic, Marxism stands in permanent opposition as a force for change, a continuing critique exposing the fictive character of representation, the mystification of its methods, and the false consciousness of our acceptance (see Mepham, 1979). It is this commitment to the critical review of the dominant that is the key identifying characteristic of arguments to be labeled Marxist in the dialectical tradition.[8] The business of scholarship is emancipation through the change of consciousness (see McLellan, 1986, as well as Russell, 1979).

The individual in Marxism through the 1950s was a product of the dominant ideology without recourse in the absence of liberating efforts. There has been a subsequent reclamation of the individual in Hall's recognition that folks are not "cultural dopes" and de Certeau's notions of opposition and resistance. As a collectivist, dialectical argument, however, the individual will always appear momentarily in the margins between sets of oppositions whether those oppositions are class, gender, ethnicity, race, or similar ideological distinctions.

Continental structuralism. In its strong statement, the individual as a practical force of history, an initiator of knowledge and action, a self-defining intelligence, disappears within continental structuralism.[9] In its place is a semiconscious expression: the individual "as a living, working, and speaking being who is subject to death, desire and language as law" (Bannet, 1989, p. 158). Our understanding of the individual will not be found in the examination of people but in the study of the structures that produce the ideological framework in which individuals appear.[10] Human science in latter-day structuralism is both an empirical and a critical activity that documents structures (such as the characters and narratives of our media; see Hodge & Kress, 1988) and their ideological consequences, thereby empowering emancipatory movement or at least temporary refurbishment for those scholars who resist utopianism.

American functionalism. Within our media studies, American functionalism appears in press theory (e.g., McCombs & Shaw, 1972) and in uses and gratifications theory (e.g., Rosengren & Windahl, 1972). American functionalism, most readily identified with Talcott Parsons's (1951) later structural functionalism[11] and Robert Merton's (1957) less ambitious design, is concerned with a system of interdependent collective variables that define social life. The system is dynamic in that change in one variable effects change throughout. The system emphasizes the collective in that variables appear in (either as a consequence of or within the scope of) collective endeavors.

The individual is defined as a part of a social system beyond his or her personal control, although choice among socially determined parts-to-be-played is sometimes recognized. The ontology of the individual is described in a variable-analytic manner through ordained characteristics such as education/occupation/income of father/mother/self, class of birth, attained class, gender, race, religion, dialect, ethnicity, and political and social memberships, all of which converge to answer the question of who I am (e.g., Frazer, 1981).

Coming out of a foundational empiricist tradition, American functionalism rejects a critical stance. It has, nonetheless, been a very optimistic theoretical frame in that science can be put to progressive work moving toward social integration (Isajiw, 1968).

Critical Forms

Critical theory and cultural studies represent the two most widely cited critical forms of the conjunctive model.[12] Both critical theory and cultural studies are holist and historicist in that it is the unities of actual circumstances that produce the ideologies of practical action. Or in the Marxist phrase, social being produces social consciousness (Thalheimer, 1936). The unreflective individual, given the decline of family-centered life, is necessarily a product of the untempered influences of social institutions: the media, the school, the workplace, the practices and sites of consumption (Williams, 1991; Wolin, 1992). Subjectivity denies autonomy in this formulation. As Alexander (1992) puts it in his comment on worthy friends and immoral enemies: "Actors are not intrinsically either worthy or moral: They are determined to be so by being placed in certain positions on the grid of civil culture" (p. 291).

Much of the critical form in the 1980s and 1990s is concerned with managing the triumvirate of identity, subjectivity, and agency. In the early going, the focus was primarily on the enforcement of subjectivity with its themes of media-inspired dominance, repression, and subjugation (Grossberg, 1991, 1993).

The adoption by cultural studies of (a) Althusser's ideology-is-everywhere offering subjectivity as a necessary part of the presentation of self and not a categorical evil, as well as (b) Gramsci's concept of hegemony as a loose reality-forming confederation of interrelated ideologies, opened the space of analysis to change and personal expression (Turner, 1990). The individual is still a collective enterprise but one who can now exploit the cultural system while yet its subject (Canfield, 1990; Newcomb, 1991). To dominance, repression, and subjugation have been added the themes of resistance, opposition, and emancipation in the absence of revolution (Morley, 1980).

In the presence of Habermas, critical theory has retained its philosophical character, its critical attack, and its conceptualization of a repressive subjectivity. It maintains its "ideal of an emancipated individual in an emancipated society" (Szahaj, 1990, p. 54) in which the autonomous subject returns.

Cultural studies offer a more modest outcome of a fully contextualized subject who, whether in an enlightened and reflective understanding or more directly through practical knowledge, can work the margins and free play spaces for at least political gain if not redemption (de Certeau, 1984).

Summary

The conjunctive model retains its strong statement in current objectivist sociology and similar sociological expressions in other disciplines. Like the attribute model, it is most effective in variable-analytic approaches that "atomize" the individual into separate independent influences. It is common in "quantitative" investigations to see the two models combined in studies that make use of "demographic and psychographic," "etic and emic," or "exogenous and endogenous" variables.

The conjunctive model has also been characteristic of traditional critical and cultural analyses. Here the emphasis has been on the effect of cultural "totalities" (as opposed to separate elements) in producing the subject. British and American cultural studies have begun a salvage effort on the concepts of identity and self. This effort, on the American side, has paralleled if not been connected to a reclamation of Peircean semiotics, pragmatism, and symbolic interactionism in what might be a fin de siècle return to the beginnings of this century (Wexler, 1991; Wiley, 1994).

Such efforts have also attempted to reclaim action as a significant semiotic component in the makeup of the self. The conjunctive model on the whole lacks any notion that forms of behavior—particularly forms of interaction—have a signifying dimension that directs meaning and the possibilities by which the self can be made known or knowable. As will be seen next, however, what one "is" may depend as much on what one can or cannot do within various arenas of localized social activity as it depends on the kinds of macroscopic variables that characterize more traditional sociological inquiries. Within cultural studies, at any rate, the working model of the individual has moved noticeably closer to the situated model discussed next.

Situated Model

In the situated model, we change the view from the collective producing the subject to that of the individual finding her or his means of expression in the resources of culture and society. And media change from a repressive agent of the ideological apparatus to the means of the circulation of meaning resources in society (Becker & McCall, 1990). John Hall (1992), for example, proposes a cultural structuralism referencing "diverse configurations of institutionalized meanings, recipes and material objects that may be differently drawn on by various actors within the same social arena or society" (p. 279). It is a significant existential shift that positions the agency of the acting identity in every explanation.[13]

This identity ranges from James's concept of a moral force whose will creates the circumstances of its success, to Goffman's unprincipled choice in which the role to be played is the only substance of identity, to Alford's (1991) use of Kohut (1977) and Lacan (1977) to illuminate the incomplete self's closure in the other. In any case, whatever the identity, its material expression is always within the boundaries of meanings supplied by culture and society (Wagner, 1981). The individual is a socially derived presentation. The actualized self is underdetermined and probabilistic but sociologically everywhere addressable (for a media-based study, see Fry, Alexander, & Fry, 1990). The answer to who I am appears out of a kaleidoscope of social meanings that define the "who" I can be. As Hewitt (1989) remarks, the acting subject "fills the empty container of a role with commitment and energy, making it possible for the situated individual to act with force and direction" (p. 150).

In the situated model, the three components of identity, agency, and subjectivity are brought into more equal footing, although agency is not yet immanent. In the attribute model, the emphasis was on identity as defined by the sum of the traits. In the conjunctive model, the emphasis was on subjectivity with the individual being a cultural production. Here, we have an identity with continuity and a semblance of independence and autonomy that materializes a culturally produced subjectivity in, at least, partial response to personal motive and desire.

Agency, although acknowledged, remains domesticated under the ready control of global motivations, values, or structures of desire. Motivation, organic or conditioned, stands as the determinant of choice. The individual remains comfortably in the hands of the analyst as choice is deprived of its immanence and local operation has no epistemological value. We have a "Nintendo" person whose surface variations to the buttons we push belie the fixed code of their determination.

Inquiry, within the situated model, concerns the discovery and critical analysis of the symbols and meanings that provide for the subjectivities to be materialized as well as the discovery and operational analysis of the motivations that effect that materialization. Symbols, meanings, and motivations are the explanatory targets for the answers to the questions: What are they? How do they develop? How do they function? What are their consequences? Why do they effect those results? What is the manner of their improvement?

The situated model more clearly brings into play the potential influences of action in the overall constitution of the self. This starts a significant change from the nearly complete dependence on discourse that characterizes the cognitivism of the attribute model and the critical theory and cultural studies of the conjunctive (Durfee & Rodier, 1989). (It will be extended in the model that follows.)

The move toward action is significant but not radical as the self is equated with social roles and the prescriptions for action that they command. The situated model makes no provisions for the need to interpret or coordinate role performances. Particular social roles tend to be treated as virtual realities that stand autonomously from the individuals that perform them. To engage any role is, thus, the means by which to engage social forces and to perpetuate their influences. If there is an agency behind the role, it is principally just along for the ride.

We are finally ready to move to our last model. In this activative model,[14] still greater shifts occur in the action (rather than discursive) conceptualization of the self. The activative model sees language and action as necessarily intertwined. This more performance-oriented semiotic approach holds it necessary to incorporate action strategies to manage the various indeterminacies created through sign practices. Here, self-discourse does not determine action, but the action of the self frames its discourse in meaningful ways. The two create a collective context of meaning production (Traudt, Anderson, & Meyer, 1987).

Just as the relationship between identity and subjectivity separated the situated model from the previous two, the containment of agency we found in the situated model will separate the situated from the activative individual, as follows.

Activative Model

In the activative model, the individual is considered an artful co-conspirator who materializes collective resources of action in local and partial performances within the realm of his or her own agency (Anderson & Meyer, 1988). The individual both activates some collection of the social resources of meaning (signs and interpretations) made available by the situation, and is activated in turn within the framework of those meanings (Jensen, 1991).

The work site of this model is clearly within the semiotic domain (Kerby, 1991). The activative model positions itself in the center of the tension between the collective and the self. It grants both the necessity and the apriority of the collective forms of existence but recognizes that those forms will be improvisationally materialized in local action that will express those forms partially and metaphorically and can express those forms comically, ironically, or even oppositionally. Given a way to be, the agent must yet perform *how to be that way* within the contingencies (local circumstances) of that performance. Rather than determinants of action, collective symbols and interpretations stand as resources for lives to be lived.

The activative model is a pastiche of existentialism (Kierkegaard, 1958; Sartre, 1956), hermeneutics (e.g., Caputo, 1987), and social semiotics (e.g., Anderson & Meyer, 1988), American pragmatism (particularly James, 1983), and the interpretive turn (Taylor, 1991). It returns immanence to agency and fully historicizes the acting agent. But at the same time it insists that meaningfulness is a collective achievement and that each of us is born into and continually contributes to a system of meanings that are the stuff of life. The agent is neither free nor autonomous but is altogether implicated (Aboulafia, 1986; Ricoeur, 1992). The self, according to Wagner (1981), is the "product of human action" (p. 78).

We also see a shift from the self as monad to the self as dyad accompanied by a shift from monologic action to dialogic participation. The dyadic nature of the self in the activative model suggests that the self exists principally *as* relationship rather than just *in* relationship.

In the activative model, social actors are seen as supervising their own and others' actions to bring into being some larger, collective line of activity. What one actor does makes sense principally in relation to the larger line of action—or social routine—that actors attempt to manifest.

Such lines of action are open to continuous negotiation in what they mean. For example, reading a newspaper may be as much a demonstration of social consciousness as it is an act of resistance to a domestic dispute. What the same action can or might mean depends on interpretations of action contexts that are often incomplete, indeterminate, and intermittent.

All action, then, discursive or otherwise, is seen as dialogic in its nature (Pearce, 1994). Actors working together produce themselves and their meanings in various constellations of enacted social forms of behavior. Given the constant shifts that can arise, it becomes clearer as to why the activative model necessitates the presence of choice and agency as analytical devices. Each juncture in action can pose social actors with unexpected challenges that cannot be anticipated by social prescriptions for roles. The multiple meanings that can be produced require management and managers. Although social forces, institutions, and roles may pose the initial conditions in which actors make themselves known, such prescriptions often do not identify how such actions are to be brought into being.

The business of inquiry takes a radical turn under this model. It forces the recognition that inquiry is not a method of discovery or a critical analysis but instead a complicitous partner in the meaningful systems in which we live (e.g., McPhail, 1994). Inquiry (science, criticism, journalism, all forms of discursive claim) is part of the reality-producing enterprise (Anderson, 1992; Caputo, 1992).

A Comparison of Models

The models that we have been discussing are intended to represent the gathering places of communities from which people write. Their definitions are both elastic and permeable (this is the heuristic escape clause). They are, however, intended to discriminate the various places we have traveled from Descartes's independent and autonomous ego.

Historically, the initiation of conjunctive and attribute arguments begins in the writings of Durkheim and Comte, respectively (Alexander, 1982). The conjunctive had a more rapid development with the expansion of sociology and Marxist thought. The turn of the twentieth century gave us the foundations of the situated and activative models, the dominant force of positivism, as well as American behaviorism and developmental and cognitive psychology.

The failures of the positivist project and of classical Marxism, evident by the late 1950s but still not recognized in many intellectual communities, have accelerated the return of the repressed (Hardt, 1989). The postmodern scholarly landscape is excessive, distracting, and contradictory, and our attempts to tidy it up will not prevail, but they might provide a moment's respite.

We will then consider the four models as distinguished across the issues that appear to create their boundaries. Those issues are identity, subjectivity, and agency, the body as an element of theory, the place of action relative to discourse, the reigning theory of the self, the level of explanation, the position on the unity of science (with its attendant implications for materialism and reductionism), the position on the questions of multiple domains of reality, and, finally, the purpose of inquiry. Table 12.1 presents a capsule statement for each of the models across these issues; the paragraphs that follow provide additional comment.

Identity

The theoretical recognition of a core identity with continuity and independence occurs in the situated and activative models. In the situated model, identity is the local, materializing force of social forms. That force brings a unique set of conditions and abilities to that expression. The activative model adds an activating component in that the character of social forms must first be activated before they can be acted upon (brought into play before they can be performed). This component references the improvisational nature of social expression in the relationship between identity and subjectivity. The attribute model deliberately rejects a core identity and substitutes an identity defined by the weighted sum of the set of human defining traits. The conjunctive model has had little to say about identity concentrating its interest on subjectivity, although identity is now entering into the discussion.

Subjectivity

Subjectivity is the crucial topic of the conjunctive model and is central to both the situated and the activative forms. With identity missing in the former, subjectivity becomes the only means of referencing the person. Both of the latter models must struggle with the relationship between identity and subjectivity (issues of alienation, deception, conflict, and so on). The attribute model conflates identity and subjectivity into a technical sum, the value of which is objective (although it can be misread).

Agency

Agency is ordinarily rejected in the attribute model, which follows from its rejection of identity (no agent available). With the rejection of agency, the issues of freedom, autonomy, and choice also disappear from this model.

Table 12.1 *A Comparison of Models of the Individual*

Issue	Models			
	Attribute	Conjunctive	Situated	Activative
Identity	Sum of the traits	Expressed in subjectivity	Acting force	Activating and acting force
Subjectivity	Not usually addressed	Influence intersection	Frame of expression	Frame of expression
Agency	Usually deterministic	Within a given subjectivity	Nonimmanent selection	Constrained immanence
Body	Physical substrate of cognitive traits	Object of desire/ subjugation	Reality check and symbolic object	Present and at issue
Action	Operational variables	Social practices	Agents of social roles	Agency in action routines
Theory of self	No unified entity	Contained in subjectivity	A willing agent	Active and activated agent
Level of claim	Transcendent and foundational	Historical, global, and ideological	Global roles locally produced	Historical, local, and ideological
Unity of science	Generally accepted	Sociological yes, critical no	No	No
Domain of argument	Holds materialism as ideal	Material, semiotic, both	Semiotic	Semiotic
Purpose of inquiry	Discovery and explication	Discovery and explication, illumination and critique	Discovery or illumination and critique	Illumination, critique, and construction

More contemporary forms of the conjunctive model accept the necessity of choice but see choice making as defined by the subjectivity in place. Once a subjectivity is known, agency disappears as an explanatory element. Agency is a theoretical necessity for both the situated and the activative models and is a particularly animated element of the activative. The difference between them is across the issue of immanence. Most situated forms see agency as explained by global determinants (organic and conditioned motivations). The activative model insists on the existentialist claim that forms are always in the process of becoming in action, and that each life expression is a creative act (the idea of a local, uncaused cause) that is under influence but not determination.

The Body

The body appears in the attribute model most effectively as the physical substrate of cognitive traits (sometimes called identity theory) such as in right brain-left brain traits. The body may appear (in rejection of identity theory) as the vessel of the mind or as the socialization object of certain traits (e.g., the "short man" syndrome). The body is much more operative in the other models as object and symbol and often has standing as an agent in its own right. Reality, for example, appears to James (1983) as a "muscle tension."

Action

Forms of action have meaning in all of the models discussed, but the sources of those meanings vary from model to model. In the attribute model, the meanings ascribed to the self's lines of activity are determined by the scientific procedure itself. Action is contained in the operationally defined variables, which are the antecedents of separately defined criterion variables that verify or disconfirm scientific hypotheses. Comment is bounded by the protocol. The significance of action beyond observed outcomes lies outside the scope of such investigation.

In the conjunctive model, action has been given only the most rudimentary analysis, primarily in the underdefined catchphrase *social practices*. Lines of action are treated primarily as evidence of the presence of various social forces at play on the individual. If there is an agency present, such agency is most often attributed to ideological forces or to rudimentary forms of psychological drive theory.

The situated model begins to incorporate action as a necessary component in understanding not only what the self is but how the self is. Action is a part of the social process by which individuals are able to create and constitute the very conditions in which their selves may thrive. Actions and their meanings become part of the overall mosaic of social meanings with which individuals must grapple so as to know themselves and others.

At the same time, the situated model keeps a firm hand on agency. Roles, their meanings, and their means of enactment are the primary resources of explanation. Where there is the concept of the self-as-role performance, analyses tend not to extend beyond effects produced at monad and monologic levels of action.

The activative model attempts to rescue action as a viable signifying system that restructures both the nature of self and the meanings for the lines of action the self enacts. Lines of action, while often associated with various social roles, also require attendance to larger, collective, and coordinated social actions beyond which any one individual participates. The individual self is given a significant role to play: interpreter and manager of meaning.

In the activative model, the meaning of what any one individual says and does arises more in the relationships between self-and-other and the ways those utterances or other actions fit together in various patterns of interaction. It is collective action that makes room for the self to emerge in its myriad ways, and it is this same collective action that sustains or alters the self-in-progress.

Theory of Self

The independent and autonomous self is (a) able to engage reality under her own control; (b) able to think her own thoughts about her own experiences and her own ideational activity unmediated by collective accomplishment; (c) able to represent her own experience and ideation in her own knowledge; (d) able to make her own judgments about the value of her experience, ideation, and knowledge; (e) able to literally and entirely declare her own experience, ideation, and knowledge; (f) able to direct her own activity from her own engagement and knowledge; and (g) able to enact her own hitherto unknown personage. Although we may think of ourselves in that way, no model of theory accepts that formulation. In some form of each model, each ability is somehow compromised, weakened, or outright rejected. Nonetheless, presence of the independent and autonomous self will not disappear from the foundation of our theorizing. If nothing else, we need it as a foil for explaining what is a genuine theory of the self.

In the attribute model, this Cartesian self becomes a series of "*self* hyphens" (self-concept, self-esteem, self-recognition) but remains true to form in science's claims to objectivity. The conjunctive model has its uses of objectivity and the stance of the critic (How is the Marxist critique not simply a disguised element of the bourgeois project?). Despite these needs, members of both sets of practitioners have been stern in their repudiation of the Cartesian ideal.

Scholars associated with either the situated or the activative models by their retention of some form of identity and agency must necessarily have a more relaxed view. The self is an accountable element in their theory and they do not have to view themselves as some kind of "special case."

Level of Claim

Level of claim refers to the location of validity—in history or beyond, global or local, foundational or ideological. Attribute arguments are beyond history (transcendent) and foundational (based on an objective reality). Conjunctive arguments can be historical or not and foundational or not. Most contemporary European conjunctive arguments are historical and ideological. Situated arguments are historical, global in their reach although locally invested and just beginning to address the issue of ideology. Activative arguments are historical, regional (communities of meaning and interpretation), locally invested, and openly ideological.

Unity of Science

Only the attribute and the sociological form of the conjunctive models would accept the unity of science hypothesis. All other arguments specifically reject it.

Domain of Argument

It follows from their position on the unity of science that analysts of the attribute and sociological conjunctive ilks would hold materialism as the ideal and argue for the material reality of their "objects of explanation" (even cognitive states or social forces). Some Marxist conjunctive arguments make use of both semiosis and materialism; others are wholly semiotic. Both situated and activative arguments speak of material practices that are effective semiotically. There are materially real things done but their work is semiotic.

Purpose of Inquiry

Discovery and explication for the purpose of prediction and control are the purposes of attribute arguments and some traditional conjunctive sociology. A critical stance enters other forms of conjunctive sociology and is the heart of the critical forms. Situated arguments often contain an element of critique but may be satisfied with a claim to discovery. Activative arguments work discovery and critique and reflexively recognize their own part in the reality construction process.

Cognitive and developmental psychology and American functional sociology as well as those locations that seek to emulate those disciplines are common disciplinary homes for discovery (finding what's there) and explication (prediction and control) arguments. Marxist cultural studies, critical theory, and symbolic interactionism make use of discovery (illumination and interpretation) and critique (reformation and emancipation) arguments. And interpretive sociology, ordinary language theorists, hermeneutics, and hermeneutic ethnography make use of discovery, critique, and construction (knowledge production) arguments.

Conclusions

More than anything, our conclusions begin and end with the recognition that terms such as *the individual, the person,* and *the self,* as well as *identity* and *subjectivity* remain in contested grounds. The means by which their contested character is laid to rest are boundary setting for communities of theory and scholarship alike.

A community's definition of the self is a high-value resource, a linchpin connection in the structure of argument emblematic of its place of construction. It is no wonder that the debates around the self are serious and often bloody. It would be folly, postmodern as we are, to sound some reconciliatory note.

Notes

1. This epistemological requirement is called methodological individualism (Nagel, 1961). It holds that collectives do not exist as entities with supraindividual characteristics but must be explained by the individual elements they contain.

2. Levin (1992), Levine (1992), and Wegner and Vallacher (1980) provide overviews. An interesting read across two decades of thought is given in a comparison of Gergen's 1971 text with his 1991 book.

3. This test was suggested to us by Lawrence Grossberg (1993), who was quoting O'Hanlon (1988).

4. Subjectivity should not be read as the "effect of the subject," that personal opinion opposite of objectivity; rather, it is the "effect of the collective," which positions each individual at the site of ethnic, race, class, and gender (and so on) distinctions.

5. The alternative to multiple domains of explanation is the unity of science. This belief that inhabits modernist social science holds that all science reduces to a common foundation usually identified with physics.

6. Ross (1992) writes, for example, "Strictly speaking there is no such thing as the self—at least not in scientific psychology" (p. 1). A bit later on the same page, he legitimizes the claim: "This insistence that self is not an entity, that it must not be reified, is in line with the usage found in the contemporary research literature on which this book is based" (p. 1).

Part of this conceptualization can be seen as psychology's move to define itself in the face of nineteenth-century models of the individual, which held to an essentialist self.

7. The majority of Marxist argument has held that there can be an authentic (nonideological) representation that their methods will reveal. In this regard, Marxist thought shares the same goal as

that of objective empiricism—liberation through truth. Anderson's sense of this postmodern, post-Soviet space is that there is a greater acceptance by Marxist and other critical scholarship of an all-encompassing nature of ideology but that some ideologies are less exploitative than others and all can benefit from critique (see, for example, Gurnah & Scott, 1992).

8. The obvious problem of where a liberated scholarly elite comes from, having been exquisitely trained in bourgeois ideology, is the subject of the critique advanced by Lyotard (1984).

9. Continental structuralism is most closely identified with Saussure (1910/1959), Piaget (1970), and Lévi-Strauss (1967) and culminates in the enigmatic figures of Foucault and Lacan. Structuralist figures can become poststructuralist figures as did Barthes, and structuralism is often combined with Marxist analysis as in the work of Baudrillard (1981). It is, perhaps, Derrida's (1978) attack on logocentrism that marks the beginnings of poststructuralism. The American strain of structuralism is identified with Harrison White (1963) and his students (Mullins, 1973) as well as linguistic studies of which conversational analysis is communication's most apparent structuralist branch. American structuralism typically lacks the ideological component common to continental structuralism.

10. The usual line of argument cited here includes Lenin (1960), Lukacs (1971), Gramsci (1971), and Althusser (1984).

11. Parsons's early work, *The Structure of Social Action* (1937), was much more in line with the situated individual model described under that heading, but it clearly changed in his later writings (Mennell, 1974). Parsons's work was under regular critique by his student Merton (e.g., 1948) as well as others. In addition, the tenor of the times was much more in line with the conjunctive model, although Parsons openly resisted behaviorism both theoretically in his writings and politically at Harvard (Mullins, 1973)—perhaps an example of social forces at work.

12. *Critical theory* is the name given to the tradition initiated by the "Frankfurt School" (M. Hockheimer, T. Adorno, H. Marcuse) and most famously continued in the theory of communicative action developed by Habermas. *Cultural studies* generally refers to the diverse efforts of Richard Hoggart, Raymond Williams, Stuart Hall, and the Birmingham Centre in the field of British cultural studies and its equally diverse American representation found in James Carey, Lawrence Grossberg, and Horace Newcomb, among others.

Although an outsider might consider critical theory and cultural studies in the same kind of work, they clearly identify themselves as belonging to different intellectual communities. And, indeed, critical theory is much more in the German philosophical tradition while British cultural studies present an ethnological heritage colored by French structuralism and continental Marxism.

Finally, both critical theory and cultural studies, as Marxist enterprises, are deeply influenced by the failure of class conflict as the theoretical engine of Marxism. The road to recovery offered by cultural studies appears to be the more vital one.

13. The model of the situated self draws heavily on American pragmatism and semiotics, symbolic interactionism, and interpretive sociology. The central figures in American pragmatism are C. S. Peirce, W. James, J. Dewey; in symbolic interaction, they are G. H. Mead, H. Bloomer; in interpretive sociology, they are M. Weber, W. Park, C. Cooley, W. I. Thomas. It is the use of these scriptures that clearly delineates the situated model from the current movement of cultural studies.

14. The term *activative* represents equally the failure of the authors to find a better term and the notion that the individual is both activated (called into material presence through action) and activating (calling the necessary meanings for action into place).

References

Aboulafia, M. (1986). *The mediating self: Mead, Sartre and self determination.* New Haven, CT: Yale University Press.

Alexander, J. C. (1982). *Theoretical logic in sociology: The antinomies of classical thought: Marx and Durkheim* (Vol. 2). Berkeley: University of California Press.

Alexander, J. C. (1992). Citizen and enemy in symbolic classification: On the polarizing discourse of civil society. In M. Lamont & M. Fournier (Eds.), *Cultivating differences: Symbolic boundaries and the making of inequality* (pp. 289-308). Chicago: University of Chicago Press.

Alford, C. F. (1991). *The self in social theory.* New Haven, CT: Yale University Press.

Allen, R. C. (1987). Reader oriented criticism and television. In R. C. Allen (Ed.), *Channels of discourse: Television and contemporary criticism* (pp. 74-112). Chapel Hill: University of North Carolina Press.

Althusser, L. (1984). *Essays on ideology*. London: Verso.

Anderson, J. A. (1987). *Communication research: Issues and methods*. New York: McGraw-Hill.

Anderson, J. A. (1992). On the ethics of research in a socially constructed reality. *Journal of Broadcasting and Electronic Media, 36*, 353-357.

Anderson, J. A., & Meyer, T. P. (1988). *Mediated communication: A social action perspective*. Newbury Park, CA: Sage.

Bannet, E. T. (1989). *Structuralism and the logic of dissent*. Chicago: University of Illinois Press.

Bartky, S. (1995). Foucault, femininity and the modernization of patriarchal power. In J. P. Sterba (Ed.), *Social and political philosophy* (pp. 453-467). Belmont, CA: Wadsworth.

Baudrillard, J. (1981). *For a critique of the political economy of the sign* (C. Levin, Trans.). St. Louis, MO: Telos.

Becker, H. S., & McCall, M. (Eds.). (1990). *Symbolic interaction and cultural studies*. Chicago: University of Chicago Press.

Bourdieu, P. (1978). Sport and social class. *Social Science Information, 17*, 819-840.

Burgoon, J. K., & Le Poire, B. A. (1992). Effects of communication expectancies, actual communication, and expectancy disconfirmation on evaluations of communicators and their communication behaviors. *Human Communication Research, 20*, 67-96.

Canfield, J. V. (1990). *The looking glass self: An examination of self-awareness*. New York: Praeger.

Caputo, J. D. (1987). *Radical hermeneutics: Repetition, deconstruction and the hermeneutic project*. Bloomington: Indiana University Press.

Caputo, J. D. (1992). On being inside/outside truth. In J. L. Marsh, J. D. Caputo, & M. Westphal (Eds.), *Modernity and its discontents* (pp. 45-64). New York: Fordham University Press.

de Certeau, M. (1984). *The practice of everyday life* (S. F. Rendall, Trans.). Berkeley: University of California Press.

Derrida, J. (1978). *Writing and difference* (A. Bass, Trans.). Chicago: University of Chicago Press.

Durfee, H. A., & Rodier, D. F. T. (1989). The self and its language. In H. A. Durfee & D. F. T. Rodier (Eds.), *Phenomenology and beyond: The self and its language* (pp. 1-10). Dordrecht: Kluwer Academic.

Ellis, R. (1986). *An ontology of consciousness*. Dordrecht, the Netherlands: Martinus Nijhoff.

Frazer, C. F. (1981). The social character of children's television viewing. *Communication Research, 8*, 307-322.

Fry, V. H., Alexander, A., & Fry, D. L. (1990). Textual status, stigmatized self, and media consumption. In J. A. Anderson (Ed.), *Communication yearbook 13* (pp. 519-544). Newbury Park, CA: Sage.

Gergen, K. J. (1971). *The concept of self*. New York: Holt, Rinehart & Winston.

Gergen, K. J. (1991). *The saturated self*. New York: Basic Books.

Gramsci, A. (1971). *Selections from the prison notebooks* (Q. Hoare & G. Nowell-Smith, Eds.). London: Lawrence and Wishart.

Grossberg, L. (1991). Strategies of Marxist cultural interpretation. In R. K. Avery & D. Eason (Eds.), *Critical perspectives on media and society* (pp. 126-162). New York: Guilford.

Grossberg, L. (1993). Cultural studies and/in new worlds. *Critical Studies in Mass Communication, 10*, 1-22.

Gurnah, A., & Scott, A. (1992). *The uncertain science: Criticism of sociological formalism*. London: Routledge.

Hall, J. R. (1992). The capital(s) of culture: A nonholistic approach to status situations, class, gender, and ethnicity. In M. Lamont & M. Fournier (Eds.), *Cultivating differences: Symbolic boundaries and the making of inequality* (pp. 257-285). Chicago: University of Chicago Press.

Hansen, C. H., & Krygowski, W. (1994). Arousal-augmented priming effects: Rock music videos and sex object schemas [sic]. *Communication Research, 21*, 24-47.

Hardt, H. (1989). The return of the "critical" and the challenge of radical dissent: Critical theory, cultural studies and American mass communication research. In J. A. Anderson (Ed.), *Communication yearbook 12* (pp. 558-600). Newbury Park, CA: Sage.

Hewitt, J. P. (1989). *Dilemmas of the American self*. Philadelphia: Temple University Press.

Hodge, R., & Kress, G. (1988). *Social semiotics*. Ithaca, NY: Cornell University Press.

Isajiw, W. (1968). *Causation and functionalism in sociology*. New York: Schocken.

James, W. (1983). *The principles of psychology*. Cambridge, MA: Harvard University Press.

Jensen, K. B. (1991). When is meaning? Communication theory, pragmatism, and mass media reception. In J. A. Anderson (Ed.), *Communication yearbook* (Vol. 14, pp. 3-32). Newbury Park, CA: Sage.

Kerby, A. P. (1991). *Narrative and the self*. Bloomington: Indiana University Press.

Kierkegaard, S. (1958). *Journals* (A. Dru, Trans.). London: Collins.

Kohut, H. (1977). *The restoration of the self*. New York: International Universities Press.

Lacan, J. (1977). *Ecrits* (A. Sheridan, Trans.). New York: Norton.

Lacan, J. (1988). *The seminar of Jacques Lacan* (1st American ed.). New York: Norton.

Lenin, V. (1960). *Selected works*. Moscow: Foreign Languages Publishing House.

Levin, J. D. (1992). *Theories of the self*. Washington, DC: Taylor & Francis.

Levine, G. (Ed.). (1992). *Constructions of the self*. New Brunswick, NJ: Rutgers University Press.

Lévi-Strauss, C. (1967). *Structural anthropology* (G. Weidenfeld, Trans.). Chicago: University of Chicago Press.

Lewis, H. D. (1982). *The elusive self*. London: Macmillan.

Lindlof, T. (1988). Media audiences as interpretive communities. In J. A. Anderson (Ed.), *Communication yearbook 11* (pp. 87-107). Newbury Park, CA: Sage.

Lukacs, G. (1971). *History and class consciousness*. London: Merlin.

Lyotard, J. (1984). *The postmodern condition: A report on knowledge* (G. Bennington & B. Massumi, Trans.). Minneapolis: University of Minnesota Press.

Marx, K. (1959). *Capital* (Vol. 1). New York: Modern Library. (Original work published 1867)

McCombs, M. E., & Shaw, D. L. (1972). The agenda-setting function of mass media. *Public Opinion Quarterly, 36*, 176-187.

McLellan, D. (1986). *Ideology*. Minneapolis: University of Minnesota Press.

McPhail, M. (1994). The politics of complicity: Second thoughts about the social construction of racial equality. *Quarterly Journal of Speech, 80*, 343-357.

Meltzer, B. N., Petras, J. W., & Reynolds, L. T. (1975). *Symbolic interactionism: Genesis, varieties and criticism*. London: Routledge & Kegan Paul.

Mennell, S. J. (1974). *Sociological theory: Uses and unities*. New York: Praeger.

Mepham, J. (1979). The theory of ideology in *Capital*. In J. Mepham & D. Rubin (Eds.), *Issues in Marxist philosophy* (Vol. 3, pp. 141-174). Brighton, England: Harvester.

Merton, R. K. (1948). Discussion of Talcott Parsons' "The position of sociological theory." *American Sociological Review, 13*, 164-168.

Merton, R. K. (1957). *Social theory and social structure*. Glencoe, IL: Free Press.

Meyers, P. N., Jr., & Biocca, F. N. (1992). The elastic body image: The effect of television advertising and programming on body image distortions in young women. *Journal of Communication, 42*, 108-133.

Morley, D. (1980). *The 'Nationwide' audience: Structure and decoding*. London: BFI.

Mullins, N. C. (1973). *Theories and theory groups in contemporary American sociology*. New York: Harper & Row.

Nagel, E. (1961). *The structure of science*. London: Routledge & Kegan Paul.

Newcomb, H. M. (1991). On the dialogic aspects of mass communication. In R. K. Avery & D. Eason (Eds.), *Critical perspectives on media and society* (pp. 69-87). New York: Guilford.

O'Hanlon, R. (1988). Recovering the subject: Subaltern studies and histories of resistance in colonial South Asia. *Modern Asian Studies, 22*, 189-224.

Parsons, T. (1937). *The structure of social action; a study of social history with special reference to a group of recent European writers*. New York: McGraw-Hill.

Parsons, T. (1951). *The social system*. London: Tavistock.

Pearce, W. B. (1994). Recovering agency. In S. Deetz (Ed.), *Communication yearbook 17* (pp. 34-41). Thousand Oaks, CA: Sage.

Piaget, J. (1970). *Structuralism* (C. Muschler, Trans.). New York: Basic Books.

Popper, K. R., & Eccles, J. C. (1977). *The self and its brain*. Berlin: Springer-Verlag.

Ricoeur, P. (1992). *Oneself as another*. Chicago: University of Chicago Press.

Rosengren, K. E., & Windahl, S. (1972). Mass media consumption as a functional alternative. In D. McQuail (Ed.), *Sociology of mass communications* (pp. 166-194). Harmondsworth: Penguin.

Ross, A. O. (1992). *The sense of self: Research and theory*. New York: Springer.

Russell, K. (1979). Science and ideology. In J. Mepham & D. Rubin (Eds.), *Issues in Marxist philosophy* (Vol. 3, pp. 185-196). Brighton, England: Harvester.

Sartre, J. P. (1956). *Being and nothingness* (H. E. Barns, Trans.). New York: Philosophical Library.

Saussure, F. de. (1959). *Course in general linguistics*. New York: McGraw-Hill. (Original work published 1910)

Segal, J. M. (1991). *Agency and alienation: A theory of human presence*. Savage, NY: Rowman & Littlefield.

Silverman, K. (1983). *The subject of semiotics*. Oxford: Oxford University Press.

Szahaj, A. (1990). Actuality of the Frankfurt School's critical theory of society: The Polish reception. In P. v. Engledorp Gastelaars, S. Magala, & O. Preuss (Eds.), *Critics and critical theory in Eastern Europe* (pp. 53-60). The Hague, the Netherlands: University Press Rotterdam.

Taylor, C. (1991). The dialogic self. In J. F. Bohman, D. R. Hiley, & R. Shusterman (Eds.), *The interpretive turn: Philosophy, science, culture* (pp. 304-314). Ithaca, NY: Cornell University Press.

Thalheimer, A. (1936). *Introduction to dialectical materialism: The Marxist world-view* (G. Simpson & G. Weltner, Trans.). New York: Covici Friede.

Traudt, P. J., Anderson, J. A., & Meyer, T. P. (1987). Phenomenology, empiricism, and media experience. *Critical Studies in Mass Communication, 4*, 302-310.

Trujillo, N. (1993). Interpreting November 22nd: A critical ethnography of an assassination site. *Quarterly Journal of Speech, 79*, 447-466.

Trujillo, N., & Ekdom, L. (1985). Sportswriting and American cultural values. *Critical Studies in Mass Communication, 1*, 262-281.

Turner, G. (1990). *British cultural studies: An introduction*. Boston: Unwin Hyman.

Wagner, R. (1981). *The invention of culture* (rev. ed.). Chicago: University of Chicago Press.

Wegner, D. M., & Vallacher, R. R. (Eds.). (1980). *The self in social psychology*. New York: Oxford University Press.

Wexler, P. (1991). *Critical theory now*. London: Falmer.

White, H. C. (1963). *An anatomy of kinship: Mathematical models for structures of cumulated roles*. Englewood Cliffs, NJ: Prentice Hall.

Whitt, L. A., & Slack, J. D. (1994). Communities, environments and cultural studies. *Cultural Studies, 8*, 5-31.

Wiley, N. (1994). *The semiotic self*. Chicago: University of Chicago Press.

Williams, R. (1991). Base and superstructure in Marxist cultural theory. In C. Mukerji & M. Schudson (Eds.), *Rethinking popular culture* (pp. 407-423). Berkeley: University of California Press.

Wolin, R. (1992). *The terms of cultural criticism*. New York: Columbia University Press.

Index

226

About the Authors

James A. Anderson is Professor and Chair of the Department of Communication at the University of Utah. His research interests are in the epistemological foundations of communication theory and the application of social action approaches to the study of communication. His most recent book is *Communication Theory: Epistemological Foundations*.

Mary Ellen Brown is Assistant Professor in the Department of Communication at the University of Missouri, Columbia. Her research interests are in the cultural analysis of television audience reading practices, particularly in relation to gender politics. She is the author of *Soap Opera and Women's Talk: The Pleasure of Resistance* and has edited *Television and Women's Culture: The Politics of Pleasure*.

Donal Carbaugh is Professor of Communication and Faculty Affiliate in American Studies at the University of Massachusetts, Amherst. His current research involves cultural analyses and comparative studies of American, American Indian, Finnish, and Russian communication systems. His research has been published in over a dozen academic journals and includes the books *Situating Selves, Talking American: Cultural Discourses on Donahue* and the edited book *Cultural Communication and Intercultural Contact*.

Kenneth J. Gergen is the Mustin Professor of Psychology, Swarthmore College. He is the author of *Toward Transformation in Social Knowledge, The Saturated Self*, and *Realities and Relationships: Soundings in Social Construction*. He is a central exponent of social constructionism in the social sciences.

Debra Grodin is Visiting Scholar at the University of Washington, Northwest Center for Research on Women, and formerly a faculty member of the Department of Communication at the University of Louisville. Her research has been published in *Critical Studies in Mass Communication, Text and Performance Quarterly*, and the *Journal of Communication*. Her current research interest is in how self and community are experienced in the context of mediated culture.

Autumn Grubb-Swetnam received her Ph.D. in communications at the University of Kentucky in 1994. Her research interests include media and cultural studies, social change, and feminist theory. Currently, she administers the internal and external video communication needs of Morehead State University.

Thomas R. Lindlof is Associate Professor of Telecommunications at the University of Kentucky. He received his Ph.D. from the University of Texas at

Austin. He is the editor of *Natural Audiences: Qualitative Research of Media Uses and Effects* and author of *Qualitative Communication Research Methods*. He has published extensively on mediated communication processes, audience theory, and qualitative research methodology.

Sheila McNamee is Associate Professor and Chair of Communication at the University of New Hampshire. She has published several articles exploring conceptualizations of research as social intervention. She has also written on social constructionist approaches to family therapy.

Patricia J. Priest received her Ph.D. in mass communication from the University of Georgia in 1992. In the summer of 1993, she traveled through Argentina on a Fulbright-Hays grant to study women's issues, particularly women's efforts to effect social change. She is currently a freelance writer who has published in the *Washington Post* and *Electronic Media*. She is the author of *Public Intimacies: Talk Show Participants and Tell-All TV*.

Gerard T. Schoening is Assistant Professor of Communication at LaSalle University. His current interest is in the relationship between social action and visual communication. Recent theoretical research on social action theory in mass media has been published in *Communication Theory* (along with James Anderson) and *The Electronic Journal of Communication*.

Wendy Simonds is Assistant Professor in the Institute of the Liberal Arts at Emory University. She is author of *Abortion at Work: Ideology and Practice in a Feminist Clinic*, *Women and Self-Help Culture: Reading Between the Lines*, and coauthor (with Barbara Katz Rothman) of *Centuries of Solace: Expressions of Maternal Grief in Popular Literature*.

Timothy A. Simpson is a doctoral student in communication and cultural studies at the University of South Florida. His dissertation research examines the discourses of historical preservation, cultural memory, identity, and community that surround Ybor City, Florida, a national historic landmark district located in Tampa, Florida.

Sherry Turkle is Professor of the Sociology of Science at the Massachusetts Institute of Technology. She holds a joint doctorate in sociology and personality psychology from Harvard University and is a licensed clinical psychologist. She is the author of *Psychoanalytic Politics: Jacques Lacan and Freud's French Revolution*; *The Second Self: Computers and the Human Spirit*; and *Life on the Screen: Identity in the Age of the Internet*.

Suzanna Danuta Walters is Assistant Professor of Sociology at Georgetown University and is the author of two books, *Lives Together/Worlds Apart: Mothers and Daughters in Popular Culture* and *Material Girls: Making Sense of Feminist Cultural Theory*. She has lectured and written extensively on feminist theory and popular culture, and is currently working on a study of contemporary representations of lesbians and gays.